Management and Organizations in Transitional China

China's 30-year market transition and its integration into the world economy provide a unique opportunity for exploring the nature of large-scale economic and political transformation and the mechanisms underlying organizational behavior during such a transition. *Management and Organizations in Transitional China* explores how managers and firms cope with transition-related challenges by adapting to, manipulating, or even creating the complex institutional environment. This book examines the way transitional institutions shape individual decisions and organizational strategies, the mechanisms that promote the diffusion of innovative management practices and economic policies, and the formation and evolution of interfirm networks.

Based on a comprehensive review of the studies on market transition, this book investigates how firms manage their relationship with important stakeholders in the environment. It highlights the importance of network-based strategies for institutionally less-advantaged actors (like private firms, foreign entrants, and entrepreneurs) to establish legitimacy, gain institutional support, and mobilize financial resources. Moreover, this book studies the mechanisms that facilitate the adoption of innovative management practices and economic policies in the transitional context, comparing the mainstream diffusion theories and evaluating the relative potency of the diffusion drivers. Furthermore, *Management and Organizations in Transitional China* provides empirical analyses using longitudinal data of alliance formation, network evolution, and the effect of both alliance formation and network evolution on firm decision-making and performance.

Combining theory, data analysis, and rich contextual description to provide a comprehensive understanding of the organizational transition process, this book will appeal to scholars and practitioners in general management, organizational studies, international business, entrepreneurship, and related disciplines.

Yanlong Zhang is an Assistant Professor of Management at Guanghua School of Management, Peking University, China.

Lisa A. Keister is Gilhuly Family Professor of Sociology at Duke University, USA.

Routledge Studies in International Business and the World Economy

For a full list of titles in this series, please visit www.routledge.com

Management and Organizations in Transitional China

Yanlong Zhang and Lisa A. Keister

Routledge
Taylor & Francis Group

NEW YORK AND LONDON

First published 2016
by Routledge
711 Third Avenue, New York, NY 10017

and by Routledge
2 Park Square, Milton Park, Abingdon, Oxon OX14 4RN

Routledge is an imprint of the Taylor & Francis Group, an informa business

© 2016 Taylor & Francis

The right of Yanlong Zhang and Lisa A. Keister to be identified as authors of this work has been asserted by them in accordance with sections 77 and 78 of the Copyright, Designs and Patents Act 1988.

Library of Congress Cataloging-in-Publication Data
Names: Zhang, Yanlong, 1980– author. | Keister, Lisa A., 1968– author.
Title: Management and organizations in transitional China / by Yanlong Zhang and Lisa A. Keister.
Description: First Edition. | New York : Routledge, 2016. | Series: Routledge studies in international business and the world economy ; 65 | Includes bibliographical references and index.
Identifiers: LCCN 2016002385 | ISBN 9781138813014 (cloth : alk. paper) | ISBN 9781315748429 (ebook)
Subjects: LCSH: Organizational change—China. | Organizational behavior—China. | China—Economic policy. | Management—China.
Classification: LCC HD58.8 .Z43 2016 | DDC 302.3/50951—dc23
LC record available at http://lccn.loc.gov/2016002385

ISBN: 978-1-138-81301-4 (hbk)
ISBN: 978-1-315-74842-9 (ebk)

Typeset in Sabon
by Apex CoVantage, LLC

Contents

Tables and Figures

Tables

Figures

1 Introduction
The Chinese Context

Introduction

It has now been four decades since China launched its reform and opening up policy in 1978, which is guided by the principle of "crossing the river by feeling the stones." This large-scale and profound social change has attracted scholarly attention from multiple disciplines. Not only has China become a natural laboratory for testing the theories on economic development, policy making, and business strategies, but it has also become a place where an increasing number of new phenomena emerge every day that beg new models or theoretical frameworks to explain their emergence, successes, and failures. In order to achieve economic growth, which is regarded as crucial to the political survival of the regime, the state has been willing to incorporate wisdom from various models of the state and build new capacities. Some of the adjustments have made observers believe that the Chinese state will eventually evolve into a system that is similar to western capitalism. However, the reform process is not as linear as transitional theorists have portrayed. Although reformers at different times made great efforts to promote economic development and improve the nation's strength, the content of the waves of reforms has been continuously reformulated: from the four modernizations, to the building of a socialist market economy, to the construction of a *xiaokang* society, and then to the realization of Chinese dreams. There have been successes and failures, but what is most remarkable is simply how far China has moved toward a market economy and how the reform process has maintained its relevance despite the changing challenges the economy has faced (Naughton, 2007). From a state-building perspective, these changes in the overarching political and economic goals, as well as the practical policy choices, are responses to the challenges that arose during the marketization and globalization processes. These responses were neither well planned nor unified under one ideology, and were often reactive to the challenges the regime faced at each moment (Gao, 2009).

The capitalist system, at the empirical level, is less coherent than it is assumed to be. It is often a loose conglomeration of institutions, ideas, and policy prescriptions from which policy makers pick and choose based on the prevailing political, economic, social, historical, and institutional conditions in a nation. As a result, the specific policy structure is far from uniform, and varies greatly across countries. Other developing countries embraced western styled capitalism by adopting pro-market economic policies as prescribed in the Washington Consensus and implementing political democratization. Unlike these other countries, China adopts similar neoliberal economic policies, but appears to have remained in its traditional Leninist form (Gao, 2009; Krug & Hendrischke, 2008; Nee, 1992; Zheng, 2004). The coexistence of a vibrant market economy with a powerful authoritarian state contradicts the prevailing model in two ways. First, economic liberalization does not go hand in hand with political democratization. Whereas the country's economy is increasingly open to the global market, its political system has not changed much in the past three decades. Second, although the market's power has substantially increased during the reform era, the state has not relinquished its control over the economy; instead, state intervention is still active and influential and can be easily identified in many economic sectors (Blanchard & Shleifer, 2001; Fligstein & Zhang, 2011; Hall & Soskice, 2001; Yeung, 2003). Such paradoxical coexistence does not lead to serious conflicts between the political and economic doctrines. Compared with the local states in other developing or transitional economies, the Chinese local states play the role of a "helping hand" and promote the market development in the local economy (Jin, Qian, & Weingast, 2005). In many cases, the authoritarian state actively uses its political power and institutional resources to implement pro-market policies. At the same time, the authoritarian state has been very cautious in expanding the neoliberal ideas to new fields; it tries to ensure that market institutions are nothing more than policy tools for the state (Gao, 2009).

In light of these complexities, some scholars have argued that instead of asking how rapidly and in what respects China is moving toward western styled capitalism, a more important issue that needs to be clarified first is whether China is moving toward capitalism or away from it, and if the latter, then is China on a collision course with western capitalism? Unlike early scholarly work which generally viewed China as an additional example of emerging economies that would follow the past development trajectory of advanced economies (Guthrie, 1998; Nee, 1989, 1992; Peng, 2003), later scholars contended that China's current trajectory is not in the direction of capitalism; rather the current trajectory is toward central management (Lin, 2011). It is suggested that China has coopted western capitalism and emulated many of its overt features; now it poses an unprecedented and profound challenge to western capitalism that scholars, policy consultants, and policy makers have only begun to grasp (Meyer, 2011).

Presenting a comprehensive review on the future of Chinese capitalism is not the goal of this book; however, we do believe that such discussions allow us to better understand the myriad of organizational and management phenomena in the Chinese context. Borrowing insights from theories that are originally developed at individual or national levels, we can achieve a more comprehensive understanding of management issues across institutional domains representing various levels of marketization, state control, and the penetration of foreign social and economic influences, and we can directly examine the effect of social, political, and economical forces on different economic outcomes (Nee & Opper, 2009). In fact, many scholars have taken this initiative and extended this framework to the study of organizations.

Transition or Transformation?

Early theories that aim to shed light on the nature and mechanics of China's social and economic transformations and their impact on economic actors have paid considerable attention to the interaction between political power and market forces, and tried to explain the rationale behind economic actors by embedding them into the institutional contexts defined by the relative potency of state versus market. The new institutional sociology approach developed by Nee is among the early scholarly attempts to understand the mechanism and direction of this social economic transformation (Brinton & Nee, 1998; Nee, 2005). Applying this theory to interpret the socioeconomic changes that occurred in former socialist transitional economies, theorists foresee that economic liberalization may result in transformative change in the direction of more relative autonomy between the political and economic sphere, which is quite similar to the situation in established market economies. Theorists predict that the value of political capital will decline as a consequence of progressive marketization; meanwhile, power will shift from redistributors to producers and the emergence of a market economy in departure from state socialism (Nee, 1989, 1992; Nee & Opper, 2009).

Instead of simply assuming the existence of institutions, the new institutionalism approach aims to articulate the mechanisms that govern how institutions operate, i.e., the way institutions facilitate or constrain social actions. This theory calls for the integration of both formal and informal institutional conditions into the analysis of the rationale underlying individual or firm-level decisions. *Formal institutions* here are defined as laws and well-codified rules that are often formulated and enforced by the state, whereas *informal institutions* refers to norms that tend to be monitored and enforced through the approval and disapproval of various social contacts, such as friends, relatives, acquaintances, and even strangers (Nee, 2005). This approach deals directly with behavior where uncertainty and transaction costs are high, which happen to be common institutional features of transitional economies. Moreover, it facilitates explicit analysis of interactions between large-scale social change and micro behavior (Keister, 2009; Keister & Zhang, 2009).

The early development of this approach was mainly focused on the organizational dynamics that lead to China's rapid economic growth, especially

in the rural sectors. Nee (1992) argued that similar to transitional economies in Eastern Europe and the former Soviet states, the transitional context
is characterized by a variable degree of state intervention and heterogeneous
levels of market development. During the early transition period, these societies tend to have weak markets, poorly specified property rights, and institutional uncertainty. These conditions not only lead to changes in the resource
allocation mechanism (i.e., the changing balance between the market allocation and bureaucratic allocation, which changes the relative importance of
the state bureaucratic allocation), but also give rise to new organizational
forms that can more effectively cope with the uncertainties in the environment. It was argued that the introduction of market mechanisms gradually
promotes the shift of power from redistributors to direct producers. As a
result, the traditional state-owned enterprises, with a closer relationship to
the bureaucratic redistributors, lost power to firms with hybrid and private
ownership forms (Nee, 1992, 2005). In addition, due to the higher economic efficiency in an increasingly competitive market, hybrid and privately
owned firms may construct various informal institutional arrangements that
function as alternative governing mechanisms (Borys & Jemison, 1989).
Such arrangements, ranging from informal lending networks to private
capital to new start-ups to distribution networks, may present significant
challenges to the remaining state control, and may constitute an important
reform momentum from below (Keister, 2009; Nee, 1992).

This market power thesis also suggests that the spread of markets and
the changing structure of property rights increasingly favor private firms;
business successes will be less dependent on the particularistic relationships
with the redistributors (Nee, 1992; Nee & Opper, 2009). For instance,
through in-depth interviews with more than 155 Chinese officials and
industrial firm managers in 1995, Guthrie (1998) concluded that powerful economic actors began to pay more and more attention to formal
rules, laws, and regulations, which are important elements of an emerging
rational-legal market. This finding supports the idea that an institutional
system is being constructed by the Chinese state. The respondents from the
large industrial organizations increasingly saw social connections as unnec-
essary and dangerous because the new regulations prohibited the use of
social relations to bypass official procedures. However, the complexity of
the transitional context and the non-linear development of marketization
made some theorists revise their initial predictions. They argue that the
original market power thesis cannot be interpreted as a complete devalua-
tion of political connections. Such connections are found to be functional
in many types of economies, including the mature markets (Boisot & Child,
1988, 1996). A more refined argument is that political capital matters for
firms that seek legitimacy in the transitional as well as advanced economies. However, the value of such resource is greater in institutional domains
where government agencies can still exert significant influence over economic activities (Nee & Opper, 2009).

In addition to the power shift, the new institutional sociology also maintains that when the rewards for producers are increasingly based on their performance rather than their connections to the redistributors, positive incentives are created for entrepreneurial activities and innovators. Therefore, as marketization proceeds and market competition intensifies, it can be expected that firms will invest more in innovations, which is regarded as an effective way to extend firms' profit margins. Moreover, as the market institution becomes better established, the price signals function as better indicators, which allow entrepreneurs to identify the emerging market needs and invest in productive activities (Nee & Opper, 2009). Such predictions have received much support in the entrepreneurship literature. It is indicated that entrepreneurship existed in nearly all transitional economies before the 1980s, although it was not widespread. During the transition process, many states have relaxed the restrictions imposed on private entrepreneurs (Davis, 1999; Peng, 1997). When it comes to the Chinese case, ideological discrimination against private ownership was abolished, private enterprises have become important pillars of the nation's economy, private entrepreneurs are allowed to join the communist party, and entrepreneurship and innovation are regarded as important means to boost economic growth during the recent economic slow-down.

This new institutional sociology perspective was echoed by developments in the strategic management literature exploring how organizations make strategic choices during fundamental institutional transitions (Hoskisson, Eden, Lau, & Wright, 2000) and later led to the emergence of an institution-based perspective (Peng, 2003). Scholars argue that previous literature offers less useful knowledge about how organizations resist old rules, incorporate new routines, and develop new capabilities. They believe that institutions can facilitate strategy making by allowing firms to react to and play a more active role in an institutional environment. If firms have adaptive ability and agency, that allows them to move beyond institutional constraints (Hoskisson et al., 2000; Oliver, 1991). It was argued that firms operating in the transitional context often respond to the institutional environment in a way that is quite different from the expectations of the reformers. The transition process is often not smooth; the abolishment of old institutions can create new opportunities for new entrants who can benefit from the market-based institutions but adversely affect the interests of the incumbent groups who may resist the new rules of the game (Peng, 2003).

According to this perspective, market-oriented institutional transitions can be depicted as a process of evolving from one exchange mode to another. A relationship-based transaction mode tends to fit the needs of a less complex economic system, where the number of transactions and variety of economic activities tend to be low. Relationships can also function as important market-supporting institutions in this context because information about the trustworthiness of the transaction parties is readily available and social sanctions tend to remain effective in this context. As the transition proceeds, the scope, complexity, and scale of economic transactions will experience tremendous growth. Therefore, social relations can no longer effectively function as market-supporting institutions due to their high embeddedness, localized nature, and lack of formal sanctioning mechanisms. Third party enforcement mechanisms are thus needed to ensure the successful functioning of the increasingly complex and competitive market system. At this stage, more codified institutions are established to reduce the uncertainties and costs associated with market exchanges. And the end state of the institutional environment during transition will be a rule-based, impersonal exchange system, which is generally regarded as the underpinning mechanism of successful modern economies involved in the complex contracting necessary for modern economic growth (North, 1990; Peng, 2003). The transition process, according to this perspective, will begin with a predominantly relationship-based transaction structure and then may gradually move to a second, rule-based structure.

However, the evolution of China's economic, social, and political system has presented a more complex picture to scholars who wish to use a single unified theoretical model to characterize the essence of this profound, large-scale social change. During the transition, we see the state gradually unleash market power and allow domestic private and foreign investors to play a bigger role in the economy, and meanwhile gradually integrate China into the global economy. We see the state resembles a development state: it made important changes to the existing institutions to win the competition for floating capital and to design and promote industrial policies to encourage the development of strategic industrial sectors so that the nation can climb up the global value chain (Gao, 2009). These complexities have made proponents of the institutional-based view realize that the two-stage framework is relatively simplistic. They acknowledge that institutions are composed of multiple dimensions that are interconnected, mitigating or reinforcing each other. Consequently, the institutional transitions may achieve progress at different speeds along different dimensions (Zhou & Peng, 2010). In order to better understand the way that firms respond to different levels of institutional transition, it is necessary to explore the contingencies that affect firms' strategic choices, from relation-based strategies to market-based strategies.

The contingency approach generally focuses on the impacts of three factors. The first factor is the extensiveness and effectiveness of institutions that promote fair competition. These institutions include the developed factor and product market, in which price-setting mechanisms are primarily market driven and are free from bureaucratic control; the factor and product market can effectively coordinate transactions of raw materials and other production factors as well as the sale of the final product (Lee, Peng, & Barney, 2007; Zhou & Peng, 2010). The second factor is the effectiveness and efficiency of the judicial system, which reduces the transaction costs for litigation and helps producers enforce contracts or protect their legal rights. The well-functioning market-supporting institutions will increase the confidence of the trading partners and provide effective sanctioning mechanisms that ensure trading parties will fulfill their legal obligations. This will further enhance the willingness to expand business transactions to new .exchange partners and explore emerging business opportunities (Wright, Filatotchev, Hoskisson, & Peng, 2005; Zhou & Peng, 2010). The third factor refers to the development of institutions that help facilitate the flow of information and improve the quality of information (North, 1990; Zhou & Peng, 2010). These institutions include independent auditing and accounting agencies, which provide reliable information to economic actors. These institutions reduce information asymmetry and mitigate the uncertainties associated with impersonal exchanges. They also encourage firms to go beyond their immediate local market to expand their business to other sectors or regions. This revised perspective thus advises managers, especially those from multinationals operating in both developed and emerging economies, to carefully observe the development of formal institutions, informal norms, firms' own resources, and industry contexts, all of which are crucial to the development of business strategies (Zhou & Peng, 2010).

A Network Capitalism?

In contrast to theories that assume a transition process from a network-based transaction mode to a more impersonal market-based transaction mode, other scholars adopted a more dialectic view of the relationship between the use of relation-based strategies and the development of formal institutions. It was argued that the prevalence of social relations (or *guanxi* in Chinese) is believed to originate from weak institutional support, such as insufficient legal protections and market mechanisms (Chen, Chen, & Huang, 2013; Lovett, Simmons, & Kali, 1999; Xin & Pearce, 1996). *Guanxi* is regarded as a mechanism that regulates economic transactions in the absence of a state institution for that purpose. Just as Stark (1992) suggested, one way to spread risks in an uncertain environment with few well-specified property rights is to include current and former state officials in one's economic network. Therefore, managers cultivate personal connections to substitute for reliable government and an established rule of law (Xin & Pearce, 1996). Luo and Chen (1997) argued that *guanxi* provides the lubricant for the Chinese to get through life and heavily influences Chinese social behavior and business conduct. *Guanxi* provides a balance to the cumbersome Chinese bureaucracy by giving individuals a way to circumvent rules through the activation of personal relations. Developing, cultivating, and expanding one's *guanxi* has become a common preoccupation and a form of social investment (Wall, 1990). Since China began economic reform and opened the door to the outside world in 1979, *guanxi* has become even more important (Luo, 1997). For firms lacking marketing experience, distinctive competencies, or distribution channels, it is very important to cultivate *guanxi* to compensate for their deficiencies (Xin & Pearce, 1996). Eventually, they can build a *guanxi* network of their own, which could help them gain access to and expand their local markets (Luo, 1997). In other words, a firm could enhance its performance by benefiting from the *guanxi* network it has established.

Because institutions are often situation specific, the institutional characteristics of a country should be evaluated with regard to a specific phenomenon rather than in terms of general arrangements (Ahlstrom & Bruton, 2006; Busenitz, Gomez, & Spencer, 2000; Orru, Biggart, & Hamilton, 1991). It thus follows that the use of *guanxi* will be more prevalent for the newer, smaller businesses or those under private ownership. For instance, studies indicate that entrepreneurial firms in emerging economies face the risks of being domiciled in environments that are unpredictable and volatile, where property rights are uncertain and markets for goods and capital are in a very nascent stage (Bruton & Ahlstrom, 2003; Lockett & Wright, 2002). Moreover, entrepreneurs with strong network ties to state firms and state bureaucrats as sources of raw materials, marketing outlets, and official protection will be greatly advantaged (Parish & Michelson, 1996).

The extensive use of network resources has been a common strategy for entrepreneurs in many countries, including those with advanced economies. Network ties have played a significant role in western economic life for a long time, and evidence has increasingly indicated the rapid growth of economic networking in recent years and even the rise of a network form of organizations (Keister, 2009; Lazerson, 1995; Podolny & Page, 1998). In addition, there is evidence that entrepreneurs in transition economies rely on strategies that their counterparts in established capitalist economies also use (Peng, 2000). Among the more common strategies are the use of personal networks, prospecting, and boundary blurring. Using personal networks allows economic actors to cope under conditions of uncertainty (Keister, 2009). The "network approach to entrepreneurship" is basically developed in an advanced economy context. This literature assumes that network resources, networking activities, and network support are heavily used to establish new firms. The network of the entrepreneurial firms provides access to relevant market information, which allows for the discovery and exploitation of profitable opportunities. The network also helps firms in the early phase to access, mobilize, and deploy resources in order to exploit the opportunities they have spotted. Moreover, a venture has to deal with the liability of newness. The more innovative it is, the greater challenges it faces when acquiring support from stakeholders or legitimacy in a local community. Network ties can help organizations overcome legitimacy barriers (Aldrich & Fiol, 1994; Elfring & Hulsink, 2003; Van de Ven, 1993).

In addition to the facilitation of entrepreneurial activities, social networks can serve as an alternative governance mechanism above autonomous firms to coordinate their activities or help them overcome environmental hazards (Granovetter, 1995). In most emerging economies, although firms remain legally independent, a myriad of economic and social ties connect firms into business groups. These ties enable member firms to coordinate their actions in product markets or the markets for inputs. Many groups span a diverse set of industries, and most of them are connected to an extended family or a non-family holding entity. Such groups are evident in many emerging economies and control a substantial proportion of some countries' productive assets and account for a large share of the countries' firms (Khanna & Rivkin, 2001, 2006). Scholars who uphold a political economy perspective regard business groups as means to foster state control and advance industrial development. They are devices of the state to achieve both political and economic policy objectives. The state can promote or nurture the formation and growth of business groups by direct investment in the establishment of large business groups in specific industries that are regarded as the backbone to a nation or a local region's economy (Khanna & Fisman, 2004; Yiu, Lu, Bruton, & Hoskisson, 2007). The state can also provide critical resources, such as funds and subsidies, business licenses, technology, land, and information to foster or develop business groups that the state considers strategic (Guthrie, 1997; Keister, 1998, 2001; Tsui-Auch & Lee, 2003). For instance, Chinese business groups often function to fill ownership voids because their institutional traits are distinct from those of other types of state-owned shareholdings. Business groups are thus expected to play a more important role in the corporate governance and hence to positively impact the performance of state-owned listed companies in China's transition economy (Ma, Yao, & Xi, 2006). Some scholars believe that business groups based on particularistic relationships are a transient phenomenon in emerging economies. During market-oriented transition, family and prior social ties could improve group performance by providing informal norms that strengthen the intermediation within business groups, and family relationships could reduce strategic restructuring and generate performance benefits (Keister, 2009). Consistent with the market transition theory, researchers found that the positive contribution of family members rises up to a threshold, after which additional family members tend to adversely affect group performance. However, this is not because of the decline of the marginal contribution of additional family involvement to the group's efficiency, but because high family control may discount the legitimacy of these firms in the eyes of foreign investors (Luo & Chung, 2013).

However, such a view of foreign investors toward business organizations may be an unfair and distorted response to Asian capitalism as a result of ethnocentrism, which is defined as a western-based view of the proper organization and functioning of a market economy. Biggart and Hamilton (1992) argued that American economic thinking is largely based on the neoclassical economic tradition, which regarded competition between autonomous economic actors as a necessity of mature capitalism. In contrast with the U.S., which has institutionalized competitive individualism in its market structure, Asian economies are organized through networks of economic actors that are believed to be natural and appropriate to economic development. Asian nations thus have institutionalized policies and practices that originate from a network vision of market relations (Hamilton, 1996; Hamilton & Biggart, 1988). Biggart and Hamilton (1992) contended that the western academic and popular conceptualizations of Asia, particularly those based on the neoclassical model, are biased portrayals of Asian economic dynamics. Analysts who uphold such a western perspective may conclude that Asia's network capitalism is just a result of market imperfections, and therefore that the vibrant capitalism of the region has been artificially induced and maintained (Hamilton & Feenstra, 1998). Biggart and Hamilton (1992) believe that the successful network structure of Asian capitalism suggests the neoclassical model to be not a general theory of capitalism, but rather an ethnocentric model developed from western experience and applicable only to western economies. Such an argument does not intend to negate the utility of neoclassical economics, rather, it tries to point out that such a theory may be limited to settings where its institutional assumptions are in force (Biggart & Hamilton, 1992).

Such a view is also held by Boisot and Child (1996). They argued that China's economic growth makes people believe that its economic system is moving toward market capitalism. However, China has distinctive political, institutional, and cultural characteristics, and such factors can give rise to different modes of economic organization. They proposed a C-space framework to analyze the difference between the modernization process of China and Europe. This framework is associated with the extent to which transaction related information can be diffused and shared within a target population and to how far it can be codified. Codification refers to the selection and compression of data into stable structures. The movement toward greater codification corresponds to a shift from a high context to low context system. It stimulates and facilitates but does not guarantee decentralization and the development of large-scale markets. Using the codification/diffusion framework, Boisot and Child (1988) argued that China would have been inhibited in decentralizing from bureaucracies to markets because it had not built up a stable codified bureaucratic order from which to decentralize. The Chinese system is still reproducing the model of organization specific to the relations between the ministries, governments at various levels, and the enterprises within their hegemony. Transactions between governmental bodies and their enterprises that are conducted at arm's length through markets are still managed through personal interactions.

Therefore it is not the presence of networking that makes China distinctive; rather it is the depth and nature of the embeddedness that makes it different from others. Through the implicit and dynamic relationships, this network capitalism helps handle complexity and uncertainties. Networks have greater capacities for generating and transmitting new information, and interpersonal trust offers a cushion against possible various risks. The networks of the emergent Chinese capitalism thus are qualitatively different from those within the western market system (Boisot & Child, 1996).

A Corporatist State?

Whereas the new institutionalism theories postulate that market institutions will become mature and eventually play a greater role in the transitional economy, the state corporatist approaches emphasize that the state will continue to be prevalent and relevant. It is argued that China's rapid industrial growth in the 1980s was largely due to favorable fiscal contracts, which created incentives for local bureaucracies and officials who dominated the industrial development of their jurisdictions (Oi, 1992, 1999; Walder, 1995; Wong, 1992). The highly decentralized fiscal administrative system and the resulting entrepreneurial behaviors of the local government contribute to the improvement of the financial performance of the rural industrial enterprises (Park, Rozelle, Wong, & Ren, 1996; Walder, 1992, 1995). New terms such as local government entrepreneurship (Walder, 1995, 1998), local state corporatism (Oi, 1992, 1999), and corporate culture (Unger & Chan, 1995; Weitzman & Xu, 1994) were invented to describe the nature of these activities and patterns of government-enterprise relationship. Although they vary in their approaches, all these explanations converge on the same institutional variable—the decentralized fiscal reform which lead to the intensified fiscal interests of local government in the local enterprises' financial performance. This factor explains the entrepreneurial behavior that was observed among rural officials frequently in the 1980s (Byrd & Gelb, 1990; Oi, 1992, 1999; Walder, 1995; Wong, 1988, 1992).

Oi (1992, 1999) believed that the impressive rural industrial growth between 1978 and 1988 is in large measure a result of active local government intervention in the business affairs of their enterprises. She uses the phrase "local state corporatism" to summarize the workings of a local government that coordinates economic enterprises in its territory as if it were a diversified business corporation. Nee (1992) also acknowledged that although local corporatism may exacerbate the macro economy, this institutional arrangement represents a locally efficient solution to the problem of incomplete market structures and institutional foundations for a market economy. Weitzman and Xu (1994) argued that China's township and village enterprises are vaguely defined cooperatives and concluded that the success of China's transition from central planning to a market economy was due to the existence of a corporatist culture. The corporative capacity of China is larger than that of the East European countries. Lin (1995) pointed out that this local coordination perspective allows us to understand how and why locally embedded socio-cultural institutions coordinate rather than compete with each other in order to compete more efficiently in the external or global market.

Instead of treating the corporative character as an exogenous factor, corporatists (Oi, 1992, 1999; Unger & Chan, 1995; Walder, 1995, 1998) believe that the formation of local state corporatism is a direct result of the macrolevel fiscal institutional change in the 1980s. They argued that fiscal reform has assigned local governments (county, township, and village level in this argument) property rights over increased income and has created strong incentives for local officials to pursue local economic development. Fiscal reform gives local governments the rights over the income flow of their firms. They can decide as a corporation how to use profits from its various enterprises and how to redistribute income. They can control the operation of their enterprises through the selection of management personnel and through control over the allocation of scarce production inputs, provision of services, and investment and credit decisions. In this process local governments have taken on many characteristics of a business corporation, with officials acting as the equivalent of a board of directors.

It is argued that the relationships between levels of government and between government and enterprises have changed substantially as a consequence of fiscal reform. First, the fiscal contract system cut off the local fiscal reliance on higher-level government; local governments are permitted to maintain any fiscal residuals and are also responsible for local fiscal deficiencies. Local governments in the new fiscal regime are no longer central agents who collect taxes for the ministry of finance (Wong, 1992); instead they are economic actors with independent fiscal interests. Second, fiscal reforms have served the function of clarifying the rights of local governments over assets they administer and reallocating property rights downward within government hierarchies. This explains why fiscal reform provides all governments and enterprises with the same incentives although their outcomes are different. Higher-level governments have larger capability in economic coordination; they often control many enterprises and have various non-financial interests in them. The fiscal contract system does not weaken such capability and the financial pressure higher-level governments felt is weak. Things are different in lower-level governments: the fiscal contract hardened their budget, and their economic interests are directly linked to the financial performance of enterprises in their jurisdiction, therefore the financial pressure they felt is larger. In addition, they often control a much smaller number of enterprises and have fewer non-financial interests in them (Walder, 1995). Kornai's (1992) analysis has overlooked the above issues, but these organizational characteristics contribute to the tightening budget constraints of both governments and firms. In his theory, Walder (1995, 1998) highlighted the importance of local governments and the rule of entrepreneurial local political actors in shaping the trajectory of transition.

Krug and Hendrischke (2008) further developed the theory of local state corporatism by introducing the coevolution perspective into the analysis. They pointed out that unlike the coevolution between macro- and microlevel institutions in the new classical theory, the interaction between micro- and macro-institutions proceeds in a reverse mechanism. That is, the increasing use of microlevel institutions created demand for and increased the effectiveness of macrolevel institutions. In this coevolution model, the macrolevel government often initiates the coevolution by creating an institutional space at the lower levels by decentralizing the decision-making power, reducing direct interferences from the higher levels, and refraining from the temptation of early institutionalization of local practices. With such incentives and autonomy, local governments began to explore new systems in coordinating local economic activities and competed with each other for limited resources and markets. When local institutional reform yields positive outcomes in terms of economic growth, the macrolevel government has the incentive for coevolution in the form of reduced or selective interference. Ultimately, this coevolution path enables local differentiation and adaptation to specific circumstances and defines the overarching framework of a national business system.

The local state corporatist approach diverges from new institutionalism in its prediction about the future of economic coordination in transition economies. Whereas the new institutionalist approach implies that transition will ultimately lead to a market-based capitalism similar to western capitalism, state corporatism suggests that transition is better conceived of as a transformation. In other developing societies, marketization often causes clientelism not to disappear but only to mutate from traditional to modern forms. With the increase of national-level economic integration and state intervention, local elites come to assume the role of bridge ties and mediators. This economic and political mediation between the still segmented sectors gives rise to a government-based political patronage. Therefore, a revisionist market transition perspective also suggests that local administrators may well continue to hold onto considerable local power—not despite but because of marketization (Parish & Michelson, 1996). This suggests the reforms might eventually create new forms of organizing economic activity that are unique and perhaps well suited to the context. The unique histories and experiences of transition economies may produce unprecedented forms of coordination (King & Szelényi, 2005; Parish & Michelson, 1996; Stark & Bruszt, 1998; Walder, 2003; Zhou, Li, Zhao, & Cai, 2003).

Judging from a state-building perspective, corporatist policies, in addition to the function of coordinating economic activities, are indispensable for the state to maintain proper social order in a society with increasingly divergent interest groups. Gao (2009) argued that as private entrepreneurs and their business organizations gained power in the economic sphere, they developed a propensity for asserting their interest in politics and using their business associations to pursue their individual and collective goods. Because democratization is not an option for the state, corporatist mechanisms become a good compromise in this context. Instead of seeking autonomy from the state, corporate groups in China are embedded in the state, and the state can strengthen or relax its control over these groups by manipulating the leadership of these groups, the allocation of resources, and so forth (Dickson, 2003). Meanwhile, various sector-based associations are established and can influence the policy-making processes to differing extents based on their institutional distance from the state. It was argued that over the past two decades, the policy-making process at various levels began to be more incorporative of diversified interests voiced by the newly emergent social groups. This process helped the state to reduce political risks. However, the corporatist model encouraged the maintenance of strong links among business and political elites, and this may have lead to the misuse of political power in achieving private economic gains. In some cases, this may have created tension and conflict that weakened the legitimacy of the party state (Gao, 2009).

Overview of the Chapters

As Meyer (2011) has mentioned, framing the Chinese system in terms of the familiar capitalist system or an emerging alternative model is crucial in order to anticipate how western and Chinese economies will interact and move forward. Although western observers wish to see a more congenial China where western business communities can extend their reach, the reality might be that China and western capitalists may identify more profound differences than prima facie similarities. Instead of anticipating the convergence of the systems in the future, we may need to question the assumption that China will eventually evolve toward a familiar form of capitalism.

Therefore, it is important to continue scholarly investigation to address the fundamental problems associated with China's transition process. Specifically, we need to understand whether the economic order that emerged from the previous system is capitalist as understood by western observers, or does it require its own specific designation? If there emerges a distinctive system, then what kind of roles does the state play in its operation (Boisot & Child, 1996), and how do the state and the business community interact to promote further evolution of the business as well as the political system?

In this book, we present a set of empirical studies that relate China's distinctive institutional characteristics to the behaviors and strategies of individual entrepreneurs, firms, and crucial entities with other organizational forms. We pay special attention to the mechanisms through which government intervention and intergovernmental competitions shape the trajectory of economic development, and the ways that government and firms are connected and interact. These intervention and coordination mechanisms, we believe, are important elements of China's emerging economic order. The book as a whole should be read as an initial attempt to advance the research that its subject richly deserves, its purpose at this stage being to highlight the importance of the aforementioned bigger questions rather than to offer comprehensive and adequate answers.

In this introductory chapter, we have mentioned that scholars from multiple disciplines have devoted tremendous effort to understanding the nature and mechanisms underlying this transition. We presented an overview of the transition processes and critical review of the literature on organization and management issues in the transition context. We focused on studies that investigate how the transitional institutional context conditions the behaviors of organizations and managers, how organizations, managers, and entrepreneurs adapt to this change by adopting new management practices and strategies, and how organizational networks form and evolve as the transition proceeds.

With this introduction to the Chinese institutional context during the reform era, we then move to the discussion of how institutional factors conditioned firms' strategies in handling relationships with various stakeholders in their environment. In Chapter 2, we explore the evolution of firms' networking strategies from a longitudinal perspective. We noticed that although the importance of interorganizational networks to business success has attracted considerable research attention, relatively little research has explored the changing patterns and significance of networks (networking) over time during the institutional transformation. In this chapter, we fill such a gap by developing an institutional embeddedness argument to explain these processes and analyzing archival and survey data to study these processes empirically. We find that the importance of state ties has declined somewhat, whereas ties with market actors have become more important. Determinants of networking investment have shifted from managers' perceived importance of network ties to a firm's immediate institutional environment. Finally, the impact of networking on performance has decoupled over time. These findings deepen our understanding of the coevolution processes between the institutional environment and firms' networking strategies.

In Chapter 3, we change the subjects of our study and investigate how foreign entrants use various political strategies to gain legitimacy and seek survival in an emerging economy context. We develop a neo-institutional framework explaining the observed heterogeneity in Foreign Invested Enterprises' (FIE) use of political strategies in the transitional context. We argue that the relative potency of the dual institutional pressure from both home and host countries conditions FIEs' choices. Three levels of institutional factors—country of origin and cultural distance at the country level, local marketization and rank of cities at the regional level, and ownership type and resource dependence at the firm level—strongly affect the adoption of a wide range of corporate political strategies. In addition, FIEs use foreign and domestic business associations as collective venues to strengthen firm-government relations. Member firms are more likely to employ multiple types of strategies, and compared with foreign business associations, domestic business associations are more effective in helping firms gain opportunities to interact with political actors.

In addition to discussing strategies adopted by domestic and foreign corporations, we diverted our attention to the strategies taken by the nascent entrepreneurial context and explore how entrepreneurs use connections to business as well as political actors to mobilize financial resources in less-developed regions. In Chapter 4, we analyze large-scale household survey data and find that entrepreneurs' access to debt-financing sources is conditioned by the resources embedded in their social networks. Business and political contacts increase entrepreneurs' access to formal financial resources, and urban contacts increase access to informal resources. However, the effects of business and bureaucratic ties are contingent on the level of institutional trust in a region and on firms' stages of development. Regarding access to formal sectors, business ties are more effective for older firms and for firms in high-trust regions, whereas bureaucratic ties are more effective for younger firms and for firms in low-trust regions.

The second theme of this book is to investigate how Chinese firms adopted innovative management practices, and how intergovernmental interactions promote the establishment of premarket economic policies. In Chapter 5 we argue that adaptation to radical change is central to research in organization theory, and some of the most dramatic examples of environmental change have occurred recently in China. In this chapter, we study the relative importance of organizational and environmental factors in producing innovative managerial responses. We find that strategic choice predicted innovation in the early stages of reform, but environmental factors increased in salience over time. Intrafirm support, communist party connections, and a market orientation produced innovation early in reform. Simple imitation of others was also salient in early years. As reform progressed, managers increasingly imitated other profitable firms but also drew on their own experience. Our results inform an understanding of both the process by which innovation occurs and firm behavior in transition economies.

We then turned our attention to the collaborative relationships between public and private entities. Specifically, in Chapter 6 we focus on public-private partnership, which has gained popularity during the liberalization reforms in infrastructure sectors around the world. As China is integrated into the world economy, China's private sector becomes a major force that redefines the landscape of the local infrastructure markets. Despite widespread adoption of the pro-market policies, cities differ greatly in the extent to which they allow the private sector to participate in these sectors. Building on the literature of policy diffusion and innovations, we argue in this chapter that the internal characteristics of cities, pressure from neighboring and structurally equivalent peer cities, and influence from provincial governments as well as policy research communities strongly affect the extent of local liberalization reforms. We consider the effects of these factors on the adoption of a set of Public-Private Partnership (PPP) arrangements that represents different levels of private involvement. We find generally robust support for our arguments, using an analysis of projects with private participation in Chinese prefecture cities. The results also reveal interactive relationships between diffusion mechanisms: the increasing influence from peer cities undermines the influence of neighbor cities, and the growing influence from provincial governments also reduces the effectiveness of epistemic influence and peer pressure.

The last substantive section of this book relates to the formation and evolution of business groups in China. The two chapters in this section study the impact of this special governance system on firms' performance from a longitudinal perspective. Chapter 7 describes the changing relationship patterns in the conventionally defined business groups. We note that the interfirm relations developed in business groups during economic transition are central to China's reform and are becoming an important part of the country's emergent economic structure. Using an original dataset that includes direct observations of firms' economic choices, we explore the process by which these interfirm lending and trade ties emerged and evolved in the early stages of reform. Initially, information from sources external to the network dominated the formation and direction of exchange relations. Firms turned to their prior connections, took advantage of market position, and drew on bureaucratic power to develop alliances. Over time, internal influences gained importance, and managers increasingly drew on internal nontrade relations and other indicators inside the business group to identify lending and trade partners. This chapter contributes to an understanding of organizational adaptation to a major economic transition and of interfirm alliance formation more generally. The findings reveal that firms select exchange partners of known reputation and solicit relations that reduce uncertainty, even when there is a cost involved.

In addition to the study of conventionally defined business groups, we also explored the structure and impact of state-led business groups, which were established on the basis of China's decentralized state-owned asset management system. In Chapter 8, we focus on the publicly listed firms and argue that the emergence and development of Chinese stock markets enables firms to expand their control over multiple firms across different business sectors. These cross-holding relationships give rise to a special network pattern in the stock market, allowing us to investigate the structure of the interconnected corporate world and the mechanisms that underlie its changes. In this chapter, we reconstruct the cross-holding networks based on published information of the 10 largest shareholders of the listed firms. We examine the changes in cross-holding network patterns from 1996 to 2012. We then investigate the impact of the ultimate owners' status, the diversification of the business groups, and the group governance structure on member firms' performance. This study allows us to better understand how governments maintain or transform their control power over the backbones of the nation's economy in the new institutional context.

In the last section of this book, we briefly summarize the findings yielded from the multiple studies incorporated in this book. We discuss what we learned about the Chinese experience and explore its theoretical as well as practical implications. We argue that our study sheds light on the issue of how a vibrant market economy coexists with a powerful authoritarian state and how this coexistence influences the nature and pace of China's economic modernization. The answer to this question not only helps us understand the change process in other transitional or emerging economies but also is theoretically useful to understanding changes in industrialized economies.

References

Ahlstrom, D., & Bruton, G. D. (2006). Venture capital in emerging economies: Networks and institutional change. *Entrepreneurship Theory and Practice, 30*(2), 299–320.

Aldrich, H. E., & Fiol, C. M. (1994). Fools rush in? The institutional context of industry creation. *Academy of Management Review, 19*(4), 645–670.

Biggart, N. W., & Hamilton, G. G. (1990, Auguest). The Western bias of neoclassical economics: on the limits of a firm-based theory to explain business networks. In *Networks and Organizations Conference*, Harvard Business School.

Blanchard, O., & Shleifer, A. (2001). Federalism with and without political centralization: China versus Russia. *IMF Staff Papers, 48*(4), 8.

Boisot, M., & Child, J. (1988). The iron law of fiefs: Bureaucratic failure and the problem of governance in the Chinese economic reforms. *Administrative Science Quarterly, 33*, 507–527.

Boisot, M., & Child, J. (1996). From fiefs to clans and network capitalism: Explaining China's emerging economic order. *Administrative Science Quarterly, 41*, 600–628.

Borys, B., & Jemison, D. B. (1989). Hybrid arrangements as strategic alliances: Theoretical issues in organizational combinations. *Academy of Management Review, 14*(2), 234–249.

Brinton, M. C., & Nee, V. (1998). *The New Institutionalism in Sociology*. New York: Russell Sage Foundation.

Bruton, G. D., & Ahlstrom, D. (2003). An institutional view of China's venture capital industry: Explaining the differences between China and the West. *Journal of Business Venturing, 18*(2), 233–259.

Busenitz, L. W., Gomez, C., & Spencer, J. W. (2000). Country institutional profiles: Interlocking entrepreneurial phenomena. *Academy of Management Journal, 43*, 994–1003.

Byrd, W., & Gelb, A. (1990). Why industrialization? The incentive for rural community governments. In W. A. Byrd & Q. Lin (Eds.), *China's Rural Industry: Structure, Development and Reform* (pp. 358–388). New York: Oxford University Press.

Chen, C. C., Chen, X. P., & Huang, S. (2013). Chinese Guanxi: An integrative review and new directions for future research. *Management and Organization Review, 9*(1), 167–207.

Davis, D. (1999). Self-employment in Shanghai: A research note. *The China Quarterly, 157*, 22–43.

Dickson, B. J. (2003). *Red Capitalists in China: The Party, Private Entrepreneurs, and Prospects for Political Change*. Cambridge, UK: Cambridge University Press.

Elfring, T., & Hulsink, W. (2003). Networks in entrepreneurship: The case of high-technology firms. *Small Business Economics, 21*(4), 409–422.

Fligstein, N., & Zhang, J. (2011). A new agenda for research on the trajectory of Chinese capitalism. *Management and Organziation Review, 7*(1), 39–62.

Gao, B. (2009). The Rubik's cube state: A reconceptualization of political change in contemporary China. *Research in the Sociology of Work, 19*, 409–438.

Granovetter, M. (1995). Coase revisited: Business groups in the modern economy. *Industrial and Corporate Change, 4*(1), 93–130.

Guthrie, D. (1997). Between markets and politics: Organizational responses to reform in China. *American Journal of Sociology, 102*(5), 1258–1304.

Guthrie, D. (1998). The declining significance of guanxi in China's economic transition. *The China Quarterly, 39*, 254–282.

Hall, P. A., & Soskice, D. W. (Eds.). (2001). *Varieties of Capitalism: The Institutional Foundations of Comparative Advantage*. New York: Oxford University Press.

Hamilton, G. G. (1996). *Asian Business Networks* (Vol. 64). Berlin and New York: Walter de Gruyter.

Hamilton, G. G., & Biggart, N. W. (1988). Market, culture, and authority: A comparative analysis of management and organization in the Far East. *American Journal of Sociology, 94*, S52–S94.

Hamilton, G. G., & Feenstra, R. (1998). The organization of economies. In M. C. Brinton & V. Nee (Eds.), *The New Institutionalism in Sociology* (pp. 153–180). New York: Russell Sage Foundation.

Hoskisson, R. E., Eden, L., Lau, C. M., & Wright, M. (2000). Strategy in emerging economies. *The Academy of Management Journal, 43*(3), 249–267.

Jin, H., Qian, Y., & Weingast, B. R. (2005). Regional decentralization and fiscal incentives: Federalism, Chinese style. *Journal of Public Economics, 89*(9), 1719–1742.

Keister, L. A. (1998). Engineering growth: Business group structure and firm performance in China's transition economy. *American Journal of Sociology, 104*(2), 404–440.

Keister, L. A. (2001). Exchange structures in transition: Lending and trade relations in Chinese business groups. *American Sociological Review, 66*(3), 336–360.

Keister, L. A. (2009). Organizational research on market transition: A sociological approach. *Asia Pacific Journal of Management, 26*(4), 719–742.

Keister, L. A., & Zhang, Y. (2009). 8 organizations and management in China. *The Academy of Management Annals, 3*(1), 377–420.

Khanna, T., & Fisman, F. (2004). Facilitating development: The role of business groups. *World Development, 32*, 609–628.

Khanna, T., & Rivkin, J. W. (2001). Estimating the performance effects of business groups in emerging markets. *Strategic Management Journal, 22*, 45–74.

Khanna, T., & Rivkin, J. W. (2006). Interorganizational ties and business group boundaries: Evidence from an emerging economy. *Organization Science, 17*(3), 333–352.

King, L. P., & Szelényi, I. (2005). Post-communist economic systems. In N. J. Smelser & R. Swedberg (Eds.), *The Handbook of Economic Sociology* (pp. 205–229). Princeton, NJ: Princeton University Press.

Kornai, J. (1992). *The Socialist System: The Political Economy of Communism: The Political Economy of Communism*. New York: Oxford University Press.

Krug, B., & Hendrischke, H. (2008). Framing China: Transformation and institutional change through co-evolution. *Management and Organization Review, 4*(1), 81–108.

Lazerson, M. (1995). A new phoenix?: Modern putting-out in the Modena knitwear industry. *Administrative Science Quarterly, 40*, 34–59.

Lee, S.-H., Peng, M. W., & Barney, J. B. (2007). Bankruptcy law and entrepreneurship development: A real options perspective. *Academy of Management Review, 32*(1), 257–272.

Lin, N. (1995). Local market socialism: Local corporatism in action in rural China. *Theory and Society, 24*(3), 301–354.

Lin, N. (2011). Capitalism in China: A centrally managed capitalism (CMC) and its future. *Management and Organization Review, 7*(1), 63–96.

Lockett, A., & Wright, M. (2002). Venture capital in Asia and the Pacific Rim. *Venture Capital: An International Journal of Entrepreneurial Finance, 4*(3), 183–195.

Lovett, S., Simmons, L. C., & Kali, R. (1999). Guanxi versus the market: Ethics and efficiency. *Journal of International Business Studies, 30*, 231–247.

Luo, X. R., & Chung, C. N. (2013). Filling or abusing the institutional void? Ownership and management control of public family businesses in an emerging market. *Organization Science, 24*(2), 591–613.

Luo, Y. (1997). Guanxi and performance of foreign-invested enterprises in China: An empirical inquiry. *MIR: Management International Review, 37,* 51–70.

Luo, Y., & Chen, M. (1997). Does guanxi influence firm performance? *Asia Pacific Journal of Management, 14*(1), 1–16.

Ma, X., Yao, X., & Xi, Y. (2006). Business group affiliation and firm performance in a transition economy: A focus on ownership voids. *Asia Pacific Journal of Management, 23*(4), 467–483.

Meyer, M. W. (2011). Is it capitalism? *Management and Organization Review, 7*(1), 5–18.

Naughton, B. (2007). *The Chinese Economy: Transitions and Growth.* Cambridge, MA: MIT Press.

Nee, V. (1989). A theory of market transition: From redistribution to markets in state socialism. *American Sociological Review, 54,* 663–681.

Nee, V. (1992). Organizational dynamics of market transition: Hybrid forms, property rights, and mixed economy in China. *Administrative Science Quarterly, 37,* 1–27.

Nee, V. (2005). The new institutionalisms in economics and sociology. In N. J. Smelser & R. Swedberg (Eds.), *The Handbook of Economic Sociology* (pp. 49–74). Princeton, NJ: Princeton University Press.

Nee, V., & Opper, S. (2009). Bringing market transition theory to the firm. *Research in the Sociology of Work, 19,* 3–34.

North, D. C. (1990). *Institutions, Institutional Change, and Economic Performance.* New York: Cambridge University Press.

Oi, J. (1992). Fiscal reform and the economic foundations of local state corporatism in China. *World Politics, 45,* 99–126.

Oi, J. (1999). *Rural China Takes Off: Institutional Foundations of Economic Reform.* Berkeley, CA: University of California Press.

Oliver, C. (1991). Strategic responses to institutional processes. *Academy of Management Review, 1,* 145–179.

Orru, M., Biggart, N. W., & Hamilton, G. G. (1991). Organizational Isomorphism in East Asia: Broadening the New Institutionalism. In Walter W. Powell & Paul J. DiMaggio (Eds.) *The New Institutionalism in Organizational Analysis* (pp. 361–389). Chicago and London: The University of Chicago Press.

Parish, W., & Michelson, E. (1996). Politics and markets: Dual transformation. *American Journal of Sociology, 101,* 1042–1059.

Park, A., Rozelle, S., Wong, C., & Ren, C. (1996). Distributional consequences of reforming local public finance in China. *The China Quarterly, 147,* 751–778.

Peng, M. W. (1997). Firm growth in transition economies: Three longitudinal cases from China, 1989–1996. *Organziation Studies, 18,* 385–413.

Peng, M. W. (2000). *Business Strategies in Transition Economies.* Thousand Oaks, CA: Sage.

Peng, M. W. (2003). Institutional transitions and strategic choices. *Academy of Management Review, 28*(2), 275–296.

Podolny, J. M., & Page, K. L. (1998). Network forms of organization. *Annual Review of Sociology, 24,* 57–76.

Stark, D. (1992). Path dependence and privatization strategies in East Central Europe. *East European Politics and Societies, 6,* 17–54.

Stark, D., & Bruszt, L. (1998). *Postsocialist Pathways: Transforming Politics and Property in East Central Europe.* Cambridge, UK: Cambridge University Press.

Tsui-Auch, L. S., & Lee, Y.-J. (2003). The state matters: Management models of Singaporean Chinese and Korean business groups. *Organization Studies, 24*(4), 507–534.

Unger, J., & Chan, A. (1995). China, corporatism, and the East Asian model. *The Australian Journal of Chinese Affairs, 33,* 29–53.

Van de Ven, H. (1993). The development of an infrastructure for entrepreneurship. *Journal of Business Venturing, 8*(3), 211–230.

Walder, A. G. (1992). Property rights and stratification in socialist redistributive economies. *American Sociological Review, 57,* 524–539.

Walder, A. G. (1995). Local governments as industrial firms: An organizational analysis of China's transitional economy. *American Journal of Sociology,* 263–301.

Walder, A. G. (1998). *Zouping in Transition.* Cambridge, MA: Harvard University Press.

Walder, A. G. (2003). Elite opportunity in transitional economies. *American Sociological Review, 68,* 899–916.

Wall, J. A. (1990). Managers in the people's republic of China. *Academy of Management Executive, 4*(2), 19–32.

Weitzman, M. L., & Xu, C. (1994). Chinese township-village enterprises as vaguely defined cooperatives. *Journal of Comparative Economics, 18*(2), 121–145.

Wong, C. P. (1988). Interpreting rural industrial growth in the post-Mao period. *Modern China, 14,* 3–30.

Wong, C. P. (1992). Fiscal reform and local industrialization: The problematic sequencing of reform in post-Mao China. *Modern China, 18,* 197–227.

Wright, M., Filatotchev, I., Hoskisson, R. E., & Peng, M. W. (2005). Strategy research in emerging economies: Challenging the conventional wisdom. *Journal of Management Studies, 42*(1), 1–33.

Xin, K. K., & Pearce, J. L. (1996). Guanxi: Connections as substitutes for formal institutional support. *Academy of Management Journal, 39*(6), 1641–1658.

Yeung, W.-C. (2003). *Chinese Capitalism in a Global Era: Towards a Hybrid Capitalism.* New York: Routledge.

Yiu, D. W., Lu, Y., Bruton, G. D., & Hoskisson, R. E. (2007). Business groups: An integrated model to focus future research. *Journal of Management Studies, 44*(8), 1551–1579.

Zheng, Y. (2004). *Globalization and State Transformation in China.* New York: Cambridge University Press.

Zhou, J. Q., & Peng, M. W. (2010). Relational exchanges versus arm's-length transactions during institutional transitions. *Asia Pacific Journal of Management, 27,* 355–370.

Zhou, X., Li, Q., Zhao, W., & Cai, H. (2003). Embeddedness and contractual relationships in China's transitional economy. *American Sociological Review, 68,* 75–102.

2 Institutional Changes, Stakeholder Salience, and Network-Based Strategies

As more firms filed their annual reports, the financial details of the A-share listed companies became public. Statistics show that there are nine firms that posted over 100 million yuan business entertaining expenses. Among these nine firms, China Railway Construction Corporation Ltd (CRCC) reported that their entertaining expenses in 2012 were 837 million yuan. The total of the top ten companies on the list amounts to 2.9 billion yuan. During a telephone interview, the CEO of CRCC argued that "is that number big? Other firms have even higher entertaining expenses, they just manipulated their books." A small business owner commented that "from my point of view, the entertaining expenses are necessary for business growth, as long as they are legal, we should allow it. If there is no such expenses, then it is difficult to maintain good relations with major clients." The Dean of Fudan University's economics school argued that "in order to get more business opportunities, firms may use some resources to build their guanxi network, this may bring them financial benefits. Most shareholders are willing to pay such costs." Other people disagree, they claim that firms should use the precious capital more strategically, and invest more in product innovation, technology improvement, hiring talent, or expanding markets rather than on networking or luxurious consumption.

—Ye Huang, *International Finance News*, 2013–5–7

The study of network-based strategies has been one of the leading themes in strategy research on emerging economics in general and in Asia in particular (Guillen, 2000; Khanna & Palepu, 1999, 2000; Park & Luo, 2001; Peng, 2003; Peng & Heath, 1996; Peng & Luo, 2000; Peng & Zhou, 2005; Perotti & Gelfer, 2001; Spicer, McDermott, & Kogut, 2000; Xin & Pearce, 1996). Extant research has documented the extensive utilization of a network and the significant impact of strategic networking on firm performance (Li, Meng, Wang, & Zhou, 2008; Luo, 2003; Park & Luo, 2001), market benefits (Davies & Walters, 2004), and competitive advantages (Tsang, 1998; Yeung & Tung, 1996). Whereas most studies conclude that networking has played an important role during the market transition, there are disagreements regarding whether the significance of social networking and its impact on firms' performance will persist over time.

Another school of researchers who subscribe to institutional theories stress that institutional conditions are important contingent factors which shape the relative costs and benefits of firms' strategic choices. In their view, neither network-based strategies nor institutional contexts are static. In fact, they interact with each other and coevolve in the process of market transitions. For example, Xin and Pearce (1996) argue that social networks function as substitutes for formal institutional support, which is characterized by the state's remnant control of resources and opportunities (Li et al., 2008), personalized bureaucratic administrations (Boisot & Child, 1996), government intervention in firms' operations (Ahlstrom, Bruton, & Lui, 2000), and weak legal protection of property rights (Hoskisson, Eden, Lau, & Wright, 2000; Peng, 2003). These institutional imperfections make market transactions costly and uncertain. Managers thus often seek and utilize social connections with various stakeholders to gain legitimacy or seek institutional support. Some firms further utilize social networking as a strategic mechanism to overcome competitive and resource disadvantages in underdeveloped markets (Park & Luo, 2001).

Following the logic of this institutional substitution thesis, a reasonable inference is that with the development of a market economy and the emergence of successfully functioning market supporting institutions, the importance of social networks should decline (Guthrie, 1998; Peng, 2003). During the institutional transition, as the transaction structure shifts from relationship-based and personalized exchanges to rule-based and impersonal exchanges, networks and connections that were once regarded as imperative for business success will no longer seem as important (Peng, 2003). However, this theoretical proposition has received little support from empirical studies. For example, whereas Guthrie (1998) finds the declining significance of networks, others have the opposite findings during the very same market transition in China (Wank, 1999; Yang, 1994, 2002). In fact, most empirical research indicates the prevalence and persistence of social networking in social and economic life, from interorganizational relationships (Keister, 2002; Luo, 2003) to daily social and economic interactions (Bian, 2002; Lin, 2011; Potter, 2002; Wank, 1999, 2002; Yang, 1994). Evidence from other transitional economies shows that even foreign firms have relatively stable network relationships over time (Stark & Vedres, 2006). Moreover, social networking is prevalent in other institutional contexts, including developed market economies (Granovetter, 1985; Hamilton & Biggart, 1988; Uzzi, 1997) or in multinational business (Ahlstrom, Bruton, & Yeh, 2008; Dyer & Nobeoka, 2000).

These inconsistencies challenge the expectation that with the change in the institutional environment, network-centered strategies will automatically transform into market-centered strategies (Peng, 2003). The logic of this two-stage model is flawed because, for one thing, it is unclear whether the rule-based, impersonal exchange, which implies relatively less extensive or virtually no use of network-based strategies, is a realistic situation or just an ideal type which cannot find a real world prototype. As Boisot and Child (1996) point out, what has happened in many parts of China's economic fields is that the system continues to reproduce a model of organization specific to the relations between the governmental authorities and the enterprises within their hegemony. The impersonal abstract order associated with a decentralization to markets has yet to replace the much more concrete personalized order that delegation within a patrimonial system can allow. In fact, in many Asian cultures, regardless of their progress toward the mature market system, the high embeddedness of business transactions in relational networks is widely documented (Ahlstrom et al., 2008). Even in the developed economies, there is ample evidence that suggests that individuals' economic activities as well as firms' business strategies are also highly embedded in various relational networks (Burt, 1992; Granovetter, 1985; Gulati, 1995; Uzzi, 1999).

In addition, the argument that institutional transition shapes the evolution of network-based business strategies has failed to consider the complexity of the institutional environment and the variety of firms' network-based strategies. Institutional factors have many dimensions, which are closely connected and may change at different speeds. It is suggested that the evolution of the economic institution is not one-dimensional as assumed in the market and hierarchies perspective, in which the policy options are located along a single dimension with the state at the one extremity and market-oriented firms at the other end. China may evolve along a distinct trajectory in which the competitive market coexists with a less codified institutional context, which gives rise to network capitalism (Boisot & Child, 1996). Regarding the variation of firms' networking strategies, extant theoretical arguments on the role of social networks in the transitional economies do not differentiate between different types of networks. They often attempt to make general statements about whether networking as a whole will decline or persist. The lack of scrutiny of the change in the salience of key stakeholders, i.e., suppliers, governments, buyers, and customers, contributes to the inconsistent or even conflicting findings regarding the trend of networking. As the market system becomes more complex, the interests of different stakeholders can be inconsistent with one another. Thus, in different sectors or locations, the power, legitimacy, and urgency of different stakeholders' claims can vary substantially, which demands that firms' leaders pay more attention to these changes and respond to these changes effectively and efficiently. It is necessary to borrow from the stakeholder theory and study how the salience of various stakeholders changes over time and how firms adapt their networking strategies based on their understanding and judgment of the environmental constraints and their impact on stakeholder salience (Agle, Mitchell, & Sonnenfeld, 1999).

Given the aforementioned limitations, it is necessary to use a refined theoretical framework, new data, and solid methods to revisit important issues, such as: (1) Has the network-based strategy changed over time with the progress of market transition? (2) Did the network-based strategy continue to be effective in a changed market and institutional context? Theoretically, we borrow insight from institutional, resource dependence, and stakeholder theories and argue that the dual transition processes, i.e., the institutional transition from a command economy to a market economy and changing patterns of resource allocation and dependence relations have shaped the salience of different stakeholder groups in the emerging context (Agle et al., 1999; Mitchell, Agle, & Wood, 1997). Such changes give some stakeholders' claims increased legitimacy, power, or urgency over others, and thus demand that managers use various resources to satisfy such demands. More importantly, we argue that the improvement of stakeholder relations can be achieved through multiple means. When the overall market-supporting institution is still imperfect, managers may resort to particularistic ties to cultivate and maintain quality stakeholder relations, whereas when institutional quality improves, managers may not have to use the old ways to handle such relations. Alternative means, such as compliance with institutional requirements, improvement of product or service quality, or collective lobbying can emerge to be important ways that allow firms to effectively manage stakeholder relations (Ahlstrom et al., 2008). In terms of performance implications, such evolutions may suggest that the effectiveness of networking with different stakeholders in improving firms' performance may change over time; moreover, when the institutional development reach to a higher level, then the impact of an individual-based networking strategy on firms' performance may diminish.

Institutional Change, Resource Reallocation, and Stakeholders' Salience

Our first question is how institutional changes have affected the salience of stakeholders during the economic transition. Scholars often attribute the prevalence of networking in transitional economies to the institutional imperfections in the transitional societies (Davies et al., 1995; Guillen, 2000; Khanna & Palepu, 1999, 2000; Li et al., 2008; Luo, 2003; Park & Luo, 2001; Peng, 2003; Peng & Heath, 1996; Xin & Pearce, 1996; Yeung & Tung, 1996). It is argued that if the market system functions well and the legal infrastructure is effective, firms can rely on formal structures to pursue rule-based, impersonal transactions. In contrast, where formal institutions are ineffective or even absent, informal constraints will play an important role in facilitating relationship-based, personal exchanges (North, 1990). In this light, "in the absence of the state and formal rules, a dense social network leads to the development of informal structure with substantial stability" (North, 1990: 38).

Managers who attempt to use a network-based strategy to advance firms' interests often face an important decision, which is to identify the important stakeholders in their environment. Mitchell and colleagues (1997) proposed three criteria to differentiate the importance of stakeholder groups. The first criterion is the legitimacy of a stakeholder's claim on a firm based upon contract, exchange, legal title, legal right, moral right, at-risk status, or moral interest in the harms and benefits generated by company actions (Agle et al., 1999). The second criterion is a stakeholder's power to influence the firm's behavior. Agency theory and resource dependence theory are particularly helpful in explaining why power plays such an important role in the attention managers give to stakeholders. According to agency theory, the use of incentives or monitoring can force agents to act in ways that are consistent with the principle's interests. Managers are expected to attend to those stakeholders that have power to punish or reward them. Resource dependence theory also argues that those who control resources that are needed by firms can differentiate themselves from other stakeholders. The third criterion, urgency, is defined as the degree to which stakeholder claims call for immediate attention. It is based on the time sensitivity, i.e., the degree to which managerial delay in responding to the claim or relationship is unacceptable to the stakeholder; and criticality, i.e., the importance of the claim or the relationship to the stakeholder (Mitchell et al., 1997).

The legitimacy, power, and urgency of various stakeholders are in fact closely associated with the institutional context and the resource allocation patterns. Naughton (1996) argues that China's market transition is a process of "growing out of the plan," in which the old institutions associated with the command economy were gradually phased out, whereas the new market-oriented infrastructure and rules started to exert more influence on economic activities. The transition process is far from smooth: in some fields, the old system coexists with the new ones, which leads to a "dual track system," whereas in other fields, the old system is dismantled before an effective new system is established, which gives rise to the emergence of various "institutional voids" (Khanna & Palepu, 2000). In this context, firms can hardly rely on well-defined institutional solutions to gain raw materials, financial capital, sales channels, or legal protection. Various stakeholders seem to have the power to demand immediate attention of the managers, regardless of the legitimacy of these claims. Networks thus quickly entered almost every field of organizations' life and firms tended to hold a diffusive view of networking. The use of *guanxi* not only enables firms to gain resources and institutional protection from the state agencies, but also gives them an alternative way to minimize the risks and uncertainties in various economic transactions (Park & Luo, 2001; Peng, 2003; Xin & Pearce, 1996).

With the progress of market building and market development, the institutional environment evolves. Figure 2.1 shows the temporal change of the provincial marketization index at two different time points. The

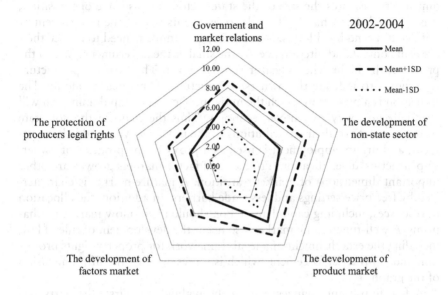

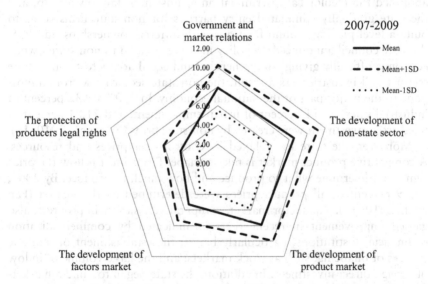

Figure 2.1 Change of Institutional Environment in Two Different Time Periods

Source: Fan, 2011, *Chinese Marketization Index (2011), NERI report.*

marketization index is created by the National Economic Research Institute (Fan, Wang, & Zhu, 2010). Published annually since 2001, this index comprises 19 indicators of institutional arrangements and policies in five major areas of the market-oriented reforms. The government and market dimension measures the size of the state sector. At this stage of transition, it is believed that China still needs to reduce its size of the government at both central and local levels. Meanwhile, governments need to reduce their areas of control and interference. So the smaller the government's size in the province, the higher the indicator value they get. The ownership structure is designed to indicate the ownership structure of the local economy. The transition is a process in which the initial public ownership domination will gradually give way to a mixed economy. Thus the share of the non-state sectors in terms of their contributions to the industrial value added, investment, and urban employment is used as a proxy to the progress of ownership structure diversification. Product and factor markets growth are other important dimensions of market transition. A mature market is characterized by free price settings and less trade barriers. In addition, the allocation of resources, including capital and labor, should also follow market mechanisms. A well-functioning market also needs the development of rule of law, including the establishment of a legal framework for property rights protection and contract enforcement, which is represented by the fifth dimension of the graph.

A few important changes need to be highlighted. First, the party has abolished the ideological discrimination against non-state ownership, and the state gradually eliminated entry barriers for non-state firms so as to build a level playing ground for firms with different ownerships. In 2005, the state council announced 36 policy measures related to non-state-owned economy, officially giving comprehensive and equal access to the non-state sector to all industries. As a result, the non-state sector grew from almost none to the major part of the national economy. In 2007, 69.32 percent of industrial sales, 78.11 percent of urban employment, and 71.81 percent of fixed asset investment were created by non-state firms (Fan et al., 2010: 16).

Moreover, the state has relaxed its control over prices and resources. A competitive product market is taking shape. Firms must follow the price signals to determine what to produce and how much to produce. By 2007, 93.19 percent of all product prices were determined by the market (Fan et al., 2010: 16). The factor market, comparatively slower in progress, also gained improvement in recent years as indicated by commercialization of financial institutions, particularly banks; the establishment of multiple sources of financing, such as stock markets; and the large volume of inflow of foreign direct investment. In addition, the state began to build a market-friendly institutional framework in the mid-1990s, and this process was greatly accelerated by China's accession to the WTO in 2001. By the end of 2007, China had revised some 3,000 parts of domestic laws and regulations in accordance with WTO rules and promulgated a series of new domestic laws and regulations to fulfill its WTO commitments (Biukovic, 2008). By 2007, when the five-year transitional period of China's membership in the WTO ended, the entry barriers for all foreign companies (e.g., banks) were officially eliminated.

The passage of new laws and policies and the growth of the market forces, on the one hand, have filled much of the institutional void, and therefore have reduced the uncertainties caused by the imperfect institutional framework. On the other hand, actors' interests and the resources they controlled became differentiated. This differentiation in turn leads to the changes in resource dependence relations among different actors. As World Bank (2002) noted: "As time goes by, the economy is likely to feature more complex transactions involving more transaction parties, which is a trend consistent with the broad historical patterns associated with economic development around the world." Correspondingly, firms' networking strategies might also undergo a change from diffusive to a targeted mode. As rational actors, organizations will figure out what kinds of relationships need networking, and what kinds of relationships need simple market transactions. They will also figure out the right combination of using firms' own capability and networking to advance their interests.

Consequently, market building and market development leads to changes of resource dependence relationships and transaction mode. As resource dependence theory (Pfeffer & Salancik, 1978) maintains, the power relationship between organizations largely determines their relative bargaining status, and therefore the necessity of networking utilization. Organizations with important and scarce resources have power over others that need those resources. The dependent organization is thus at a power disadvantage. On the other hand, dependent organizations have various strategic choices, including networking, to manipulate or mitigate any power disadvantage. Cultivating and maintaining a network with powerful parties is such an option to mitigate disadvantage in the Chinese context (Walder, 1986; Xin & Pearce, 1996). In other words, networking serves as a weapon of the weak (Zhang & Keh, 2010). As such, networking utilization/practice will be most likely found in relationships in which the two sides have asymmetric power and one side is dependent on the other. Market transition shifts power from the government to market actors and differentiates the power relationships among market actors. Organizations can then choose either simply to buy or network based on power relationships (White & Liu, 2001).

The Evolution of Networking Strategies

As the market transition started, traditional institutions were dismantled while the new institutional building was still underway. This created a complex institutional environment in which firms found it difficult to predict the trend of change or encountered different logics when doing business with different parties. As a result, networking strategies in the initial stages of market transition tend to show no clear patterns, in other words, networking is the result of idiosyncratic decisions that are largely driven by firm leaders and lack an identifiable pattern. Baffled by such dramatic institutional changes and the chaotic environment, firms wander in the wilderness in choosing a business model and strategy (Newman, 2000; Peng, 2003). The absence of effective formal constraints lead some organizations to seek informal constraints to govern economic exchange. The use of personal connections or *guanxi* is part of the traditional Chinese business culture. When formal constraints lost their effects, this informal or traditional business strategy quickly revived. If practitioners of the networking strategy benefit greatly from their effective ties with regulatory agencies or resource providers, then other firms quickly imitate their strategy and begin to cultivate and utilize the network-based strategies to gain economic advantage or institutional security in the highly uncertain institutional context (DiMaggio & Powell, 1983). As time passed, the adoption of network-based strategies therefore became widespread, affected almost all arenas of social life and organizational exchange, and prevailed in all transaction relationships. This diffusive networking strategy makes some observers feel that networking is "essential to gaining approval for or access to just about everything" (Tsang, 1998: 64).

However, as institutions change and the social structure evolves, the networking strategy becomes more targeted. On the one hand, market development has made big strides, with an emerging competitive market and the construction of the legal infrastructure taking shape (Fan et al., 2010). When the institutional environment is more stable and the market-oriented rules are more developed, a firm needs to figure out what kinds of economic relationships require networking, as well as what kinds of relationships need simple market transactions. Firms have accumulated more experience to assess the relative importance of various stakeholders (Newman, 2000), and thus are more capable of making rational choices. This implies that the necessity and practices of networks will become more targeted. In other words, when the key issue in the early stage is whether firms should increase their networking investment, the key issue in the later stage is with whom should firms network and how to satisfy the demand of the salient stakeholders in the environment.

Important stakeholders in the environment can be grouped into two categories, those related to the state, and those related to the market. Networks with state agencies and with market actors are widely regarded as crucial to business success in transitional economies (Park & Luo, 2001; Peng & Luo, 2000). The former includes relationships with government agencies and state banks, whereas the latter refers to relationships with suppliers, distributors, customers, and business partners (cf. Fong & Chen, 2007). The institutional transition and market development have brought significant changes to the resource dependence relations between firms and their stakeholders. The shift in the power balance between firms, state agencies, and other market actors will lead to changes in firms' valuations on their relationships with various actors.

Regarding firms' relations with the governments, scholars found that, in the early stage of market transition, Chinese executives rated the state regulatory power as the most influential, most complex, and least predictable among all environmental factors (Tan & Litschert, 1994). Managers thus have to maintain a "disproportionally greater contact" with government officials (Child, 1994: 154) to seek opportunities and avoid threat (Peng & Luo, 2000; Xin & Pearce, 1996). As transition has proceeded, the state's control of resources and industries, intervention in business operations, and regulatory uncertainty have declined (Haveman, David, Greenwood, Oliver, Sahlin, & Suddaby, 2008; Naughton, 2007; Peng & Zhou, 2005). Moreover, the previous unilateral dependence of firms upon government is replaced by mutual dependence between business and government, because government officials have started to rely more on business organizations to generate revenues, create job opportunities, and develop the local economy (Lin, 1995; Kennedy, 2007).

These changes alter the power relationship between business and government and lower the necessity for business to actively network with government officials, resulting in the changes in the nature of business-government relations. If networks with government officials had been a necessity for business survival and success in the early stage of market transition, it becomes optional today. Business executives have discretion regarding whether they should gain competitive advantage from the market or by catering to government officials (Ahlstrom et al., 2008).

In terms of the firm–bank relationships, the state exerted tight control over banks in the early stage of market transition—all banks were essentially owned by the state. Later on, the state reformed the banking system and pushed forward the rapid commercialization of state banks. Since the late 1990s, some state-owned banks started to be corporatized and listed in the stock market. In 2005 and 2006, three out of the four biggest state banks went public. Although the connections between banks and the state remain strong—the head of these banks was still appointed by the government (Lin, 2011)—these banks have become more market-oriented. At the same time, more domestic commercial banks emerged, and foreign firms also entered the banking sector. In addition, the capital market (e.g., stock markets, venture capital, etc.) develops gradually, and provides firms with alternative ways of financing. These changes reduced firms' reliance on state banks. Consequently, the necessity of networking with transformed state banks should have also declined.

As the state-centered institutional logic is gradually replaced by the market-oriented institutional logic, firms rely increasingly on the market to survive and succeed (Kim, Kim, & Hoskisson, 2010). However, the progress of market development does not necessarily exclude relationship-based, personal exchanges, as market efficiency logic maintains (Davies & Walters, 2004; Guthrie, 1998). Social networks not only allow firms to "get by," i.e., overcome uncertainties and risks in the market, but also enable some to "get ahead," i.e., to get an upper hand in market competition.

When the market becomes increasingly competitive, particularly the product market, and customers have more choices than ever before, companies have to make great efforts to satisfy customers (Davies & Walters, 2004). This means that the resource dependence relationships between the focal firm and market actors (particularly customers) become more important. However, China's market transition is characterized by incremental and uneven changes in different arenas (Hoskisson et al., 2000; Wright, Filatotchev, Hoskisson, & Peng, 2005). Due to the lack of independent law enforcement, the deficiency of supervision mechanisms, and frequent law changes, many commercial laws, although enacted, have not been strictly enforced (Luo, 2006; World Trade Organization, 2006). There is still no established market information system to disclose codified and accurate market information (Boist & Child, 1996). Established business ethics and norms are still absent in large, opportunism is prevalent in some fields, and a low level of social trust further increases the risks associated with business transactions (Luo, 2006; Zhang & Keh, 2010). This can be attributed to the long tradition of untrustworthy legal and political systems, the lack of independent law enforcement, the deficiency of supervision mechanisms, and frequent law changes (Luo, 2006). The ineffective legal system and market institutions provide weak external governance and create high uncertainty in market transactions. Under such circumstances, firms still need to rely on network-based strategies and use reliable social connections to reduce the risks and uncertainties in market transactions.

In addition, when the market, especially the product market, becomes increasingly competitive, and customers have more choices than ever before, companies have to make greater efforts to manage their relationships with market actors, customers in particular (Davies & Walters, 2004). The intensified market competition is likely to push firms to adopt all available means to survive or gain an advantage, among which relying on networks with market players to access information, acquire resources, and safeguard economic transactions is a popular choice. Luo (2003) finds that when competition intensifies, firms tend to rely more on managerial networks to achieve a competitive advantage. Through this network-based strategy, some can acquire more favorable terms or benefits than others—in effect they can use ties to buffer themselves from competitive forces.

To empirically test these ideas, we used data from surveys conducted by the World Bank group at different times. The 2005 data is from World Bank's Investment Climate Survey, and the 2012 data is from its Enterprise Survey. Both surveys were based on random samples of Chinese firms. They both asked respondents to provide their evaluations of the impact of various ties on their operation. This information was solicited with the following question: "please indicate to what extent the following factors affect your company's operation and growth?" They were required to rate the severity of the impacts using a Likert 5-point scale from not at all to very high. The results in Table 2.1 show that from 2005–2012, the relations with basic infrastructure or utility service providers, i.e., providers of electricity, communication, and transportation, became less influential to firms'

Table 2.1 The Severity of the Following Factors' Impact on Firms' Operation and Growth (2005, 2012)

	2005						
	Average	*Small*	*Medium*	*Large*	*Cities at prov. level*	*Prov. capitals*	*Other cities*
Electricity	2.01	1.78	2.01	2.25	2.33	2.27	2.15
Communication	1.33	1.27	1.34	1.38	1.38	1.47	1.33
Transport	1.84	1.72	1.79	2.00	1.79	2.10	1.89
Customs	1.26	1.12	1.20	1.45	1.67	1.48	1.33
Tax Administration	1.67	1.57	1.61	1.82	1.68	1.87	1.73
Access to information on laws and regulations	1.64	1.55	1.62	1.75	1.71	1.84	1.67
Unstable economic and administration policies	1.81	1.70	1.74	2.00	1.86	2.07	1.89
Access to finance	2.31	2.18	2.31	2.43	1.90	2.44	2.41
	2012						
Electricity	1.49	1.43	1.51	1.55	1.37	1.49	1.54
Communication	1.29	1.31	1.27	1.29	1.29	1.29	1.29
Transport	1.53	1.49	1.52	1.57	1.45	1.54	1.52
Customs	1.27	1.24	1.25	1.31	1.35	1.24	1.26
Tax Administration	1.72	1.67	1.70	1.80	1.65	1.59	1.91
Access to information on laws and regulations	1.34	1.35	1.34	1.34	1.37	1.28	1.42
Unstable economic and administration policies	1.28	1.28	1.26	1.29	1.31	1.23	1.32
Access to finance	1.82	1.76	1.83	1.87	1.68	1.75	1.95

operation and growth. The relations with banks and government agencies also weighed less on the viability of firms during this period. By comparing the answers provided by entrepreneurs at two times, we find that access to information regarding laws and regulations, the stability of economic and administrative policies, and access to finance have been less important to firms' continuous operation in 2012 as compared to 2005. However, in two out of the eight dimensions, customs and tax administration, we see no significant changes in their impact on firms' operation. This on the one hand shows that not all elements in the external environment have achieved significant improvement over the years, and on the other hand, that firms may still need to pay close attention to the relations with these stakeholders or government agencies.

The Changing Antecedents of Networking Investments

A second question we address is what factors have affected firms' strategies in allocating networking investments among the relations with different actors? Newman (2000) argues that organizational learning is significantly affected by the market and institutional environment. When they operate in an environment with significant environmental uncertainties, firms' strategy making may heavily rely on the idiosyncratic knowledge of managers who assess the importance of stakeholders based on their values or experience. In the early stage of market transition, firms' relationships with the state agencies and business partners are less formalized. The volatility and the particularistic nature of these inter-organizational ties make it difficult to manage the networking effort through a routinized plan or strategy. The management of the networking effort therefore relies much on managers' judgment of whether a particular stakeholder is a worthwhile network connection. If managers perceive networks with government officials as critical for business survival and success, they tend to invest more in cultivating such ties. In contrast, if they regard market relationships as more crucial, they will devote more resources to networking with market players. In this light, managerial preferences or judgment would be the main determinant of networking investments.

As the market environment become more stable, organizational learning will be improved accordingly. Firms may choose more appropriate business models and in a more rational way. When it comes to our case, we argue that the determinants of firms' network effort (e.g., firms' investment in a specific type of relationship) in a relatively more developed institutional environment will differ from those in a highly uncertain context. With the establishment of new market institutions, the enforcement of laws and regulations becomes more transparent, and the institutional environment becomes relatively stable and predictable. These conditions allow firms to shift to a more rational networking management strategy, in which firms' networking efforts are affected less by managers' individual preferences but more by organizational characteristics, such as firms' market position or their immediate institutional environment.

In order to test this changing antecedents thesis, we used data from a repeated cross-sectional survey in which the researchers studied the determinants of firms' networking investments at different times. The networking investments were operationalized as the percent of entertaining expenses in the total operational costs of firms. This is a typical accounting item, which covers expenditures on meals, gifts, and other social activities. We then constructed models to estimate the impact of firm characteristics, e.g., firm age, firm size, industry, location, etc., and managers' perception of the stakeholder salience on firms' networking spending. We find that in 2004, organizational level variables have only limited predictive power, whereas the most significant factor that determines firms' networking spending is managers' evaluations of stakeholder salience. To test the robustness of this finding, we used data from World Bank's 2004 investment climate survey.[1] In this survey, the researchers asked firms to report three types of expenditures in 2004, including business travel expenses, entertaining expenses, and conference expenses. We then computed the percentage of entertaining expenses in the firms' total sales revenue and used it as a dependent variable. The results indicate that firm characteristics are only weakly associated with the expenses, whereas managerial characteristics, such as education tenure and positional power, have significant impact on the outcome variable. This lends support to the argument.

We also argue that as the transition proceeds, the market mechanisms become dominant in resource allocation, and the institutional environment becomes relatively stable and predictable. Under such conditions, firms' networking strategies can be more based on the well codified knowledge about the influence of firms' market positions and corresponding bargaining status on their performance. They will be more strategic in choosing the appropriate target to network with and make investments wisely (Park & Luo, 2001; Peng & Luo, 2000). Therefore, organizational characteristics will shape a firm's networking investments. In order to support this idea, we used data from the China Enterprise Survey conducted by the World Bank Group (see Appendix for more information about the survey) in 2012. In this survey, the researchers asked respondents to recall the instances that they are expected to give gifts or make informal payments to facilitate business matters. The module designed multiple statements related to different public service units or government agencies. We classified the sampled firms according to firm size, which reflected firms' market position and can be a proxy of firms' vulnerability when facing various environmental pressures or challenges. The firms were grouped into small, medium, and large categories according to the number of employees they had at the time when the survey was conducted.

The results (Table 2.2) show that the variation of firm sizes is systematically associated with the probability of giving gifts in different occasions. However, contrary to our expectations, the data suggests that larger firms were more likely to give gifts or make informal payments to get things done. For instance, fifteen percent of large firms reported that they have received at least one gift giving request, whereas this proportion is less than ten percent in the small firm group. Moreover, for large firms, 11.5 percent of the public transactions are expected to be expedited by giving gifts or making informal payments, whereas this percentage is around nine percent in the small firms group. Similar patterns can also be found when firms try to get help from tax officials, get an operating license, get a construction permit, get electrical connection, or ask public officials to get things done. The reason that large firms rather than small firms are more likely to make more investments to get things done can be that the types and volume of resources that large firms need may be very different from small family

Table 2.2 Percentage of Firms Expected to Give Gifts in Various Public Transaction Processes

	Region		Firm Size		Location			Industry		
	EA & Pacific	China	Small (5–19)	Medium (20–99)	Cities at prov. levels	Prov. capitals cities	Other cities	Manuf.	Services	Constr.
% of firms that have ever given gifts	27.4	11.6	9.9	12.4	11.9	17.6	26.5	10.8	12.4	10.1
% of transactions where a gift or informal payment was requested	20.2	9.9	9.2	10.2	10.2	16.2	30.9	8.5	11.3	9.4
Gift giving is expected when meeting with tax officials	17.9	10.9	9.7	11.2	11.4	16.0	32.9	10.1	11.7	9.4
Gift giving to secure government contracts	29.7	42.2	53.0	34.5	4.8	19.5	43.9	33.1	51.0	58.2
value (% of contract value)	2.4	0.2	0.1	0.4	0.0	0.1	0.6	0.2	0.3	0.9
get an operating license	20.0	7.8	4.7	7.8	0.4	9.7	13.8	8.6	7.2	7.3
get an import license	22.9	19.2	19.2	22.8	10.3	n.a.	24.2	18.8	19.7	n.a.
get a construction permit	33.4	18.8	0.0	18.4	1.4	25.0	26.8	18.0	22.1	3.5
get an electrical connection	26.8	3.0	0.6	3.6	0.1	4.9	15.7	3.2	2.6	25.1
get a water connection	25.9	6.2	1.7	12.3	4.1	12.1	13.2	8.1	3.4	n.a.
ask public officials "to get things done"	23.0	10.7	9.4	12.0	8.0	13.0	14.0	9.3	12.1	13.9

firms. They may have to get separate or commercial grade resource supplies, which often involves administrative approval. Moreover, as firms' size reaches a certain standard, the tax preparations tend to be more complex. They therefore need more assistance from the regulatory agencies. However, sizes can also bring firms advantage: when competing for government contracts, larger firms are less likely to use gift giving or informal payments as means to secure government contracts.

A second factor affecting firms' networking investments industry. Firms in different industries face different market conditions and institutional rules. The manufacturing industry was the first to adopt the market logic and rules and to develop a more sophisticated market infrastructure. In contrast, in the real estate industry, state officials still hold the power of land use and determine the construction projects associated with urban development. Therefore, firms facing distinct environments may strategically determine their networking efforts. Our data lend support to this argument. We compared firms in manufacturing industries and service industries, and developed a separate column for the construction industries, which were included in the service industry during the survey. The data show that compared to firms in manufacturing industries, those in service industries are more likely to experience gift giving requests. Moreover, the market transactions in service industries involve more gift giving activities: in 11.3 percent of the public transactions, firms are required to give gifts or make informal payments, and this percentage is 8.5 percent in manufacturing industries. A more striking difference is associated with firms' attempts to secure government contracts. In service industries, 51 percent of firms use network-based strategies to obtain government contracts, whereas in manufacturing industries this percentage dropped by 18 percent. In particular, the construction firms stand out in terms of both extensity and intensity of networking investment. It is indicated that 58 percent of construction firms have to use gifts or informal payments to secure government construction contracts, and on average, they spend nearly one percent of the contract amount on networking activities. This percentage is only 0.2 and 0.3 among manufacturing firms and service firms in general.

A third factor is firm location. The local market environment can vary across regions. Due to different paces of market reform and economic development, the regional market and institutional environments differ substantially (Fan et al., 2010). Whereas market institutions are largely developed in one region, they may still be absent or ineffective in other regions. Even within the same region, the institutional environment would differ because of the existence of various special arrangements. In China's hierarchical administrative system, cities are divided into six political statuses: independent planning cities (*jihua danlieshi*), semiprovincial cities, prefecture cities, county-level cities, counties, and urban districts under prefecture. Higher political status means greater economic strength and more mature market institutions (Chan, 1997; Wong, Heady, Woo, & Asian Development Bank,

1995). In this study, we grouped the independent planning cities with Beijing and Shanghai because, in terms of economic management power, independent planning cities are treated as being equal to provincial units; they report directly to the central government, can approve projects with large investments, and remit revenue directly to the Ministry of Finance. The central government even gives them special quotas in certain socioeconomic affairs, such as birth quotas (Chan, 1997; Solinger, 1993; Wong et al., 1995). We then created two other city groups, one consisted of provincial capitals, and the other mainly consisted of other prefecture level cities.

The data shows that, in general, firms operating in larger cities face a more favorable institutional environment. Market transactions in larger cities depend less on various networking activities. For instance, in prefecture level cities, 27 percent of firms have experienced gift giving requests, whereas this is less likely to happen in larger cities (11.9 percent in cities at the provincial level, and 17.6 percent in provincial capitals). Similarly, almost one third of public transactions in prefecture level cities involved certain types of gift giving or informal payments, whereas in the most advanced cities this proportion decreased to 10 percent. In addition, the data also suggests that in order to get necessary utility services, administrative support, or administrative approval, firms in lower-level cities are more likely to be required to give gifts or small payments. In particular, when acquiring government contracts, firms in smaller cities rely heavily on network-based strategies. More than forty percent of the firms will use networking means to get government contracts in prefecture cities. In contrast, firms in provincial capitals or higher-level cities operate in a level playing field.

The Impact of Firms' Networking Investments on Financial Performance

Previous research indicated that, in the early transition period, network-based strategies have a positive impact upon firm performance (e.g., Davies et al., 1995; Li & Zhang, 2007; Li et al., 2008), such as sales growth (Park & Luo, 2001). This is because during this period the market infrastructure is still underdeveloped; when firms cannot acquire resources or support from market means, they will use various particularistic connections to get access to resources and information, facilitate firms entering a new market, and help firms speed up administrative approvals or overcome cumbersome bureaucracy. Thus networking was critical for firm survival and success. However, with the progress of market transition, some argue that a high investment in networking should yield lower returns on firm performance. This is because first, as transition proceeds, the state controls fewer resources and relinquishes direct interventions in business operations. With the reduced resource dependence of business upon government agencies, networks with the state become less important. Second, managerial attention is a scarce resource; networking with state officials distracts a firm's attention from the market and prevents a firm from learning modern management and business strategies. Third, network practices are not cost-free and thus are a double-edged sword. Building business networks is a costly undertaking, which involves a high input of time, attention, and money (Yi & Ellis, 2000). This is particularly true in cultivating networks in transitional economies, where corruption is high and building networks often involves bribes (Wank, 1999).

Different from the diminishing significance thesis (Guthrie, 1997), some argue that in transitional economies where the influence of the state is decreasing yet the legal infrastructure is underdeveloped, networking with political as well as market actors will have positive impacts on firm performance. Forming market networks in certain sectors is particularly useful for firms to access resources and information, to deal with uncertainty in the environment, and to diversify risk (Keister, 1998; Stark, 1996). Even in a mature market economy, there is ample evidence that social networks yield positive impacts on organizations in multiple areas (Uzzi, 1996, 1999). Network ties with business partners reduce transaction costs by generating trust, channeling fine-grained information, and facilitating joint problem-solving arrangements (Uzzi, 1997).

In fact, there is ample evidence suggesting that network-based strategies have consumed much of the financial resources of Chinese firms. This issue became a hot topic in public discussion after the media revealed the high entertaining expenditures of CRCC. As the investigation went deeper, more details about firms' networking activities were exposed to the public. Statistics show that in 2012, the total entertaining expenses of 2,469 listed firms amounted to 13.79 billion yuan. Eleven firms spent more than 100 million yuan on various networking activities. Early reports indicate that CRCC ranked number one on this expense list. However, more careful studies show that in fact the number one firm should be China Life Insurance, which reported 1.42 billion yuan under the item of business entertaining expenses. Shanghai Construction Group is also among the eleven firms that have over 100 million entertaining expenses. In 2012, this firm spent 178 million yuan on networking, which is 11.12 percent of their net profit.

The accounting definition of business entertaining expenses is the expenses firms made in order to meet the reasonable production, operation, and other business related entertaining needs. For example, in order to secure contracts, firms may need to pay for clients' meals, give souvenirs or gifts, and pay for their visits or travel expenses. Some believe that it is not surprising that firms have such expenses. In a competitive market, firms need to build relationships with various stakeholders to expand their market, secure contracts, or build the brand image. Such expenses will be reasonable expenditures as long as they result in above normal business growth (Liu, 2014).

When studying the impact of entertaining expenses on firms' performance, the major difficulty is to find such items from the company's financial reports. Firms have different rules for handling entertaining expenses: some firms may list them under operating costs, whereas others may view them as sales costs. In other circumstances, firms may collect receipts for other purposes, such as training or travel, and then hide some entertaining expenses under the travel expenses and conference expenses items. In 2013, one year after the CRCC scandal, many listed firms chose not to give expenditure purposes; instead, they chose to report a lump sum amount of operation costs, sales costs, management costs, or other costs (Liu, 2014). For those who continued to report detailed expenditure items, the entertaining expenses decreased by 43 percent in 2013 and 17 percent in 2014 as compared to their 2012 expenditure (Zhou, 2015).

To empirically test the impact of firms' networking expenses on their financial performance, we used data from CSMAR (see Appendix for more information), which collected information on firms listed in both the Shanghai and the Shenzhen stock exchange. We used firms' return on assets (ROA), which measures how profitable a company is relative to its total assets, as one of the performance indicators. It equals the ratio of annual net income to average total assets of a business during a financial year. Firms' earnings before interest and tax (EBIT) are another indictor we used in measuring firms' performance. This variable is calculated as revenue minus expenses, excluding tax and interest. This indicator focuses solely on a company's ability to generate earnings from operation regardless of its tax burden or capital structure. This advantage makes EBIT especially useful in certain applications. For instance, if a researcher is comparing companies in a given industry that operate in different tax environments and have different strategies for financing themselves, tax and interest expenses would distract the researcher's attention from the core question of how effectively the company generates profit from its operations. The major independent variable used in this analysis is firms' networking related costs. Because different firms may choose different ways to list their networking expenses, we thus selected two accounting items which are often used by firms to justify networking expenditures: sales costs and management costs. Instead of using the amount of each category of costs, we used the ratio of these costs to their revenue as the indicator of the intensity of networking investment.

We started by analyzing the bivariate correlations between firms' networking spending and firms' financial performance. Table 2.3 shows the correlation coefficients in different years. The p values of the coefficients are smaller than 0.05 when their absolute values are greater than 0.05. The results show that first, the association between firms' networking spending and firms' financial performance is only significant in a few but not all years,

Table 2.3 Bivariate Correlation Between Firms' Networking Spending and Financial Performance

	2003	2004	2005	2006	2007	2008	2009	2010	2011	2012	2013	2014
ROA												
Sales Costs	−0.01	−0.05	−0.01	−0.04	0.03	−0.07	0.03	0.05	−0.01	0.09	0.07	0.08
Mgmt. Costs	−0.07	−0.02	−0.01	−0.07	0.09	0.05	−0.01	−0.03	0.01	−0.02	0.01	−0.04
EBIT												
Sales Costs	−0.01	−0.04	−0.01	−0.02	0.02	−0.02	−0.03	0.09	−0.05	−0.01	−0.01	−0.04
Mgmt. Costs	−0.02	−0.03	−0.01	−0.03	0.02	0.14	0.05	0.01	0.15	−0.01	0.01	−0.01

which indicates that such relationships cannot hold across years. Second, among the statistically significant years, we see more positive associations between firms' networking spending and firms' financial performance. We then conducted a regression analysis, which controls firms' age, size, location, and industry. The results show that when using ROA and EBIT as dependent variables, the coefficients of management costs and sales costs are negative and significant in 2006, but positive and significant in 2008, 2010, 2011, 2012, and 2013. This result does not support the declining significance thesis; instead it shows that the network-based strategy can also bring firms financial benefits in the late transitional period.

Conclusion

The changing networking strategy and the impact of networking investments on firms' financial performance in transitional economies are largely unaddressed in the current literature because of limitations in the theoretical framework and the lack of large scale surveys over time. We situate our research in China, the largest transitional and emerging economy in the world. China provides an ideal research context to test the changing patterns of the network-based strategy. This is because first, social networking, so-called *guanxi* in the Chinese context, has been widely regarded as being prevalent and crucial in governing interorganizational transactions during China's market transition. Second, in the past 30 years, China has experienced radical institutional changes. The intensity of institutional transformation in a dynamic environment also helps to capture the changes of firms' networking strategy over time. Third, China is huge and has heterogeneous market environments across regions and industries, which provide good opportunities to examine how a firm's immediate environment may shape its network strategy.

We find that as the institutional environment evolves and the resource allocation mechanisms shift from state-driven to market-driven, the salience of various stakeholders also undergoes significant changes. As a result, firms' networking strategies shift from a more diffusive pattern to a more targeted pattern. In the early period, firms tended to consider networking as necessary in almost every relationship, and thus took a diffusive view of networking; whereas in the later period, firms were more likely to give different weight to the stakeholders in the environment. Specifically, we find that firms' networking efforts were largely driven by managers' evaluations of different stakeholders' salience in the early transition period, whereas as the market system becomes more established, firms are more likely to base their networking strategy on objective indicators such as firms' industry, local environment, and firms' market status.

Based on the dynamic and structural evolution of networking importance over time, this research provides a new answer to the scholarly debate. As discussed at the beginning of this chapter, the change of the significance of the social network and its impact upon firms' performance over time still puzzles scholars. Our theoretical perspective, which incorporates ideas of institutional theory, resource dependence, and stakeholder theories helps to solve this debate. We argue that market transition (as a fundamental institutional change) coincided with changes in resource allocation mechanism. The importance of networking with certain actors has declined, whereas the importance of networking with other actors has increased.

We move beyond a unitary perspective of social networking and distinguish networking with various stakeholders. Our analyses include both the perceived importance of networking and the actual networking investments of various actors, which is rare in the current literature. We find that the patterns of social networking become more targeted along with market development and social differentiation, with waxing and waning of different types of network. Various types of networking become less correlated over time. In other words, when the market and society become targeted, a firm may choose between formal transactions or informal networks based on the nature of resource dependence and the conditions of exchange. As a result, some specific ties are valued, but not others.

Following the institutionalists' arguments, when resource allocation is more market driven, and barriers to trade and market entry are eliminated, the importance of a network-based strategy to business growth and financial performance will decline. However, contrary to their prediction, networking investments still matter in the changed market environment. The continuing/increasing importance of using networks on market relationships, particularly to win customers, suggests that impersonal and formal market transactions will not automatically follow when the market becomes competitive. Market competition might reduce the benefits achieved by utilizing a social network, but market competition alone cannot eliminate networking in business transactions. A market economy depends heavily on the development of various market supporting institutions, such as rule of law, free press, accountable government, well-governed and transparent economic entities, and business norms/ethics. In other words, a rational–legal system is a precondition for a market economy (e.g., Guthrie, 1998). Without such institutions, a market economy cannot effectively work.

More broadly, our findings deepen understanding of the relationship between social networks and institutions and social structure, and of the relationship between organizations and institutions, by doing a longitudinal study in a dynamic context. Inspired by North's (1990) argument that institutional constraints affect organizational choices, extant studies either examine the role of social networks in a transitional economy or highlight the different social networking patterns across institutional environments through comparative study. From a longitudinal angle, our study investigates the changes in social networks along with the institutional transformation in the same context. The advantage of such a study is that cultural and historical factors are constant so that we can focus on the influence of institutional changes and structural evolution.

Appendix
Data Collection and Sample

We argue that the inconsistencies that exist in previous literature can be partially attributed to the limitation of their data and methodologies. Most previous studies relied on one-time cross-sectional survey data, which makes it hard to rigorously examine the temporal changes of firms' strategies. Three are a few studies that rely on interviews in the fieldwork, but the findings and conclusions can hardly be verified or generalized to other contexts.

In order to support our theoretical argument, we draw data from multiple different sources. We hope this multi-source data can triangulate each other and yield more robust results. Our first data source is the enterprise survey conducted by the World Bank Group. The enterprise survey is one of the firm-level surveys that have been conducted since the 1990s by different units of the World Bank, including the Enterprise Analysis Unit. In each country, private contractors conducted the survey on behalf of the World Bank. For many government agencies, some of the questions, e.g., questions addressing business–government relations and bribery-related topics, may appear politically sensitive to them. Therefore private contractors rater than government agencies or organizations related to the host government are hired to collect data.

On-site interviews were conducted, during which the survey questions were answered by business owners or top managers of sampled firms. In some cases, the HR managers or accountants were asked to answer related questions. In 2012, 2,599 firms were sampled in mainland China. Regarding the industries surveyed, the manufacturing and service sectors were the primary industries of interest. In terms of firm size, any firm that was registered and had more than five employees was eligible. Service firms included construction, retail, wholesale, hotel, restaurants, transport, storage, communications, and IT. Firms that were fully owned by governments were not eligible to participate in the survey.

In order to have a representative sample, the survey adopted a stratified random sampling strategy. The strata for the survey were firm size, business sector, and geographic region within a country. Firms were divided into three size groups, small (5–19 employees), medium (20–99 employees), and large sized firms (100+ employees). The survey oversampled large firms to obtain a satisfactory sample of large firms for subsequent analyses. Sampled firms were from regions with different levels of development. This included large cities such as Beijing, Shanghai, Guangzhou, and Shenzhen, as well as independent planning cities, provincial capitals, and other prefecture cities.

Our second data source is a repeated cross-sectional survey conducted in 2004 and 2009. This research design can help researchers to better examine the changes in the practices of various networking strategies and evaluate the impact of such network-based strategy upon organizational performance over time. This survey focuses on private firms that have expanded dramatically and are more sensitive to institutional changes in China's transitional economy. Because private firms have long been discriminated against by the party's ideology and survive in a hostile institutional environment, they are more sensitive to the institutional changes in the environment. Furthermore, among all types of firms during China's transition, private firms face greater challenges and tend to rely more on networking to gain resources, political protection, and legitimacy (Li & Zhang, 2007; Nee, 1992; Park & Luo, 2001; Peng & Luo, 2000; Xin & Pearce, 1996). However, given the fact that these firms are operating under greater budget constraints, their networking strategy may be more efficient and thus tightly coupled to their performance. Therefore, it is easier to capture the changes in networking practices over time.

The researchers adopted a two-step sampling strategy, with purposeful sampling and random sampling being used respectively. First, six provinces were sampled purposefully: three from coastal regions and three from interior regions. A prefecture city was then selected in each province. In each prefecture, one urban district and one rural county were selected. And then in each district or county, a certain number of firms were randomly selected from the list of business registrations in the local Industry and Commerce Administration Bureau. A total of 400 firms were included in the final sample.

On-site interviews were then conducted. On-site interviews help researchers to gain access to the right respondents and ensured the correct understanding of items. A total of 239 respondents cooperated and finished the questionnaire. The response rate is 60 percent, which is within the acceptable range. The characteristics of the respondents and non-respondents were compared and no significant systematic biases were found. Among the respondents, 86.3 percent are business owners or general managers, and 13.7 percent are other top management personnel. These respondents are arguably more informative because in Chinese private firms' business owners or top managers know more business details, including firms' networking activities. Five years later, the researchers followed the sample procedure and conducted another survey. The same sampling frame was used, which yielded another sample of 400 firms, among which 179 firms responded to the survey. Independent sample T-tests were performed and all independent and control variables in the two surveys, including firm age, firm size, firm location, and industry affiliation, are largely comparable.

In addition, we also used data on China's publicly listed companies to test the impact of firms' networking investments on their financial performance.

This is because the information of listed companies is more reliable and consistent when compared to the information collected through other investigations, given the difficulty of data collection in emerging economies (Xu & Wang, 1999). Our data are from the China Listed Firm Accounting Indicators Research Database, which was collected and maintained by the GTA Information Technology Co., Ltd. (www.gtarsc.com). The database collected the accounting data disclosed by the listed companies since the early 1990s. The GTA also maintains the China Stock Market and Accounting Research (CSMAR) database, which is the primary source for information on Chinese stock markets and the financial statements of Chinese listed companies (Marquis & Qian, 2014). We therefore drew basic firm-level information from the CSMAR database. We complemented that information with corporate governance data from the WIND Info (www.wind.com.cn) database, which allows researchers to identify the actual controllers of the listed companies. There is a one-year lag between all independent and dependent variables.

Acknowledgment

We would like to thank Wei Zhao at University of North Carolina–Charlotte and Jianjun Zhang at Peking University for contributing important insights to this study.

Note

1 Data available at http://microdata.worldbank.org/index.php/catalog/661

References

Agle, B. R., Mitchell, R. K., & Sonnenfeld, J. A. (1999). Who matters to CEOS? An investigation of stakeholder attributes and salience, corporate performance, and CEO values. *Academy of Management Journal, 42*(5), 507–525.

Ahlstrom, D., Bruton, G. D., & Lui, S. S. (2000). Navigating China's changing economy: Strategies for private firms. *Business Horizons, 43*(1), 5–15.

Ahlstrom, D., Bruton, G., & Yeh, K. S. (2008). Private firms in China: Building legitimacy in an emerging economy. *Journal of World Business, 43*, 385–399.

Bian, Y. (2002). Institutional holes and job mobility processes: Guanxi mechanisms in China's emerging labor markets. In Thomas Gold, Doug Guthrie, & David Wank (Eds.), *Social Connections in China: Institutions, Culture, and the Changing Nature of Guanxi* (pp. 117–136). Cambridge, UK: University of Cambridge Press.

Biukovic, L. (2008). Selective adaptation of WTO transparency norms and local practices in China and Japan. *Journal of International Economic Law, 11*(4), 803–825.

Boisot, M., & Child, J. (1996). From fiefs to clans and network capitalism: Explaining China's emerging economic order. *Administrative Science Quarterly, 41*, 600–628.

Burt, R. S. (1992). *Structural Hole*. Cambridge, MA: Harvard Business School Press.

Chan, K. W. (1997). Urbanization and urban infrastructure services in the PRC. In C. Wong (Ed.), *Financing Local Government in the People's Republic of China* (pp. 83–126). New York: Oxford University Press.

Child, J. (1994). *Management in China During the Age of Reform*. Cambridge: Cambridge University Press.

Davies, H., & Walters, P. (2004). Emergent patterns of strategy, environment and performance in a transition economy. *Strategic Management Journal, 25*(4), 347–364.

DiMaggio, P. J., & Powell, W. W. (1983). The iron cage revisited: Institutional isomorphism and collective rationality in organizational fields. *American Sociological Review, 48*(2), 147–160.

Dyer, J. H., & Nobeoka, K. (2000). Creating and managing a high-performance knowledge-sharing network: the Toyota case. *Strategic Management Journal, 21*(3), 345–367.

Fan, G., Wang, X., & Zhu, H. (2011). *NERI INDEX of Marketization of China's Province 2011 Report*. Beijing: Economic Science Press.

Fong, E., W. Chen. (2008). Embedded entrepreneurship in market transition: resources mobilization among entrepreneurs in China. *Canadian Review of Sociology, 44*, 415–450.

Granovetter, M. (1985). Economic action and social structure: the problem of embeddedness. *American Journal of Sociology, 91*, 481–510.

Guillén, M. F. (2000). Business groups in emerging economies: a resource-based view. *Academy of Management Journal, 43*, 362–380.

Gulati, R. (1995). Social structure and alliance formation patterns: A longitudinal analysis. *Administrative Science Quarterly, 40*, 619–652.

Guthrie, D. (1997). Between markets and politics: Organizational responses to reform in China. *American Journal of Sociology, 102*, 1258–1304.

Guthrie, D. (1998). The declining significance of *guanxi* in China's economic transition. *The China Quarterly 154*(June), 254–282.

Hamilton, G. G., & Biggart, N. W. (1988). Market, culture, and authority: A comparative analysis of management and organization in the Far East. *American Journal of Sociology*, S52–S94.

Haveman, H. A., David, R. J., Greenwood, R., Oliver, C., Sahlin, K., & Suddaby, R. (2008). *The sage handbook of organizational institutionalism*. Los Angeles, CA: Sage.

Hoskisson, R. E., Eden, L., Lau, C. M., & Wright, M. (2000). Strategy in emerging economies. *Academy of Management Journal, 43*(3), 249–267.

Keister, L. A. (1998). Engineering Growth: Business Group Structure and Firm Performance in China's Transition Economy 1. *American Journal of Sociology, 104*(2), 404–440.

Keister, L. (2002). Guanxi in business groups: Social ties and the formation of economic relations. In Thomas Gold, Doug Guthrie, & David Wank (Eds.), *Social Connections in China: Institutions, Culture, and the Changing Nature of Guanxi* (pp. 77–96). Cambridge, UK: University of Cambridge Press.

Kennedy, S. (2007). Transnational political alliances: An exploration with evidence from China. *Business and Society, 46*, 174–200.

Khanna, T., & Palepu, K. (1999). *Emerging market business groups, foreign investors, and corporate governance* (No. w6955). National Bureau of Economic Research.

Khanna, T., & Palepu, K. (2000). The future of business groups in emerging markets: Long-run evidence from Chile. *Academy of Management Journal, 43*(3), 268–285.

Kim, H., Kim, H., & Hoskisson, R. E. (2010). Does market-oriented institutional change in an emerging economy make business-group-affiliated multinationals perform better? An institution-based view. *Journal of International Business Studies, 41,* 1141–1160.

Li, H. Y., Meng, Q., Wang, L., & Zhou, L. (2008). Political connections, financing and firm performance: Evidence from Chinese private firms. *Journal of Development Economics, 87,* 283–299.

Li, H. Y., & Zhang, Y. (2007). The role of managers' political networking and functional experience in new venture performance: Evidence from China's transition economy. *Strategic Management Journal, 28,* 791–804.

Lin, N. (1995). Local market socialism: Local corporatism in action in rural China. *Theory and Society, 24*(3), 301–354.

Lin, N. (2011). Capitalism in China: A centrally managed capitalism (CMC) and its future. *Management and Organization Review, 7*(1), 63–96.

Liu, S. (2014). High entertaining expenses hide in central SOE's annual reports. *Beijing Youth Daily,* April 16, 2014.

Luo, Y. D. (2003). Industrial dynamics and managerial networking in an emerging market: The case of China. *Strategic Management Journal, 24,* 1315–1327.

Luo, Y. D. (2006). Opportunism in inter-firm exchanges in emerging markets. *Management and Organization Review, 2*(1), 121–147.

Marquis, C., & Qian, C. (2014). Corporate social responsibility reporting in China: Symbol or substance? *Organization Science, 25*(1), 127–148.

Mitchell, R. K., Agle, B. R., & Wood, D. J. (1997). Toward a theory of stakeholder identification and salience: Defining the principle of who and what really counts. *Academy of Management Review, 22*(4), 853–886.

Naughton, B. (1996). *Growing Out of The Plan: Chinese Economic Reform, 1978–1993.* New York: Cambridge University Press.

Naughton, B. (2007). *The Chinese Economy: Transitions and Growth.* Cambridge, MA: MIT Press.

Nee, V. (1992). Organizational dynamics of market transition: Hybrid forms, property rights, and mixed economy in China. *Administrative Science Quarterly, 37,* 1–27.

Newman, K. (2000). Organizational transformation during institutional upheaval. *Academy of Management Review, 25,* 602–619.

North, D. (1990). *Institutions, Institutional Change and Economic Performance.* New York: Norton.

Park, S., & Luo, Y. D. (2001). Guanxi and organizational dynamics: Organizational networking in Chinese Firms. *Strategic Management Journal, 22,* 455–477.

Peng, M. (2003). Institutional transitions and strategic choices. *Academy of Management Review, 28*(2), 275–296.

Peng, M. W., & Luo, Y. (2000). Managerial ties and firm performance in a transition economy: The nature of a micro-macro link. *Academy of management journal, 43*(3), 486–501.

Peng, M., P.S. Heath. (1996). The growth of the firm in planned economies in transition: Institutions, organizations, and strategic choice. *Academy of Management Review, 21,* 492–528.

Peng, M. W., & Zhou, J. Q. (2005). How network strategies and institutional transitions evolve in Asia. *Asia Pacific Journal of Management, 22,* 321–336.

Perotti, E. C., & Gelfer, S. (2001). Red barons or robber barons? Governance and investment in Russian financial–industrial groups. *European Economic Review, 45*(9), 1601–1617.

Pfeffer, J., & Salancik, G. (1978). *The External Control of Organizations.* New York: Harper & Row, Pub.

Potter, P. (2002). Guanxi and the PRC legal system: From contradiction to complementary. In Thomas Gold, Doug Guthrie, & David Wank (Eds.), *Social*

Connections in China: Institutions, Culture, and the Changing Nature of Guanxi (pp. 176–196). Cambridge, UK: University of Cambridge Press.

Solinger, D. J. (1993). *China's Transition from Socialism: Statist Legacies and Market Reforms, 1980–1990.* Armonk, NY: M. E. Sharpe.

Spicer, A., McDermott, G.A., & Kogut, B. (2000). Entrepreneurship and privatization in Central Europe: The tenuous balance between destruction and creation. *Academy of Management Review, 25,* 630–649.

Stark, D. (1996). Recombinant property in East European capitalism. American Journal of Sociology, *101,* 993–1027.

Stark, D., & Vedres, B. (2006). Social Times of Network Spaces: Network Sequences and Foreign Investment in Hungary1. *American Journal of Sociology, 111*(5), 1367–1411.

Tan, J., R. Litschert. (1994). Environment-strategy relationship and its performance implications: An empirical study of the Chinese electronics industry. *Strategic Management Journal, 15,* 1–20.

Tsang, E. (1998). Can guanxi be a source of sustained competitive advantage for doing business in China? *Academy of Management Executives, 12*(2), 64–73.

Uzzi, B. (1996). The sources and consequences of embeddedness for the economic performance of organizations: The network effect. *American Sociological Review, 61,* 674–698.

Uzzi, B. (1997). Social structure and competition in interfirm networks: The paradox of embeddedness. *Administrative Science Quarterly, 42,* 35–67.

Uzzi, B. (1999). Embeddedness in the making of financial capital: How social relations and networks benefit firms seeking financing. *American Sociological Review, 64,* 481–505.

Walder, A. (1986). *Communist Neo-Traditionalism: Work and Authority in Chinese Industry.* Berkeley, CA: University of California Press.

Wank, D. (1999). *Commodifying Communism: Business, Trust, and Politics in a Chinese City.* New York: Cambridge University Press.

Wank, D. (2002). Business-state clientelism in China: Decline or evolution? In Thomas Gold, Doug Guthrie, & David Wank (Eds.), *Social Connections in China: Institutions, Culture, and the Changing Nature of Guanxi* (pp. 97–116). Cambridge, UK: University of Cambridge Press.

White, S., & Liu, X. (2001). Transition trajectories for market structures and firm strategy in China. *Journal of Management Studies, 38*(1), 107–142.

Wong, C., Heady, C. J., Woo, W. T., & Asian Development Bank. (1995). *Fiscal Management and Economic Reform in the People's Republic of China.* Hong Kong; New York: Published for the Asian Development Bank by Oxford University Press.

World Bank. (2002). *World development report: Building institutions for markets.* Washington: World Bank.

World Trade Organization (WTO). (2006). *Trade Policy Review Report By the Secretariat: People's Republic of China.* Geneva: WTO.

Wright, M., Filatotchev, I., Hoskisson, R. E., & Peng, M. W. (2005). Strategy research in emerging economies: Challenging the conventional wisdom. *Journal of Management Studies, 42*(1), 1–33.

Xin, K., & Pearce, J. (1996). Guanxi: Connections as substitutes for formal institutional support. *Academy of Management Journal, 39*(6), 1641–1658.

Xu, X., & Wang, Y. (1999). Ownership structure, corporate governance, and corporate performance: The case of Chinese stock companies. *China Economic Review, 10*(1), 75–98.

Yang, M. M. (1994). *Gifts, Banquets: The Art of Social Relationships in China.* Ithaca, NY: Cornell University Press.

Yeung, I. Y., & Tung, R. L. (1996). Achieving business success in Confucian societies: The importance of guanxi (connections). *Organizational Dynamics, 25*(2), 54–65.

Yi, L. M., & Ellis, P. (2000). Insider-outsider perspectives of guanxi. *Business Horizons, 43*(1), 25–30.

Zhang, J., H.T. Keh. (2010). Interorganizational Relationships in a Transition Economy: Organizational Forms, *Governance Mechanisms and Outcome. Management Organization Review,* 6(1), 123–147.

Zhou, S. (2015). The transformation of entertaining expenses of listed companies. *Security Times*, April 22, 2015.

3 Political Strategies of Foreign Entrants in the Transitional Period

Introduction

Government policies have been a significant factor influencing the market and institutional environment of firms. Many firms thus invest extensive resources and effort and take various approaches to exert influence on public policy decision-making. This phenomenon lead to the rapid growth of literature on corporate political strategies (CPS) in the last two decades (e.g., Hillman, Keim, & Schuler, 2004; Shaffer, 1995). Scholars have been focused on the question of why firms engage in various political activities. They find that CPS help a firm build better connections with the government and other political forces, gain access to markets and resources, and cope with the environmental pressure and instability (Ahlstrom, Bruton, & Yeh, 2008; Zimmerman & Zeitz, 2002).

As economic globalization proceeds, more and more firms expand their operations to multiple countries that often have very different economic or political institutions. A significant trend of this global capital flow is the fast increase of foreign direct investment in emerging economies. Differing from industrialized economies, emerging economies have not fully developed effective market institutions, and these underdeveloped institutions are characterized by an opaque policy-making process, poorly enforced contract law, and high discretion power of government officials (Boisot & Child, 1996; Peng & Luo, 2000). In such an institutional context, many foreign firms reported dissatisfaction with the business environment, they attribute this difficulty to intrusive government officials and a lack of codified laws, well developed rules, and commercial conventions (Ahlstrom & Bruton, 2001). It is thus suggested that foreign firms should learn from local private firms to establish a good relationship with the host government to gain legitimacy and facilitate business operations in emerging markets (Ahlstrom et al., 2008; Kennedy, 2007; Sanyal & Guvenli, 2000).

Previous studies have explored why firms engage in political behavior but have not adequately studied how firms engage in political behavior. We thus examine the process of political strategy formation by examining the specific decisions firms make when formulating political strategies and by exploring firm and institutional variables that affect these decisions. Whereas foreign managers generally understand the importance of establishing good business–government relationships in an emerging economy, FIEs have discretional power to undertake different strategies (Iankova & Katz, 2003). Firms' CPS can be divided into two groups: firm-based and collective-based. As for firm-based CPS, an FIE can take multiple political tactics. Some popular tactics include participating in government-organized activities on public service or investment, obtaining government awards, and hosting a visit by government officials (Ahlstrom et al., 2008; Kennedy, 2007; Liu, 2010; Wank, 2002). All these tactics help an FIE to engage and build a better relationship with the host government.

In addition to the firm-based strategy, FIEs can also take collective approaches to increase their bargaining power. An important form of collective CPS is trade associations. Trade associations play an important role in CPS in advanced democracies (Aldrich & Staber, 1988; Coleman & Grant, 1988; Hillman & Hitt, 1999; Shaffer, 1995; Schuler, Rehbein, & Cramer, 2002) and also in an international business context (Hansen & Mitchell, 2000; Jacomet, 2005). As firms pool economic and political resources, collective-oriented associational activities have advantages over firm-based political strategies by gaining higher bargaining power, lobbying more effectively, having broader public influence, and generating a positive image of the entity (Drope & Hansen, 2009; Jacomet, 2005). For example, one of the important advocacy actions of the European Chamber of Commerce in China is to lobby government agencies, government affiliated think tanks, and other key institutions to convey their policy recommendations. In 2015, they visited the State Council Development Research Center and exchanged views on the challenges China is now facing and the difficulties China is encountering in implementing the policies and strategies at local level. At the local levels, The European Chamber Shanghai actively interacted with local agencies such as the Shanghai Customs. They used this opportunity to ask the local officials to clarify the recent discussions in policy making circle regarding the possible development on taxation policies in cross-border E-commerce on the Shanghai Customs level.[1]

Although both domestic and foreign trade associations thrive in China's emerging economy, they have different implications. As the Chinese government actively participates in and supervises domestic trade associations (e.g., All-China Federation of Industry and Commerce, China Association for Enterprises with Foreign Investment), they have a close relationship with the local government (Kennedy, 2007; Liu, 2010). These associations facilitate communication with the local government, lobby on behalf of firms or industries, and pursue favorable policies (Ahlstrom et al., 2008; Deng & Kennedy, 2010). For instance, the All-China Federation of Industry and Commerce (ACFIC) is a nationwide mass organization that serves as a channel for the CPC and the government to liaise with the personages of the non-public economy and an aid of the government in administering and serving the non-public economy. This association played an important role in the nation's political consultation process. During the third plenary session of the 11th National Committee of the Chinese People's Political Consultative Conference, the ACFIC made 24 proposals and delivered eight addresses to the meeting. The proposals covered eight areas of the country's social and economic development, including promoting small- and medium-sized enterprises; encouraging healthy growth of the private sector economy; promoting further industrial structural readjustment; guiding the healthy development of various sectors; encouraging strategic new industry and low-carbon technologies; solving the problems related to farmers, agriculture, and the countryside; helping private enterprises go overseas; coordinating development of the regional economy; and creating new jobs.[2]

In contrast, foreign trade associations face more constraints in China. For example, each foreign country can register only one trade association according to Chinese law. Nevertheless, foreign trade associations (e.g., European Union Chamber of Commerce, American Chamber of Commerce) have become increasingly visible in China. These associations often have linkages with FIEs' home countries, and they actively lobby governments in both host and home countries on behalf of their members (Han, 2012; Kennedy, 2007). Among various firm-based political strategies and collective-oriented associational activities, FIEs may choose to take an active or inactive stance in firm-based political activities, or take different collective actions by joining domestic or foreign business associations. As the Chinese government is eager to attract foreign investment to stimulate economic growth, FIEs have persuasive bargaining power and may take an apolitical stance and low-involvement strategy. Some FIEs also try to keep out of politics in the host country to avoid government intervention, which is particularly sensible in China, which is characterized by horrendous corruption among government officials (Sanyal & Guvenli, 2000). Rather, FIEs tend to value and maintain a close connection with the foreign business community. In contrast, other FIEs may strive to adapt to the local institutional environment and take a high-involvement strategy. They employ extensive political tactics to engage the host government. When taking the collective-oriented associational approach, they pursue membership in the domestic business association.

Research Questions and Method

Corporate political activities (CPA) can be defined as corporate attempts to shape government policy in ways favorable to the firm or to establish legitimacy in the new environment (Baysinger, 1984). The term *legitimacy* is one of the key concepts in political science and is usually used in theoretical analysis of the validity of power associated with a ruler, a government, a regime, or an authority. According to Suchman (1995), "legitimacy is a generalized perception or assumption that the actions of an entity are desirable, proper, or appropriate within some socially constructed system of norms, values, beliefs, and definitions." Based on interview data collected from mainland China, Ahlstrom and colleagues (2008) revealed four types of legitimacy building strategies employed by private firms. In their taxonomy, individual firms may select an appropriate environment for operation. This is the simplest strategy to undertake. If firms cannot select a more favorable environment, then they need to change their own structure or practice to conform to the current environment. In this scenario firms take actions to allow themselves to meet the requirements set by constituents in the environment in order to gain recognition from the key stakeholders.

A more complicated legitimacy building strategy is manipulation. Firms may sometimes find it difficult to conform to the normative, regulatory, or cognitive demands of the local environment. They may thus seek ways to positively change factors of their environment or shape the opinions of their constituents in the existing environments. Different from the previous two types of strategies, the manipulation strategy is often a collective action. In other words, it may require the joint action of several firms. Although such collective action is difficult to coordinate or undertake, the successful implementation of such strategies can often create a significant environmental change that is favorable to member firms. The most advanced strategy is the creation of an environment. This requires firms to devote great effort and resources to create a hospitable environment for their operation. This scenario lacks established rules, norms, principles, or models (Ahlstrom & Bruton, 2008). Firms and their stakeholders therefore need to work closely to establish commonly accepted norms.

Regarding the great variation of firms' CPS practices, it is necessary to explore what factors shape FIEs' different CPS choices. In an extensive review of CPS literature, Getz (1997) contends that the CPS research should address several interconnected key questions, including *how, why,* and *who* as well as *where* and *when.* Following this guidance, our study advances understanding in these key aspects and enriches the literature of CPS in the international business context. Furthering this line of research and drawing empirical evidence in the world's largest emerging economy, China, we develop an institutional framework to examine FIEs' different strategic choices of firm-based and collective CPS to engage the host country.

First, our study extends the scope of research on *how* firms engage in CPS. Most extant studies focus narrowly on one or two firm-based political tactics in their inquiries (Schuler et al., 2002). Meanwhile, much less attention has been paid to the collective form of CPS that firms can undertake to engage the government and shape the external environment (Ahlstrom et al., 2008; Jacomet, 2005). Even fewer studies have integrated firm-based political tactics and collective-oriented political activities in the research of CPS (Hansen, Mitchell, & Drope, 2004). Extending the research scope, we examine a whole set of CPS by analyzing *not only* multiple firm-based political tactics *but also* associational activities as an important collective venue for CPS (Aldrich & Staber, 1988). We further examine the intricate relationship between these two distinct types of CPS. Our findings thus display a more comprehensive picture of CPS.

Second, we adopt a new institutional perspective (DiMaggio & Powell, 1983; Meyer & Rowan, 1977) in the international business context (Kostova & Roth, 2002; Kostova, Roth, & Dacin, 2008) to examine *why* FIEs make different choices of CPS. In the extant literature, most explanations tend to treat firms as unitary, rational, and self-interested actors with stable preferences (Jackson & Deeg, 2008). Yet a meta-analysis shows that "antecedent variables drawn from traditional theories explaining why firms engage in CPS have limited explanatory ability (accounting for 2% to 4% of the variance in CPS on average)" (Lux, Crook, & Woehr, 2011: 238). What is particularly missing in the literature is the new institutional perspective, which has not yet become a central theory guiding the CPS inquiry (Lux et al., 2011; Rodriguez, Siegel, Hillman, & Eden, 2006). This can be partly attributed to the insufficient development of the institutional perspective on organizational strategies in the international business literature (Peng, Sun, Brian, & Hao, 2009). To fill such a research gap, we adopt an institutional framework to examine the role of multi-level institutional factors in shaping FIEs' CPS.

Third, we examine *who* as well as *where* and *when* regarding CPS adoption by investigating FIEs' political strategies in a distinct research context—China's emerging economy. Whereas much of the research on international business and politics has focused on FIE–host government negotiations at the time of initial entry into a country, little research is directed toward the post-entry political strategies of FIEs (Hillman & Wan, 2005). Moreover, because dominant theories on CPS are developed in the context of western advanced democracies (Hillman & Hitt, 1999; Hillman et al., 2004), CPS of FIEs in the emerging economy receive insufficient theoretical explanations (Deng & Kennedy, 2010). As the world's largest emerging and transitional economy, China provides an interesting research site to advance our understanding of not only *who*, but also *how* and *why* in the research of CPS. An FIE bears the institutional pressure from its home and host countries, and the institutional forces underpinning both trends of globalization and localization are strong in China (Cao & Zhao, 2009). Under such "institutional duality" (Kostova & Roth, 2002), FIEs need to decide how actively they would take firm-based political tactics to engage the host government, and how they may choose among different collective actions by joining the foreign or domestic trade association. Moreover, the government played an even more crucial role in China's "politicized capitalism" characterized by extensive government interventions, a socialist legacy, an authoritarian political system, and a complex structure of governing (Nee & Opper, 2007; see also Chen, 2007). As *guanxi* are crucial to business success in China, it is also consequential to take different stances to approach the host government and choose different associational affiliations. For all these reasons, China's distinct institutional environment offers an interesting context to enrich the literature and test our institutional arguments on FIEs' political strategies.

Our empirical analysis is based on organizational data collected from a survey on FIEs in China in late 2000s. The survey collected detailed information on multiple firm-based political tactics and collective-orientated associational membership for each FIE. The vast majority of the data was collected from China's northern coastal region, including Beijing, Tianjin, Dalian, Xuzhou, and Lianyungang. This region has received sizeable foreign investment because of its coastal location and favorable policies from the central government. We focused on this region because it shares to a large extent the same cultural tradition as northern China, which helps reduce potential complications stemming from variations in regional culture. This region is also home to FIEs from a wide array of foreign countries and economies, such as western developed countries in Europe and North America and later industrialized economies in Asia (e.g., Japan, Korea, Taiwan, and Hong Kong).

Given the low social trust during the market transition and a notoriously low response rate to mail surveys in China (<10 percent per Zheng, Morrison, & O'Neill, 2006), we relied on several local research partners and utilized their extensive connections with the local business community to secure cooperation in order to collect reliable information from FIEs. We then recruited graduate students from local universities' social science and business programs to conduct face-to-face interviews with senior managers so as to complete the questionnaire. After data cleaning, 398 of 442 surveyed FIEs were retained for statistical analysis. The sample covers a wide range of FIE home countries, types of venture, city locations, and organizational dependence levels, which are ideal for conducting our test.

Individual firms can either select an environment when they make the entry decisions or conform to the rules and norms of a local market by making necessary cultural or organizational adjustments. Different from firms in other emerging economies that are more specific in relationship building, firms operating in mainland China normally consider it essential to maintain relationships with a wide range of government entities (Ahlstrom et al., 2008). Such a perception is closely associated with the transitional regulatory context, which is characterized by lack of codified law, variation in the legal system across regions, interference by bureaucrats and regulators, and arbitrary enforcement of law by regulators. As a response, firms may choose to develop organizational knowledge of local law, improve awareness of legal developments and relevant legal issues in the region, identify gaps in the law that can be sources of problems, take care not to assume homogeneity of the law across regions, designate officials to liaison with local government officials, build relationships with bureaucratic, local officials, and respond to queries about adherence to legal codes (Ahlstrom, Young, Nair, & Law, 2003).

In our study, we incorporated a few typical choices to the questionnaire. The first group of activities is undertaken typically at the firm level. That is, individual firms are the actors who initiated such legitimacy building activities. We asked if each FIE has ever taken each of four popular political tactics, including participating in government-organized public service activities, participating in government-organized investment attraction activities, winning an award from government agencies, and hosting the visits of government officials. For each of these four political tactics, we constructed a binary variable (yes = 1).

In addition to using various firm-based political activities to enhance legitimacy, individual firms may sometimes find they are unable to locate in more favorable regions, and adapting to the normative, regulatory, and cognitive demand of the inhospitable environment can be very challenging for them. This creates the need to manipulate the environment by actively shaping the opinions of their constituents in their existing environment. Because such an undertaking may require well-designed image management work and creating a favorable impression on a wide range of stakeholders, including regulatory bodies, policy makers, and society in general, it is unlikely that individual firms can afford such an investment. More importantly, a favorable environment to foreign business can be a common good; the significant externality associated with the environment manipulation efforts makes many firms unwilling to make the investment. It is therefore more appropriate to have a collective mechanism to coordinate such efforts. To measure different forms of *collective-based associational CPS*, we asked each FIE if it was (1) a member of a foreign trade association in China, or (2) a member of a Chinese regional or industry-based trade association. For each of these two variables, we used a binary coding (yes = 1). To account for the influences of known variables on firms' choices, we included several variables to control the effects of other major economic and firm characteristics. *Firm age* refers to the number of years an FIE had operated in China as of 2007. *Firm size* refers to the total number of employees. We used the logarithm transformation of these two variables to correct their skewed distributions. *Firm's market status* refers to the respondents' evaluation of their firm's position in the principal industry, including five ranked categories (1–5) from "the bottom group" to "the top three." Sampled firms were divided into four industry groups, including *heavy industry, light industry, high-tech industry*, and *service industry* (See Table 3.1).

Table 3.1 Means, SDs, and Correlation Matrix

Variables	Mean	SD	1	2	3	4	5	6	7	8	9
1 Foreign association member	0.31	0.46									
2 Domestic association member	0.43	0.50	0.26								
3 Participate in public activity	0.49	0.50	0.26	0.40							
4 Participate in investment activity	0.48	0.50	0.24	0.33	0.44						
5 Host visit by gov. officials	0.46	0.50	0.15	0.29	0.49	0.42					
6 Win gov. award	0.50	0.50	0.25	0.41	0.57	0.41	0.47				
7 Venture type	0.45	0.50	–0.09	0.21	0.23	0.13	0.24	0.19			
8 Firm age	1.61	0.89	0.15	0.18	0.19	0.04	0.06	0.34	–0.01		
9 Firm size	4.88	1.66	0.20	0.26	0.35	0.25	0.26	0.44	0.10	0.27	
10 Market status	3.87	0.87	0.13	0.11	0.18	0.11	0.21	0.24	–0.01	0.22	0.32
11 Heavy industry	0.26	0.44	0.06	–0.04	0.00	0.09	0.06	0.04	–0.02	–0.03	0.02
12 Light industry	0.38	0.49	–0.04	0.04	0.06	0.15	0.15	0.09	0.08	–0.05	0.13
13 High-tech industry	0.10	0.31	0.03	–0.03	–0.08	–0.11	–0.10	–0.09	–0.10	0.04	0.03
14 Service industry	0.25	0.43	–0.04	0.02	–0.01	–0.17	–0.15	–0.07	–0.00	0.06	–0.17
15 Asia	0.34	0.47	0.13	–0.10	–0.07	–0.02	–0.13	–0.07	–0.17	0.01	–0.02
16 North America	0.21	0.41	0.02	0.02	–0.05	–0.02	–0.02	–0.03	0.06	–0.01	–0.04
17 HK, Macao, Taiwan	0.27	0.44	–0.05	0.08	0.18	0.10	0.19	0.12	0.12	0.04	0.04
18 Europe	0.14	0.35	–0.06	0.01	–0.01	–0.03	0.00	0.02	0.01	0.00	0.05
19 Cultural distance	5.06	1.43	–0.04	0.02	–0.11	–0.04	–0.06	–0.04	0.03	–0.05	0.01
20 Municipalities	0.29	0.46	0.11	–0.05	–0.07	–0.15	–0.16	–0.08	–0.15	0.12	–0.05
21 Provincial capitals	0.44	0.50	–0.12	–0.07	–0.14	–0.08	–0.13	–0.11	–0.09	–0.05	–0.03
22 Prefectures	0.27	0.44	0.02	0.13	0.23	0.24	0.31	0.20	0.25	–0.06	0.08
23 Marketization index	8.48	0.85	–0.04	0.02	0.00	0.09	0.03	–0.01	0.14	0.08	0.11

10	11	12	13	14	15	16	17	18	19	20	21	22
0.08												
−0.09	−0.46											
0.06	−0.20	−0.27										
−0.03	−0.34	−0.46	−0.20									
−0.18	0.12	0.08	−0.12	−0.12								
0.11	−0.02	−0.08	0.20	−0.02	−0.38							
−0.05	−0.12	0.06	−0.02	0.07	−0.44	−0.32						
0.20	0.03	−0.05	−0.01	0.03	−0.29	−0.21	−0.25					
0.18	0.06	−0.08	0.09	−0.04	−0.19	0.43	−0.68	0.59				
0.18	−0.18	−0.32	0.20	0.37	−0.21	0.11	−0.01	0.12	0.11			
−0.06	0.26	0.03	−0.08	−0.22	0.22	−0.03	−0.15	−0.06	−0.02	−0.57		
−0.12	−0.10	0.30	−0.12	−0.14	−0.03	−0.08	0.17	−0.06	−0.09	−0.39	−0.54	
0.06	−0.05	−0.06	0.03	0.09	−0.26	0.10	0.08	0.12	0.10	0.15	−0.24	0.12

FIEs' CPS and Institutional Contexts

New institutional theories argue that organizational behaviors and choices are shaped by the institutional environment (DiMaggio & Powell, 1983; Meyer & Rowan, 1977). "Institutions are composed of culture-cognitive, normative, and regulative elements that, together with associated activities and resources, provide stability and meaning to social life" (Scott, 2001: 48). To gain public support, an organization strives to take legitimate actions, which are regarded as "desirable, proper, or appropriate within some socially constructed system of norms, values, beliefs and definitions" (Suchman, 1995: 574). Because an organization is cognitively, normatively, and culturally embedded in the macro environment (Dacin, Ventresca, & Beal, 1999), organizational behaviors tend to follow the "logic of appropriateness," which is often taken for granted in a given institutional environment.

Compared to firms that operate in a single country, FIEs face dual institutional pressures stemming from both the home and the host countries. Under such "institutional duality" (Kostova & Roth, 2002), characterized by the coexistence of alternative institutional logics, the taken-for-grantedness of institutionalized practices can no longer be presumed. Multiple domains of the external institutional environment and competing cognitive and normative pressures present a particular challenge to FIEs as they seek legitimacy (Kostova et al., 2008). On the one hand, FIEs bear the institutional influence from their home countries. As FIEs often face fierce competition in the international market, they also tend to cherish a global view and foreign connections. On the other hand, in the distinct local institutional environment in an emerging economy like China, they need to overcome the "liability of foreignness" and adapt to the local environment so as to fit into the host country and gain organizational legitimacy (Kostova & Zaheer, 1999).

It is sensitive for FIEs to take political actions in the host country; they thus are particularly concerned with the legitimacy of such actions and strive to take political strategies that are perceived appropriate and legitimate (Hansen & Mitchell, 2000). To what extent an FIE would launch firm-based political activities to directly engage the host government depends on its cognitive orientation and institutional background. To adopt effective political tactics to target the host government, an FIE needs to achieve a better understanding of the host country and make sense of the local institutional environment. In China, as building *guanxi* with the government is complex and subtle, it requires deep knowledge of the local culture and social norms. Similarly, an FIE's institutional background and orientation further affect its choice of collective strategy between joining a local or foreign trade association. Within a complex institutional environment, a firm desires to maintain a sensible social identity based on group affiliation, and its choice of an "appropriate" association is shaped by organizational identification and institutional linkages (Rao, Davis, & Ward, 2000).

As an FIE faces dual institutional pressure, competing institutional forces of its home and host countries provide different cognitive knowledge, social norms, and regulative policies, which prescribe different role models and scripts for organizational behaviors (Kostova et al., 2008). Under such institutional duality, an FIE's strategic choice (i.e., taking active or inactive political actions to target the host government and joining a domestic or foreign trade association) is shaped by strength and characteristics of its institutional connections to the two sides. In a sense, it reflects a tug of war between the institutional forces of an FIE's host country and those of its home country. The final result depends on which side of institutional linkages is more potent and exerts a stronger imprint on the FIE. Below we elaborate on such linkages of FIEs at country and regional levels and develop an explanation that accounts for FIEs' different choices of both firm-based and collective-oriented CPS.

Home-Country Effects

Foreign firms often learn two things when they operate in China. First, they learn that the Chinese government, especially the local government, can exert significant influence on business operations, and they pose a major challenge for firms who want to establish legitimacy. Second, they learned that there are a wide range of different practices that can be employed to build legitimacy. Whereas it is rare for a single firm to adopt all these different practices, it is also true that most international firms use more than one tactic. Different from the first movers to the Chinese markets, later entrants find that having just one contact in the higher level government is not enough to navigate through the cumbersome bureaucracy or cope with uncertainties (Ahlstrom & Bruton, 2001; Ahlstrom et al., 2008). For many firms, finding appropriate means to strengthen their relationships with key stakeholders is still a challenge. Some may choose to follow the indigenous practices surrounding building legitimacy through *guanxi*, charity, and gift giving. Empirical studies have frequently shown that international firms tried to learn from their local counterparts and adopted the localized practice. Managers reported that they watched the activities of their Chinese partners carefully to learn what they do in this regard, whereas the other managers reported more general copying of their legitimacy-building activity (Ahlstrom et al., 2008). Some firms even went beyond this and tried to take over troubled diversified SOE, hoping this would help them in getting business from the province's other state owned enterprises.

However, the degree to which firms adopt the local practices or use similar practices to enhance their legitimacy in the local market is affected by the difference of institutional background between host countries and home countries. Western developed countries in Europe and North America have acquired hegemonic political, economic, social, and cultural power in the world. They have developed sophisticated management philosophies and systems, and many of their practices are theorized as "best practices" and widely diffused internationally (e.g., Baron & Kreps, 1999). Moreover, their political systems are dramatically different from that in China, and CPS have different connotations and take different forms and strategies (Hillman, 2003; Hillman & Hitt, 1999; Hillman & Wan, 2005). Therefore, FIEs from western developed countries acquire potent cognitive and normative orientations and also strong managerial culture. They tend to maintain their connections with the foreign business community, and are more likely to resist the temptation of using localized means to engage the host government and the local business association. In contrast, firms from newly industrialized economies in Asia (e.g., South Korea and Taiwan, which account for a major part of China's FDI) are more likely to adopt localized practices. For instance, Taiwanese managers often share similar culture traditions and tend to subscribe to a similar cognitive institutional structure. This is not only due to the influence of Confucianism on the culture, but also because these markets are in transition even though they are less turbulent than that of China. Therefore it can be expected that many political actions are similar in these places and China. Based on these considerations, we expect that FIEs from western developed economies are less likely to take political tactics to engage the host government and are less likely to join a domestic trade association than joining a foreign trade association. In contrast, firms from newly industrialized nations are more likely to adopt localized political tactics and are more likely to join Chinese domestic trade associations.

In our empirical analysis, we incorporated information on FIEs' countries of origin (*FIE home country*). The vast majority of firms in our sample are from western developed economies and later industrialized economies in Asia. Among western developed countries, we distinguished North America (U.S. and Canada) from European countries, as there are considerable differences between them in political system and management culture (e.g., Guillén, 1994). We distinguished Hong Kong, Macao, and Taiwan (HMT) from the rest of later industrialized Asian economies (e.g., Korea, Japan, Singapore, etc.) because HMT have closer economic, social, and cultural connections with China.

We used multivariate probit models to test our hypotheses on the effects of institutional factors on adopting those four firm-based political tactics (H1a to H6a). Models 1–4 in Table 3.2 report the estimates on those four political tactics, respectively. As shown in the lower panel of Table 3.2, the likelihood ratio statistic rejects the hypothesis that the four equations are independent, suggesting that these equations are significantly correlated. This indicates that these equations are possibly influenced in the same direction by unmeasured effects. It thus justifies our use of multivariate probit models in analyzing these multiple political tactics.

The model results show that FIEs from western developed economies are less likely to employ political tactics to target the host government. Among the four models, Model 2 shows that compared with the FIEs from

Table 3.2 Multivariate Probit Models Predicting Adoption of Four Firm-Based Political Tactics

	M1: Participate in Public Activities		M2: Participate in Investment Activity		M3: Win Gov. Award		M4: Host Visit by Gov. Official	
	Beta	SE	Beta	SE	Beta	SE	Beta	SE
Country of origin (ref: Europe)								
North America	0.09	0.15	0.42 ***	0.12	0.26	0.41	0.26 ***	0.04
Asia	-0.11	0.32	0.57 †	0.34	-0.17	0.65	0.17	0.12
HK, Macao, Taiwan (HMT)	0.28	0.57	0.96	0.67	0.06	0.39	1.07 ***	0.21
Cultural distance	-0.04 *	0.02	0.04	0.03	0.07	0.10	-0.13 *	0.07
Marketization index	-0.71 *	0.31	0.43 *	0.17	-0.38 ***	0.07	-0.21 †	0.20
Culture × Marketization	0.02 *	0.01	-0.03 ***	0.01	-0.01	0.02	0.02 *	0.01
Control variables:								
Firm location (ref: Municipalities)								
Provincial capitals	-0.20	0.21	-0.06	0.36	0.17	0.45	0.08	0.38
Prefectures	0.38 ***	0.11	0.27	0.26	0.77	0.47	0.89 **	0.34
Venture type (ref: WFOF)	0.45 ***	0.12	-0.02	0.18	0.44 *	0.22	0.39 *	0.17
Firm age (log)	0.28 *	0.13	-0.08	0.15	0.59 ***	0.11	-0.01	0.12
Firm size (log)	0.25 ***	0.04	0.19 ***	0.01	0.33 ***	0.03	0.20 ***	0.06
Firm market status	0.17	0.13	0.09	0.14	0.26 ***	0.02	0.41 **	0.16
Industry type (ref: Service)								
Heavy industry	-0.18 *	0.08	0.39	0.42	0.04	0.24	0.21	0.24
Light industry	-0.19	0.13	0.42	0.38	-0.24	0.37	0.05	0.23
High-tech industry	-0.51 *	0.26	-0.19	0.28	-0.78 *	0.41	-0.61 ***	0.18
Constant	-0.36	1.74	-4.41 *	2.03	-0.35	0.27	-2.06	2.29
N	341							
Wald-Chi2	257				***		***	

Rho 21 0.48 ***
Rho 31 0.56 ***
Rho 41 0.52 ***
Rho 32 0.52 ***
Rho 42 0.41 ***
Rho 43 0.54 ***

Notes: † p<0.1, * p<0.05, ** p<0.01, *** p<0.001 (two-tailed tests). Cluster robust standard errors reported.

European countries, those from Asian countries (mainly later industrialized economies) are more likely to participate in government-organized invest-ment attraction activities. Model 4 shows that FIEs from HMT are more likely to host visits by government officials. Interestingly, we find that FIEs from North America are also more likely to employ these two types of tac-tics. The reason may lie in that North American FIEs are more independent and lack administrative control from the government of their home coun-tries. Thus, they more freely engage the host government. A separate t-test of coefficients in Model 4 shows that HMT FIEs are still more likely to host visits by government officials than North American FIEs. This is probably because that HMT FIEs have more extensive interpersonal connections with local government officials.

After analyzing firm-based political strategies, we examined the impact of institutional factors on joining domestic versus foreign trade associations as the collective leverage of CPS. Table 3.3 presents the results of the logis-tic models predicting FIEs being a member of domestic and foreign trade associations. Consistent with our speculation, Model 1 shows that FIEs from HMT are more likely to join Chinese domestic trade associations than European FIEs. FIEs from Asia and also North America are more likely to join foreign trade associations (Model 2). FIEs from European countries have more constraints against joining various foreign trade associations due to the broad administrative power and influence of their home countries.

The Influence of Regional Market Conditions

In addition to the general country background as discussed above, the more specific national culture of an FIE's home country and its cultural distance from the host country (here, China) can further affect an FIE's strategic choice. When the national cultures of an FIE's home and host countries are similar to each other, there is more common ground in the philosophi-cal and cultural underpinning of organizational orientation and practices. Cultural similarities also enhance communication quality and help develop mutual trust. Consequently, an FIE has fewer cultural and identity barriers to connecting with the host government and the local business circle. In contrast, a large cultural distance between an FIE's home and host countries makes it more difficult to reorient organizational identification, to acquire the subtleties of Chinese culture, and to appreciate subtle *guanxi* practices (Gamble, 2003; Taylor, Beechler, & Napier, 1996). They tend to be less active in directly engaging the local government and business community, and are more likely to use the foreign trade association as a collective lever-age in CPS.

However, the cognitive institution and the regulatory institution are closely connected. When firms operate on a level playing field, the influence of different cultures tends to diminish. In other words, the effect of cultural

Table 3.3 Logistic Regressions Predicting Trade Association Membership

	M1: Foreign Association Member only			M2: Domestic Association Member only			M3: Member of both Associations		
Independent variables									
Country of origin (ref: Europe)									
North America	0.503	0.261	*	0.024	0.251		0.043	0.031	
Asia	0.771	0.203	***	-0.012	0.146		0.039	0.056	
HK, Macao, Taiwan (HMT)	0.529	0.492		0.385	0.172	*	0.024	0.076	
Cultural distance	0.062	0.036	†	-0.073	0.024	**	-0.056	0.068	
Marketization index	-0.136	0.057	*	-0.076	0.037	*	-0.354	0.153	*
Culture × Marketization	-0.003	0.001	**	0.002	0.001	**	-0.002	0.003	
Control variables									
Firm location (ref: Municipalities)									
Provincial capitals	0.771	0.484		-0.001	0.375		0.770	0.643	
Prefectures	1.204	0.237	***	0.081	0.648		1.004	0.355	**
Venture type (ref: WFOF)	0.466	0.346	†	0.652	0.094	***	0.750	0.349	*
Firm age (log)	0.207	0.126		0.157	0.100		0.511	0.132	***
Firm size (log)	-0.025	0.220		0.164	0.147		0.450	0.107	***
Firm market status	0.301	0.244		0.144	0.083	†	0.066	0.201	
Industry type (ref: Service)									
Heavy industry	0.355	0.157	*	-0.209	0.523		-0.684	0.728	
Light industry	0.416	0.339		0.267	0.530		-0.463	0.849	
High-tech industry	0.057	0.338		0.331	0.943		-0.526	0.305	†
Constant	-1.876	2.701		-3.506	0.856	***	-0.913	3.134	
N	52			105			85		

Notes: † p<0.1, * p<0.05, ** p<0.01, *** p<0.001 (two-tailed tests). Cluster robust standard errors reported.

difference will be moderated by the quality of local regulatory institutions. The uneven economic development and fragmented market environment in China imposes different regional institutional contexts on FIEs. Laws and regulations are often interpreted by people with jurisdiction over a given industrial sector, department, or region (Peng & Luo, 2000). This implies that officials have greater discretion over key administrative decisions. Although in regions with greater exposure to foreign investments the local governments did a good job of codifying local regulations and limiting the power of officials, these locations are still exceptional. Many managers agreed that traditional networking practices, such as social eating and gift giving, are often part of the operation costs in China, especially for smaller, less connected firms (Ahlstrom et al., 2003).

In a region with a higher level of market development, its economic structure is more open to the global market, and traditional *guanxi* practices are weakened (Guthrie, 1998). In contrast, in a region with a lower level of market development, its economy is more locally oriented and inherits more traditional structures and practices of the socialist command economy. The government continues to play a central role in the local economic life. In these regions, the cognitive, normative, and regulative institutional forces all pressure FIEs to localize their practices. We therefore argue that when firms operate in more developed local markets, the impact of cultural differences tends to diminish, whereas when firms operate in less developed markets, the impact of cultural differences will be more pronounced.

To empirically test this proposition, we operationalized cultural differences among nations and regional market institutional differences using two variables. *Cultural distance* was constructed based on a Global Leadership and Organizational Behavior Effectiveness (GLOBE) study. GLOBE develops the refined cultural indexes in nine dimensions, including uncertainty avoidance, power distance, institutional collectivism, in-group collectivism, gender egalitarianism, assertiveness, future orientation, performance orientation, and humane orientation (House, Hanges, Javidan, Dorfman, & Gupta, 2004). For each society, it probes both the actual practices and situations and also the ideal situations along those nine cultural dimensions. Because these two sets of measures are highly correlated, in this study we focused on the actual practices and situations regarding cultural values. Then we computed the difference between an FIE's country of origin and China in each of these nine dimensions. We aggregated the absolute value of these differences to measure the cultural distance between each FIE home country and China. To measure various market environments across regions, we used the *marketization index* based on the index of marketization of Chinese provinces developed by China's National Economic Research Institute (Fan, Wang, & Zhu, 2011).

Regarding the main effects of the cultural differences, we find that cultural distance between an FIE's home and host countries is negatively associated with the likelihood of taking firm-based CPS. Among four models, this variable shows a significantly negative effect on the likelihood of participating in government organized public activities and on the likelihood of hosting the visits of government officials. As these tactics particularly involve private *guanxi* practices and require a deeper understanding of the local culture and norms, a larger cultural distance presents a salient barrier in this aspect. We then examined the effects of regional institutional factors. The marketization index has a significantly negative effect on the likelihood of participating in government organized public activities, winning a government award, or hosting the visits of government officials. This indicates that FIEs located in regions with a higher level of marketization are less likely to employ political tactics to engage the host government. Moreover, we find that cultural distance is negatively related to domestic trade association membership. FIEs in regions with a higher marketization level are less likely to join domestic trade associations.

We then tested whether the regional market conditions moderate the influence of cultural distance on firms' use of different political tactics. Table 3.2 and Table 3.3 summarize these results. We find that in three out of four types of firm-based CPAs, the quality of regional market institutions significantly moderate the influence of cultural distance. Meanwhile, regarding the collective-based CPAs, significant moderation effects also hold in models that estimate the joining of foreign and domestic trade associations. The results in general lend support to our theoretical hypothesis that when firms operate in more marketized regions, the influence of cultural distance will be reduced.

Business Associations as a Way to Enhance B-to-G Ties

Collective associational activities and firm-based political tactics are complementary to each other, and the former can nurture the development of the latter. Wank (1996) studied firms' *guanxi* capital investment in Xiamen city. He noticed that *guanxi* capital investment can be made in two ways. One is through the business process itself. That is, through repeated exchanges, trust emerges between two individuals, enhancing the possibility of cooperation. In addition, *guanxi* capital investments are also made by participation in associations that have been revived or newly founded in the reform era. Previous studies indicate that business associations lobby the host government to pursue favorable treatment by disseminating industry information and promoting the association agenda (Peng & Luo, 2000; Unger, 1996; Wank, 1996, 2002). Through these associations, firms can establish a communication channel with officials to better engage the host government (Ahlstrom et al., 2008). The associational process can also enhance awareness and sensitivity of CPS and offer opportunities for an FIE to imitate other members to employ more sophisticated political tactics. Scholars observed that *guanxi* investments can seek to secure favorable discretion in resources controlled by the association's sponsoring public agency.

For instance, operators assumed leadership positions in local branches and developed personal connections with officials of the industry and commerce bureau. They used these ties to seek favorable decisions in discretionary matters controlled by the Bureau. One example is that the Bureau can grant a selected group of member firms the ability to trade in valuable but scarce raw materials. In addition to the immediate economic benefits, some associations help entrepreneurs develop bureaucratic contacts. They help firm managers or owners develop connections, make friends, and exchange information through organized lectures, parties, and informal gatherings, to which high ranking city government officials are invited (Wank, 1996).

As the formal, effective institutional rules are absent in China's emerging economy, network connections with other firms and with trade associations provide important "structural support" (Xin & Pearce, 1996). In this context, foreign trade associations have an important political functions and serve as a communication channel with the government (Ahlstrom et al., 2008; Deng & Kennedy, 2010). There is evidence that FIEs utilize foreign trade associations even to a greater extent than domestic firms to achieve their political goals (Kennedy, 2007). For instance, the American Chamber of Commerce in China explicitly stated that their cooperation programs enable companies of all sizes to engage directly with industry leaders and the U.S. and Chinese governments, as well as to facilitate business opportunities in various industries. The cooperative programs offer a forum for companies to explain and demonstrate the effectiveness of their products, services, and technologies within the context of operational solutions and the Chinese government's developmental goals. The programs also promote government-to-government interaction with industry participation. The member companies often organize training programs and trade missions to the U.S. for government officials and participate in discussions with regulators as a group rather than as an individual company.[3]

Whereas previous literature recognized the importance of both firm-based and collective-based associational activities, these two types of CPS were largely treated as two distinct types of CPS, and research on the intricate relationship between these two types of activities remains scarce (Hansen et al., 2004). To extend the research scope, we further examine the relationship between associational activities (i.e., joining foreign or domestic trade associations) and firm-based political tactics. Based on the above evidence, we postulate that affiliation with a domestic or foreign business association enhances an FIE's activeness in taking firm-based political tactics to target the host government. We use M-plus to specify a path model that has a similar structure to the multivariate probit models. The only difference is that trade association memberships are endogenous to the independent and control variables, and trade association memberships in turn affect adoption of firm-based political tactics. Based on findings from the previous logistic regression and multivariate probit analyses, we allow the error terms of joining foreign and domestic trade associations to be correlated and also the

Table 3.4 Path Models Predicting the Adoption of Political Strategies

	M1: Participate in Public Activities			M2: Participate in Investment Activity			M3: Win Gov. Award			M4: Host Visit by Gov. Official		
	Beta	SE		Beta	SE		Beta	SE		Beta	SE	
Foreign trade association member	0.19	0.07	**	0.28	0.10	**	0.18	0.10	†	0.17	0.13	
Domestic trade association member	0.44	0.07	***	0.30	0.06	***	0.47	0.10	***	0.34	0.09	†
Country of origin (ref: *Europe*)												
North America	0.08	0.08		−0.11	0.17		0.23	0.12	*	0.23	0.12	*
Asia	−0.07	0.17		−0.05	0.10		−0.02	0.17		−0.03	0.16	
HK, Macao, Taiwan	0.18	0.06	**	0.03	0.09		0.16	0.03	***	0.24	0.09	**
Cultural distance	−0.05	0.08		0.08	0.06		−0.01	0.05		0.02	0.03	
Marketization index	−0.01	0.03		0.04	0.02	†	0.06	0.07		0.01	0.02	
Control variables:												
Firm location (ref: *Municipalities*)												
Provincial capitals	0.10	0.06	†	0.01	0.06		0.06	0.08		−0.02	0.07	
Prefectures	0.06	0.02	***	0.15	0.04	***	−0.01	0.04		0.07	0.03	*
Venture type (ref: *WFOF*)	0.30	0.09	***	−0.06	0.09		0.35	0.14	**	0.44	0.12	***
Firm age (log)	−0.01	0.04		−0.14	0.09	†	0.22	0.12	†	−0.16	0.04	***
Firm size (log)	0.19	0.05	***	0.11	0.05	*	0.27	0.06	***	0.08	0.05	†
Firm market status	0.22	0.06	***	0.16	0.04	***	0.17	0.10		0.36	0.08	***
Industry type (ref: *Service*)												
Heavy industry	−0.23	0.32		0.24	0.21	*	0.21	0.23		0.34	0.11	**
Light industry	−0.12	0.19		0.32	0.18	†	0.12	0.26		0.47	0.19	*
High-tech industry	−0.54	0.18	**	−0.43	0.21	*	−0.51	0.29	†	−0.24	0.17	
Constant	−2.56	0.65	***	−3.37	0.46	***	−3.64	0.83		−2.59	0.41	***

(Continued)

Table 3.4 (Continued)

Wald tests of parameter constraints:			Covariance:								
H_0: $\beta_{\text{foreign association}}$ (M1) = $\beta_{\text{domestic association}}$ (M1)	5.87 (1)	**	Cov.21	0.38	***						
H_0: $\beta_{\text{foreign association}}$ (M2) = $\beta_{\text{domestic association}}$ (M2)	0.01 (1)		Cov.31	0.28	***	Cov.32	0.22	**			
H_0: $\beta_{\text{foreign association}}$ (M3) = $\beta_{\text{domestic association}}$ (M3)	3.02 (1)	†	Cov.41	0.41	***	Cov.42	0.29	***	Cov.43	0.38	***
H_0: $\beta_{\text{foreign association}}$ (M4) = $\beta_{\text{domestic association}}$ (M4)	0.85 (1)		Model Fit Statistics: RMSEA = 0.01; CFI = 0.99; TLI = 0.97; WRMR = 0.23								

Notes: N = 358. † $p<0.1$, * $p<0.05$, ** $p<0.01$, *** $p<0.001$ (two-tailed tests). Cluster robust standard errors reported.

error terms of adoptions of four political tactics to be correlated. The model fit statistics show that the model fits the data well. The rooted mean square error of approximation (RMSEA) is 0.014, which indicates a good fit. The comparative fit index (CFI) is 0.998 and TLI is 0.969, which are greater than the conventional cut-off point of 0.90 to ensure that mis-specified models are not accepted (Hu & Bentler, 1999). Table 3.4 presents the results of the path models, which are generally consistent with H7a. We find that in all four models (M1-M4), the coefficients of domestic trade association membership are positive and significant, suggesting that being members of these associations increases FIEs' likelihood of taking all four firm-based tactics. Meanwhile, foreign association membership is significantly associated with most political tactics, excepting hosting the visits of government officials.

We then explored whether domestic trade association membership is more effective in enhancing FIE's engagement with the local government. As shown in the lower left section of Table 3.4, the Wald tests of parameter constraints reject the null hypothesis that the coefficients of foreign and domestic trade association memberships are equal in Model 1 and Model 3. This suggests that the effect of domestic trade association membership is significantly stronger than foreign association membership on FIEs in terms of participating in government-organized public activities and wining a government award. But the Wald test cannot reject a similar null hypothesis in Model 2. In Model 4, only domestic association membership is significant. Overall, these findings lend strong support to our argument.

However, the relationship between the association membership and firm-based CPS can be very complex. Our argument that associational activities can promote firm-based CPS is based both on the argument we proposed and on previous qualitative studies that focus on the function of local business associations. For example, Wank (2002) has shown how local business associations work with member firms to arrange visits by high-profile leaders so as to enhance the firms' political legitimacy. We thus tend to believe that the association membership is more likely to promote firm-based CPS not vice versa. In order to obtain empirical support for this speculation, we constructed a model using not only association membership but also used firm-based CPS as endogenous variables and explored whether firm-based CPS can promote business membership. Our results are presented in Table 3.5.

From the tables we can see that, except for the participation in investment activities, other firm-based CPS has no significant impact on association membership. Of course, we understand that this simple analysis cannot convincingly rule out the reverse causality issue. The cross-sectional research design does not allow us to do a more rigorous causality test. We thus acknowledge this issue as a limitation of our study and admit that our cross-sectional data does not allow us to make a more convincing argument about the causal directions between collective and firm-based CPS. It is possible that in certain situations, politically active firms are also more likely to

Table 3.5 The Analysis of Causal Directions Between Firm-Based and Collective CPS

	M1: Participate in public activities		M2: Participate in investment activity		M3: Acquire government recognition		M4: Host officials' visit	
	Beta	SE	Beta	SE	Beta	SE	Beta	SE
Domestic trade association member	0.44	0.07 ***	0.3	0.06 ***	0.47	0.1 ***	0.34	0.09 †
Foreign trade association member	0.19	0.07 **	0.28	0.1 **	0.18	0.1 †	0.17	0.13

	M1: Foreign trade association member	M2: Domestic trade association member
Participate in public activities	0.588	0.710
Participate in investment activity	0.678 *	0.457 **
Acquire government recognition	−0.091	0.024
Host officials' visits	0.546	0.933

adopt or promote collective CPS by joining or even organizing the domestic and foreign trade associations. We hope future studies can further explore this issue by using a more appropriate research design.

Conclusion

It is widely documented that FIEs often take various political strategies and activities to strengthen their relationships with host governments in order to improve their chances of survival and success in the new market. However, substantial variations can be observed in terms of the types of activities FIEs adopted, the effort they put into such activities, and the approaches they employed. Whereas some FIEs tend to localize their practices, others put more emphasis on a global orientation and strategy. It remains a puzzling question what factors shape FIEs' different strategy choices of forming political ties with the host government and gaining collective bargaining power or influence by joining a local or foreign trade association. Taking China's transitional economy as an example, this chapter addresses these issues. We expand the scope of CPS study by including multiple types of firm-based CPS and two types of collective CPS choices. Borrowing insights from new institutional perspectives, we investigate the influence of institutional factors at different levels on the use of firm- and collective-based CPS and explore the linkages between these two dimensions.

This study contributes to the existing literature by combining the new institutional perspective with the CPS inquiry in the international business context. We argue that as FIEs enters a new market, they face dual institutional pressure from both home and host countries. The coexistence of the competing institutional forces provides different cognitive knowledge, social norms, and regulative policies that differ greatly from each other. FIEs' strategic choices therefore depend heavily on the relative potency of these two systems. In general, we find that cultural and institutional similarities are associated with more extensive use of CPS. The likelihood of employing these political strategies is high for Asian firms. At the regional level, the quality of the market institutions determines firms' efforts in various political activities. Being in regions with higher levels of marketization reduces FIEs' reliance on these political activities.

More importantly, we studied the interactive effects between different levels of institutional factors. Previous studies have often quoted cultural distance as a major factor that inhibits international firms from better embedding themselves into the host country's social and economic system. Our study enriches our understanding of the cultural influence by arguing that the relative magnitude of such cultural influence tends to be moderated by local market conditions. Our empirical results suggest that when firms operate in an environment where production factors are distributed effectively through market mechanisms and producers' legal rights are protected by effective market supporting institutions, the influence of cultural differences tends to diminish.

In addition to the study of firm-based CPS, we also explored the influence of institutional conditions on FIEs' associational activities in the host country. We argue that just like in advanced democracies, trade associations serve as important means of coalition building. Such associational activities have advantages over firm-based political activities in several aspects and provide benefits that cannot be achieved by direct political participation. However, FIEs' joining activities are also conditioned by the specific institutional context they are embedded in. At the macro institutional level, FIEs from Asia and North America, in general, are better able to take advantage of the trade associations as compared to their European counterparts. The shorter cultural distance between the Chinese mainland and Hong Kong, Macao, and Taiwan facilitates FIEs from these regions in taking advantage of Chinese domestic associations. Regarding the regional institutional context, foreign trade associations are more popular among firms in more marketized cities, whereas in less advanced cities. foreign trade associations have limited influence; as a result, FIEs are more likely to develop a closer relationship with Chinese domestic trade associations.

Our study further advances the existing literature by specifying the connections between individual and collective dimensions of CPS. As we argued, trade associations have important political functions and serve as communication channels to the host country government; this channel helps firms strengthen their relations with the local authorities, which is often translated into better institutional support. Our results generally support this proposition. It shows that being members of trade associations, foreign or domestic, increases the extensity of firm-government interactions: first, member firms have more chances to interact with host country authorities in all four dimensions of firm-based CPS; second, member firms tend to adopt multiple types of CPS simultaneously. More importantly, we find that compared to foreign trade associations, Chinese domestic trade associations turned out to be more effective in facilitating their members' ability to build quality institutional connections with local authorities.

The evidence presented in this research has practical value to the practitioners who operate businesses in China. Many studies have pointed out the utility of the CPS in helping firms navigate the uncertain environment; some further suggest that FIEs adapt to the host country environment by emulating the practices of the domestic firms, their alliance partners, or other international counterparts (Li, Zhou, & Shao, 2009; Park & Luo, 2001; Peng & Luo, 2000). Our study highlights the importance of a good understanding of firms' immediate institutional environment. It argues that FIEs should base their strategy choices on their idiosyncratic environmental characteristics rather than blindly emulating others' activities. In addition, this study distinguished two levels of corporate political strategies (collective-level and firm-level), established the alignments between collective- and firm-level political strategies, and pointed out that associational activity can further promote the interaction between firms and states. It suggested that whereas foreign business associations can help strengthen firm-government ties, practitioners should go beyond their homophilious social circles and take advantage of local business associations, because the latter is shown to be more effective in helping foreign firms overcome environmental uncertainties, gain legitimacy in the new market, and get institutional support from host governments. That being said, we argue that although trust building, connection, and alliances with key stakeholders remain important in the current institutional context, firms should not neglect the importance of formal contracts when doing business in China. Foreign firms need to carefully stipulate contract terms with their business partners and make sure every related party understands exactly what is expected. When doing business in a new market, it is important to cultivate relations with key stakeholders, but it is also important for firms to understand their legal rights and obligations. These preparations will help firms effectively offset the potential operation risks in the new environment.

These results provide insights into FIEs political strategies in a host country that has undergone profound institutional transitions. Generalizing from the findings to FIEs in other emerging economies seems plausible. Although there are certain characteristics of the Chinese case that make it unique, many of the findings are useful as researchers attempt to understand FIEs' strategy choices in other emerging economies (Ahlstrom et al., 2008). In particular, institutional duality is evident in many transitional settings, and regional as well as sectoral variations often jointly define the institutional environment that FIEs face; therefore a better understanding of FIEs' CPS can be achieved only when various institutional factors are accounted for. Likewise, in many emerging economies, business associations serve as important intermediaries to situate FIEs in the targeted market. The extent to which these associational powers facilitate FIEs' operation in the host countries may depend heavily on the strength of country–institutional as well as regional–institutional constraints.

Appendix
Method

The majority of the research that empirically studies corporate political strategies focuses primarily on one or two firm-based political tactics. The few studies considering multiple political tactics generally treat them either as equivalent activities and use a factor analysis method to combine different dimensions, or in another extreme as independent activities regardless of the fact that they can be complementary to each other (Schuler et al., 2002). In this study, we employed multivariate probit models to estimate FIEs' likelihood of adopting a wide range of firm-based political tactics. This method allows us not only to weigh the relative importance of a set of tactics, but also to estimate the relationships between them. In terms of the structure, this model is similar to that of a seemingly unrelated regression with multiple binary dependent variables. Our study included four dependent variables; that is, we needed to simultaneously estimate four equations, each of which focuses on one political tactic. The models allow the error terms of each equation to be correlated, and the parameters are estimated using a simulated maximum likelihood estimator (in particular, the Geweke-Hajivassiliou-Keane [GHK] simulator is used), which is asymptotically consistent and equivalent to the true maximum likelihood estimator as the ratio of the square root of sample size to the number of draws tends to zero (Cappellari & Jenkins, 2003). We use the Huber-White (heteroscedasticity-consistent) estimator to calculate the standard error. We adopted a similar method to examine the relationship between collective-oriented associational activities and firm-based political tactics. We specified a path model to parse out these relationships. We used M-plus to estimate the parameters as well as possible correlations between the error terms of foreign and domestic association memberships and correlations among the error terms of those four political tactics. As for the analysis of adoption of individual or collective CPS, we recognize that an FIE can be a member of foreign trade associations only, a member of domestic associations only, or members of both associations (see Kennedy, 2007). Thus, we ran the multinomial logistic model and used firms with no association memberships as the reference category.

Notes

1 For more information, please see: http://www.europeanchamber.com.cn/en/lobby-actions
2 For more information, please see: http://www.acfic.org.cn/Web/c_000000010002 000100070004/d_1577.htm
3 For detailed cooperative programs and constitution, see: http://www.amcham china.org/about/cooperative-programs

References

Ahlstrom, D., & Bruton, G. D. (2001). Learning from successful local private firms in China: Establishing legitimacy. *Academy of Management Executive, 15*(4), 72–83.

Ahlstrom, D., Bruton, G. D., & Yeh, K. S. (2008). Private firms in China: Building legitimacy in an emerging economy. *Journal of World Business, 43*(4): 385–399.

Ahlstrom, D., Young, M. N., Nair, A., & Law, P. (2003). Managing the institutional environment: challenges for foreign firms in post-WTO China. *SAM Advanced Management Journal, 68*(1), 41–49.Aldrich, H. E., & Staber, U. H. (1988). Organizing business interests: Patterns of trade association foundings, transformations and deaths. In G. R. Carroll (Eds.), *Ecological Models of Organization* (pp. 111–126). Cambridge, MA: Ballinger.

Baron, J. N., & Kreps, D. M. (1999). *Strategic Human Resources: Frameworks for General Managers*. New York: Wiley.

Baysinger, B. D. (1984). Domain maintenance as an objective of business political activity: An expanded typology. *Academy of Management Review, 9*(2), 248–258.

Boisot, M., & Child, J. (1996). From fiefs to clans and network capitalism: Explaining China's emerging economic order. *Administrative Science Quarterly, 41*(4), 600–628.

Cao, Y., & Zhao, W. (2009). Localization in the age of globalization: Institutional duality and labor management structures in China's foreign-invested enterprises. *Research in the Sociology of Work, 19*, 165–201.

Cappellari, L., & Jenkins, S. P. (2003). Multivariate probit regression using simulated maximum likelihood. *Stata Journal, 3*(3), 278–294.

Chen, W. (2007). Does the colour of the cat matter? The red hat strategy in China's private enterprises. *Management and Organization Review, 3*(1), 55–80.

Coleman, W., & Grant, W. (1988). The organizational cohesion and political access of business: A study of comprehensive associations. *European Journal of Political Research, 16*(5), 467–487.

Dacin, M. T., Ventresca, M. J., & Beal, B. D. (1999). The embeddedness of organizations: Dialogue & directions. *Journal of Management, 25*(3), 317–356.

Deng, G., & Kennedy, S. (2010). Big business and industry association lobbying in China: The paradox of contrasting styles. *The China Journal, 63*, 101–125.

DiMaggio, P. J., & Powell, W. W. (1983). The iron cage revisited: Institutional isomorphism and collective rationality in organizational fields. *American Sociological Review, 48*(2), 147–160.

Drope, J. M., & Hansen, W. L. (2009). New evidence for the theory of groups: Trade association lobbying in Washington, D.C. *Political Research Quarterly, 62*(2), 303–316.

Fan, G., Wang, X., & Zhu, H. (2011). *NERI INDEX of Marketization of China's Province 2011 Report*. Beijing: Economic Science Press.

Gamble, J. (2003). Transferring human resource practices from the United Kingdom to China: The limits and potential for convergence. *International Journal of Human Resource Management, 14*(3), 369–387.

Getz, K. A. (1997). Research in corporate political action: Integration and assessment. *Business & Society, 36*(1), 32–72.

Guillén, M. F. (1994). *Models of management: Work, authority, and organization in a comparative perspective.* Chicago, IL: University of Chicago Press.

Guthrie, D. (1998). The declining significance of guanxi in China's economic transition. *The China Quarterly, 154,* 254–282.

Han, J. (2012). Development and governance of foreign business associations in China: A comparison of three models. *Comparative Economic & Social Systems, 12*(1), 172–180

Hansen, W. L., & Mitchell, N. J. (2000). Disaggregating and explaining corporate political activity: Domestic and foreign corporations in national politics. *The American Political Science Review, 94*(4), 891–903.

Hansen, W. L., Mitchell, N. J., & Drope, J. M. (2004). Collective action, pluralism, and the legitimacy tariff: Corporate activity or inactivity in politics. *Political Research Quarterly, 57*(3), 421–429.

Hillman, A. J. (2003). Determinants of political strategies in U.S. multinationals. *Business & Society, 42*(4), 455–484.

Hillman, A. J., & Hitt, M. A. (1999). Corporate political strategy formulation: A model of approach, participation, and strategy decisions. *Academy of Management Review, 24*(4), 825–842.

Hillman, A. J., Keim, G. D., & Schuler, D. (2004). Corporate political activity: A review and research agenda. *Journal of Management, 30*(6), 837–857.

Hillman, A. J., & Wan, W. P. (2005). The determinants of MNE subsidiaries' political strategies: evidence of institutional duality. *Journal of International Business Studies, 36*(3), 322–340.

House, R. J., Hanges, P. J., Javidan, M., Dorfman, P. W., & Gupta, V. (Eds.). (2004). *Culture, Leadership, and Organizations: The GLOBE Study of 62 Societies.* Thousand Oaks, CA: Sage Publications.

Hu, L., & Bentler, P. M. (1999). Cutoff criteria for fit indexes in covariance structure analysis: Conventional criteria versus new alternatives. *Structural Equation Modeling: A Multidisciplinary Journal, 6*(1), 1–55.

Iankova, E., & Katz, J. (2003). Strategies for political risk mediation by international firms in transition economies: The case of Bulgaria. *Journal of World Business, 38*(3), 182–203.

Jackson, G., & Deeg, R. (2008). Comparing capitalisms: Understanding institutional diversity and its implications for international business. *Journal of International Business Studies, 39*(4), 540–561.

Jacomet, D. (2005). The collective aspect of corporate political strategies: The case of U.S. and European business participation in textile international trade negotiations. *International Studies of Management & Organization, 35*(2), 78–93.

Kennedy, S. (2007). Transnational political alliances: An exploration with evidence from China. *Business & Society, 46*(2), 174–200.

Kostova, T., & Roth, K. (2002). Adoption of an organizational practice by subsidiaries of multinational corporations: Institutional and relational effects. *Academy of Management Journal, 45*(1), 215–233.

Kostova, T., Roth, K., & Dacin, M. T. (2008). Institutional theory in the study of multinational corporations: A critique and new directions. *Academy of Management Review, 33*(4), 994–1006.

Kostova, T., & Zaheer, S. (1999). Organizational legitimacy under conditions of complexity: The case of the multinational enterprise. *Academy of Management Review*, 24(1), 64–81.

Li, J. J., Zhou, K. Z., & Shao, A. T. (2009). Competitive position, managerial ties, and profitability of foreign firms in China: An interactive perspective. *Journal of International Business Studies*, 40(2), 339–352.

Liu, S. (2010). Stepping out of the "public" into the "private" sector: An analysis of the infiltration of the government into local chambers of commerce. *Chinese Journal of Sociology*, 30(1), 1–21.

Luo, Y. (2001). Toward a cooperative view of MNC-host government relations: Building blocks and performance implications. *Journal of International Business Studies*, 32(3), 401–419.

Lux, S., Crook, T. R., & Woehr, D. J. (2011). Mixing business with politics: A meta-analysis of the antecedents and outcomes of corporate political activity. *Journal of Management*, 37(1), 223–247.

Meyer, J., & Rowan, B. (1977). Institutionalized organizations: Formal structure as myth and ceremony. *American Journal of Sociology*, 83(2), 340–363.

Nee, V., & Opper, S. (2007). On politicized capitalism. In V. Nee & R. Swedberg (Eds.), *On Capitalism* (pp. 93–127). Stanford, CA: Stanford University Press.

Peng, M. W., & Luo, Y. (2000). Managerial ties and firm performance in a transition economy: The nature of a micro-macro link. *Academy of Management Journal*, 43(3), 486–501.

Peng, M. W., Sun, S. L., Brian, P., & Hao, C. (2009). The institution-based view as a third leg for a strategy tripod. *Academy of Management Perspectives*, 23(3), 63–81.

Rao, H., Davis, G. F., & Ward, A. (2000). Embeddedness, social identity and mobility: Why firms leave the NASDAQ and join the New York stock exchange. *Administrative Science Quarterly*, 45(2), 268–292.

Rodriguez, P., Siegel, D. S., Hillman, A., & Eden, L. (2006). Three lenses on the multinational enterprise: Politics, corruption, and corporate social responsibility. *Journal of International Business Studies*, 37(6), 733–746.

Sanyal, R. N., & Guvenli, T. (2000). Relations between multinational firms and host governments: The experience of American-owned firms in China. *International Business Review*, 9(1), 119–134.

Schuler, D. A., Rehbein, K., & Cramer, R. D. (2002). Pursuing strategic advantage through political means: A multivariate approach. *Academy of Management Journal*, 45(4), 659–672.

Scott, W. R. (2001). *Institutions and Organizations* (2nd ed.). Thousand Oaks, CA: Sage Publications.

Shaffer, B. (1995). Firm-level responses to government regulation: Theoretical and research approaches. *Journal of Management*, 21(3), 495–514.

Suchman, M. C. (1995). Managing legitimacy: Strategic and institutional approaches. *Academy of Management Review*, 20(3), 571–610.

Taylor, S., Beechler, S., & Napier, N. (1996). Toward an integrative model of strategic international human resource management. *Academy of Management Review*, 21(4), 959–985.

Unger, J. (1996). Bridges: Private business, the Chinese government and the rise of new associations. *The China Quarterly*, 147, 795–819.

Wank, D. L. (1996). The institutional process of market clientelism: Guanxi and private business in a South China city. *The China Quarterly*, 147, 820–838.

Wank, D. L. (2002). Business-state clientelism in China: Decline or evolution? In T. Gold, D. Guthrie, & D. Wank (Eds.), *Social Connections in China* (pp. 97–115). New York: University of Cambridge Press.

Xin, K. R., & Pearce, J. L. (1996). Guanxi: Connections as substitutes for formal institutional support. *Academy of Management Journal*, 39(6), 1641–1658.

Zhang, Y., Zhao, W., & Ge, J. (2016). Institutional duality and political strategies of foreign-invested firms in an emerging economy. *Journal of World Business*, 51, 451–462.

Zheng, C., Morrison, M., & O'Neill, G. (2006). An empirical study of high performance HRM practices in Chinese SMEs. *International Journal of Human Resource Management*, 17(10), 1772–1803.

Zimmerman, M. A., & Zeitz, G. J. (2002). Beyond survival: Achieving new venture growth by building legitimacy. *Academy of Management Review*, 27(3), 414–431.

4 Social Embeddedness and Financial Ambidexterity of Small and Micro Firms

Introduction

Entrepreneurship is widely regarded as a tool for improving economic opportunity or fostering inclusion of less-advantaged social groups in the economic mainstream (Wimborg & Landstrom, 2000). Although numerous start-ups and more-established small businesses have played an important role in economic growth and job creation in society, the potential of these entrepreneurial initiatives is significantly affected by the extent to which entrepreneurs can successfully connect to economic resources, formal and informal financial resources in particular (Casey, 2012).

Past studies show that whereas banks, credit unions, and other formal sources serve the needs of a wide array of businesses spread throughout a greater geographic area, informal financial sources, consisting of friends, relatives, network contacts, and local professional money-lenders provide immediate financial assistance to entrepreneurs via more flexible arrangements (Casey, 2012; Christensen, 1993; World Bank, 1989). When the coexistence of formal and informal financial sectors caters to the heterogeneous needs of various borrowers, the large differences in service scope and lending requirements have made it a challenge to choose the best financial source because such choices not only determine the possibility of acquiring loans but can also affect the prices and terms that entrepreneurs receive.

We argue that firms need to develop ambidextrous financial capabilities to reap the benefits of formal and informal financial resources while mitigating their negative impacts. Previous literature on organization ambidexterity has pointed out that maintaining an appropriate balance between exploration and exploitation is critical for firm survival and prosperity (March, 1991). It is argued that one of the fundamental problems facing organizations is to engage in sufficient exploitation of its primary resource pool to ensure its current viability and meanwhile to devote enough energy to exploring alternative resources to complement the primary resource pool to ensure its future viability. An ambidextrous firm that is capable of operating simultaneously to explore and exploit is likely to achieve superior performance over firms emphasizing one at the expense of the other (He & Wong,

2004; Tushman & O'Reilly, 1996). When it comes to the financial market, ambidextrous companies not only benefit from the reliable and convenient informal financial resources, but also take advantage of low-cost and large-scale financial support from the formal financial sectors (Uzzi, 1999).

Just as with other resource mobilization activities, the mobilization of financial resources can be viewed as a social process that is embedded in a social context and channeled and facilitated or constrained and inhibited by people's positions in social networks (Aldrich & Zimmer, 1986; Bruderl & Preisendorfer, 1998). Previous research on the relationship between social networks and entrepreneurial outcomes has mainly focused on structural properties, such as network size, centrality, and diversity, and relational properties such as ties (Bruderl & Preisendorfer, 1998; Granovetter, 1990; Hoang & Antoncic, 2003; Shane & Cable, 2002). Studies reveal that entrepreneurs actively utilize their social connections to obtain financial advice and access bank loans (Birley, 1985; Uzzi, 1999). These social contacts facilitate the match between investors' and entrepreneurs' preferences (Ahlstrom & Bruton, 2006; Batjargal & Liu, 2004; Burt, 1992). Moreover, the nature and composition of these social connections can affect the acquisition and pricing of commercial loans (Uzzi, 1999).

Despite the rapid growth of the literature on this subject, relatively few studies have explored the influence of the resources aspect of entrepreneurs' networks (Batjargal, 2003). It is argued that in addition to actors' own resources, the knowledge, expertise, influence, and wealth possessed by their network contacts—i.e., the actors' social resources—can also affect the outcomes of their instrumental actions (Lin, 2001). Because the volume of resources possessed by a social actor is unevenly distributed across different types and levels of positions, actors' social resources are largely determined by the types and levels of positions held by their social contacts (Lin, 1999). In support of this argument, studies find that having upward-reaching connections can help firms obtain scarce financial resources (Casey, 2012). Moreover, when firms operate in an environment characterized by high institutional uncertainties, strong personal relations with officials in state agencies function as a substitute for institutional support and help firms acquire resources to survive or even prosper in this environment (Peng, 2003; Xin & Pearce, 1996). Therefore when it comes to the entrepreneurial context, social resource differential—i.e., the uneven social resources possessed by entrepreneurs—is highly likely to significantly influence their choice of different sources (Adler & Kwon, 2002; Batjargal, 2003; Bruderl & Preisendorfer, 1998; Lin, 2001).

The Chinese transitional economy is the context of this study. During the past three decades, the Chinese financial sector has experienced substantial financial liberalization, which has led to significant institutional diversification (Laurenceson & Chai, 2003). The state-monopolized banking system has been gradually replaced by a three-tier system consisting of four specialized banks, three policy lending banks, over 100 commercial banks, and numerous rural or urban credit cooperatives (Shirai, 2002). Although financial reform made positive contributions to China's economic development, it has been less successful in providing equal access to households and entrepreneurs in different regions. The allocation of credit was always biased toward state-owned enterprises, and banks' discrimination against small borrowers is widely documented (Ayyagari, Demirguc-Kunt, & Maksimovic, 2008; Chow & Fung, 2000; Laurenceson & Chai, 2003).

Due to inadequate external financing from the formal sector, the informal financial sector has become the major source of financing for small entrepreneurs and has provided much-needed financing to small- and medium-sized enterprises and households. In 2003 the scale of informal finance was around 950 billion yuan, which accounts for 6.96 percent of the national GDP (Jiang, 2009). These resources catered to the needs of the underserved portion of the population and businesses. More than 75 percent of the debt of rural households comes from informal financial sources (He, 1999). In addition, small- and medium-sized enterprises also rely partially or fully on informal finance. Only 20 percent of small- and medium-sized firms have acquired loans from banks (Ayyagari et al., 2008). Therefore, the informal financial sector constitutes the most important external source of funds for entrepreneurs in the less-developed western regions.

In this chapter, we use data from a large-scale cross-sectional survey to explore the impact of structural, relational, and resource embeddedness on small and micro firms' financial ambidexterity. We borrow insights from the position generator method and construct new measures to distinguish and quantify entrepreneurs' social resources. In addition, we investigate the factors that condition the effects of different types of social resources on entrepreneurs' choices of financial sources. In the next section, we discuss the merits and limitations of formal and informal financial sources. We then explore how the choice of financial sources is shaped by the properties of entrepreneurs' social networks and their social resources. We next discuss the data and methods, and present results from Heckman's probit models. We conclude this chapter with a discussion of major findings and directions of future research.

The Value of Financial Ambidexterity

The major challenge for most small and micro firms (SMFs) is resource mobilization, financial resources in particular. A proper balance between formal and informal financial resources is crucial for SMFs to survive and prosper. For most SMFs, their primary source of finance is informal financial intermediaries, which provide immediate financial support to their operations. However, formal sources of finance can provide SMFs with more financial resources at relatively low price loans, which allow them to make the long-term investments that are crucial for firms' continuous growth. Therefore, in order to have reliable and efficient sources of finance, entrepreneurs need to develop ambidextrous capabilities (March, 1991) in the financial market to effectively exploit the primary financial sources and meanwhile, to explore alternative financial resources in the market.

A recent survey by the Development Research Center of the State Council shows that entrepreneurs often draw funds from a variety of sources, including formal sources, such as banks, finance companies, or credit unions, and a wide range of informal sources, such as personal funds or loans from family members or friends (Ba, 2013). Among these financial choices, banks are still the primary source of finance for many SMFs. Compared with informal sources, formal financial sources have an advantage in meeting the needs of a wide array of potential borrowers (Birley, 1985; Casey, 2012). They are more efficient than informal agents in intermediating funds over larger geographical areas and provide a relatively larger amount of capital to borrowers at a relatively lower interest rate than some informal sources, such as pawnbrokers (Besley & Coate, 1995).

However, when it comes to the extension of financial services to small entrepreneurs, financial institutions face high risks when selecting among entrepreneurs because entrepreneurs may act opportunistically toward them, and because entrepreneurs vary in their ability to identify and exploit opportunities (Shane & Cable, 2002). Formal institutions attenuate lending risk and information asymmetry mainly through imposing stringent collateral requirements and requiring borrowers to provide a well-developed business plan and carefully documented evidence showing their intention and ability for repayment (Hustedde & Pulver, 1992; Tang, 1995). Moreover, formal sources are reluctant to provide services to small businesses because many of the costs of issuing a loan are independent of the size of the transaction; only when the loan amount reaches a certain scale to cover administrative costs will the bank find it worthwhile to conduct the business. Therefore entrepreneurs who seek larger amounts of financial support are more apt to gain support from formal sources (Hustedde & Pulver, 1992; Tang, 1995; World Bank, 1989).

Entrepreneurs with a low level of wealth find it difficult to acquire debt financing via formal sources either because these people rarely have collateral acceptable to banks or because they are not regarded as creditworthy by formal financial institutions. In addition, in transitional economies such as China, there are hidden costs to acquiring loans from banks. Although the nominal interest on bank loans is lower than the informal loans, banks often impose many conditions that significantly increase the cost. For instance, some banks require firms to make a certain amount of deposit in their accounts or purchase the bank's financial products. Among the respondents, 31.8 percent report that the costs of bank loans are the highest among the alternatives. In comparison, 27.1 percent of the respondents say that small loan firms charge the highest interest, and 14.9 percent say loan sharks are in fact the most expensive means of finance (Ba, 2013).

Therefore, the majority of small entrepreneurs turn to informal sectors for financial resources (Casey, 2012; Ghate, 1992; Guiso, Jappelli, & Terlizzese, 1996). Studies show that in many developing countries, informal sources are both extensive and diverse and play an important role in solving allocation problems associated with individuals, farmers, and small enterprises. In these places social contacts such as neighbors, friends, or relatives are often the most important sources of informal credit (Ghate, 1992; Li & Hsu, 2009; Shanmugam, 1991). Other informal financial sources, such as professional moneylenders, pawnbrokers, and rotating credit associations, play a relatively less important role in many places. Studies show that professional moneylenders provided less than 20 percent of informal rural credit in sampled Asian countries; on average, they accounted for 6 percent (World Bank, 1989).

Choosing informal sources brings three advantages to borrowers. First, the costs and interest rates can be affected by the relationship between the lender and the borrower (Granovetter, 2005). Some have argued that informal relationships with financial experts result in lower costs and more convenient access to specialized knowledge and advice (Cornwell & Cornwell, 2008). Moreover, detailed personal knowledge of the client in the credit market can attenuate the information asymmetry between lenders and borrowers and reduce the costs associated with the assessment of buyers' creditworthiness (Ferrary, 2003). Studies show that few conditions of repayment are attached to loans borrowed from social contacts, and such loans are often interest free despite the fact that they are usually small and short-term (World Bank, 1989).

Second, compared to large firms, SMFs tend to favor flexibility and convenience when seeking loans. A recent survey shows that for most micro firms, the primary financial difficulty is to get short-term loans for temporary payment. Few of them need long-term or large-sum loans for project development or equipment procurement. Among the surveyed firms, 63.3 percent had short-term loans, i.e., less than one year. The amount of these loans tends to be small. Half of them seek loans ranging from 100 to 500 thousand RMB (Ba, 2013). Bank loans tend to be large, and the application process can take much longer. Therefore, informal sources of finance, such as loans from friends and family members, become a convenient financial source for SMFs.

Third, it is easier to obtain a loan from a known contact than from unrelated individuals because intimacy cultivates mutual trust (Zelizer, 2005). Lenders may feel greater assurance regarding repayment when dealing with people to whom they are related. The social relation between lender and borrower can act as an important mechanism of social sanction that protects the lender's interest. The punishment for default can be magnified in its impact through the larger networks to which both players are connected (Granovetter, 2005). In addition, lending decisions are often affected by norms of social exchange. Lenders sometimes feel it is their social obligation to assist relatives or friends in overcoming financial difficulties (Blau, 1964; DiMaggio & Louch, 1998). This consideration is driven by preexisting reciprocal obligations or by the intention to maintain and cultivate certain social relations.

Although the informal financial sector plays an important role in many developing countries, it also has some limitations. The transactions are usually highly confined to a limited geographic area or a bounded social group. To reduce default risk in the absence of tangible collateral, loans are small and short-term, and the nominal interest rate is sometimes higher than that of formal sector loans (Christensen, 1993). This is especially true in rural areas where local markets are segmented from the national market, which limits the supply of credit (World Bank, 1989).

Besides economic considerations, the borrower may also consider the social consequences of their choices. In societies with strong traditions of mutual assistance and reciprocity, accepting help from close contacts usually requires borrowers to reciprocate by providing nonfinancial services or supplying funds in turn when the lender needs to borrow in the future (DiMaggio & Louch, 1998; Tang, 1995). These traditional obligations of mutual support can be a problem for those who wish to accumulate capital; they thus may choose to borrow from sources other than their social contacts to avoid incurring reciprocal financial obligations (World Bank, 1989).

Data used in this study are drawn from a large-scale cross-sectional survey administered jointly by the Norway Institute for Applied Social Science and the Ministry of Science of Technology of China in eleven provinces in western China. The survey was conceptualized in the early 2000s and was completed in 2006. The reason the study team and the sponsors chose western China as the target region is because these places are significantly less developed than the coastal and the central areas. In order to provide information for new poverty-reduction policies, it was imperative to gain a better understanding of the social and economic life of western residents. A total of 20 universities and 2,000 college students participated in this project and conducted the field interviews. The sample frame was based on the 2000 Chinese Census that listed all neighborhood committees and townships in each province with their populations. The survey used the Probability Proportionate to Population (PPP) sampling method to select 2,772 neighborhood committees and townships. Within each selected committee or township, a residence committee or administrative village was randomly chosen. The researchers listed all households and sampled from this list. A responsible adult person in each selected household was then chosen as the respondent for the questionnaire. This person had to have good knowledge of the household in question; in most cases the responsible adult was one of the spouses in the household. A total of 41,222 interviews were completed. Because many of the small and micro businesses were not officially registered, we therefore identified the households that can be viewed as having such businesses by the types of income sources they reported. If a household reported a non-agricultural, non-wage income, then we considered this household as operating a small or micro business.

Among these households, 34 percent had borrowed money in that year, of which 58 percent borrowed from informal sources and 42 percent from formal sources. Loans from the formal sources were generally of a larger amount than loans from informal sources (16,786 yuan vs. 6,626 yuan). The average network size of the entrepreneurs was 22. The standard deviation of network size was 33, indicating a large variance in entrepreneurs' household network size (De Graaf & Flap, 1988).

Theoretical Background

Social embeddedness is regarded as the extent to which business transactions are conducted via social connections and network contacts that use various social mechanisms and cultural norms to govern business issues (Uzzi, 1997). This perspective has gained popularity in the study of self-employment, entrepreneurship, and small business formation thanks to the work of Aldrich and Zimmer (1986). The embeddedness perspective proposes competing arguments against the human capital, transactional cost, or organizational ecology theories. The argument is based on the premise that entrepreneurship is a relational task and a combinatorial problem, which is inherently a networking activity. Entrepreneurial outcomes are affected by actors' personal relations and by the structure of the overall network of relations (Granovetter, 1990). Entrepreneurs who promote this process are no longer viewed as isolated and autonomous decision makers but as actors involved in a special microcontext (Bruderl & Preisendorfer, 1998; Dubini & Aldrich, 1991). They act as organizers and coordinators of resources and use their existing social relationships to build up new businesses.

Studies on interfirm networks imply that having economic transactions embedded in the social context brings firms additional value and gives trading partners proper incentive and assurance to share the resources that can bring mutual benefits. Social ties help both parties transfer private resources, and the ties function as a self-enforcing governance mechanism that effectively reduces the likelihood of malfeasance (Portes & Sensenbrenner, 1993). The quality and quantity of resources entrepreneurs can mobilize toward the exploitation of an entrepreneurial opportunity is influenced by the structural patterns, relational qualities, and resource potential of their personal social networks (Batjargal, 2003; Kotha & George, 2012). Uzzi (1999) argues that embedding business transactions in social attachments benefits firms that are seeking financing by promoting distinctive governance mechanisms and the transfer of private information—factors that motivate banks and firms to find integrative solutions to financing problems beyond those possible through market relations, which possess different benefits. Practitioners, especially entrepreneurs, agree with this argument and complain that financial models often do not appreciate the value of bank–client relationships. This implies that there is a growing demand for a sociological theory of finance (Mizruchi & Stearns, 1994).

In the entrepreneurial context, the endowment of entrepreneurs with social resources is differentiated according to their network structure, relations, and the quantity of contacts' resources. Previous studies have identified three different types of embeddedness: structural, relational, and resource embeddedness. Granovetter defines structural embeddedness as the structure of the overall network of relations (Granovetter, 1990). He argues that structural embeddedness typically has more subtle effects on economic action. For an egocentric network, the most intuitive and frequently utilized measure of network structure is network size, which is defined as the number of direct social ties between a focal actor (ego) and other actors (alter) (Batjargal, 2003; Hoang & Antoncic, 2003). Network size affects entrepreneurs' resource-mobilization capacity by limiting the quantity and quality of information they can acquire. A larger network expands entrepreneurs' search scale and helps them locate potential investors (Batjargal, 2003). Studies show that actors with a larger network size have a higher propensity to access credit because having more ties increases one's knowledge of market information such as the availability of different loans and pricing (Uzzi, 1999). Our data indicates that a larger network is positively associated with the financial ambidexterity of SMFs. Firms with larger network are more likely to receive information from both informal and formal financial sectors. More importantly, they are more likely to have connections that enable them to mobilize and utilize resources from both sectors.

Relational Embeddedness

The effect of network size can often be attributed to the network diversity, which is closely associated with network size. As network size increases, the proportion of family members and relatives within the network decreases, which in turn improves network diversity and gives actors more heterogeneous social resources (Bian & Li, 2001; Marsden, 1987). These advantages can arguably enable entrepreneurs with larger networks to go beyond their immediate social circle to establish contact with and mobilize the resources of external investors. Therefore, to further distinguish the causal mechanism, we need to explicitly test the effects of factors that tend to be confounding with networks' structural properties.

That being said, we propose that a second type of embeddedness, relational embeddedness, is positively associated with firms' financial ambidexterity. Relational embeddedness refers to the strength of the relationships and the mutual trust attached to social ties (Granovetter, 1990). Previous studies have devoted much attention to exploring the relative value of strong versus weak ties. It has been argued that an actor embedded in a broad and diverse network can receive more help and resources compared to an actor embedded in a confined network or one that lacks basic resources. When business owners must gather information or specific knowledge on market conditions and opportunities, and if such information is unlikely to be available within the immediate social circle, then networks with many weak ties become important for success (Batjargal, 2003; Bruderl & Preisendorfer, 1998; Davidsson & Honig, 2003; Hoang & Antoncic, 2003). With regard to the acquisition of financial resources, venture capitalists and entrepreneurs can facilitate identifying each other through the use of weak ties (Batjargal & Liu, 2004). Financial studies indicate that firms with expansive networks of arm's-length ties to banks can optimize their bargaining power and acquire access to a large pool of price and loan possibilities, thereby increasing their chances at getting corporate financing (Petersen & Rajan, 1994).

However, when the major barrier to successful resource mobilization is gaining trust from or influencing the decisions of potential resource providers, then the importance of strong ties emerges. Social influence flowing through strong personal ties increases one's capacity to mobilize the actual monetary resources possessed by contacts (Cornwell & Cornwell, 2008). For example, Bian (1997) discovered that in the Chinese context, strong ties are more often used as ways to acquire scarce opportunities or influence the decisions of resource providers. Bruderl's and Preisendorfer's (1998) study in Germany found that compared with weak ties, strong ties are more effective in explaining firms' success as measured by firms' survival. Whereas strong ties increase one's ability to use contacts' resources, too many strong ties tend to confine actors in a homophilious social circle (Granovetter, 1973). For entrepreneurs residing in the distant countryside, this would significantly limit their search scale and leave little room for financial maneuvering (Batjargal & Liu, 2004).

Based on these insights, it is logical to infer that to improve firms' financial ambidexterity, entrepreneurs need to maintain a balance between strong and weak social ties. Although an expansive network of arm's-length ties can enable a firm to effectively scan the market for deals and improve broker information among banks, it lacks the embedded ties that facilitate partnering. On the contrary, whereas embedded ties promote collaboration, a network with embedded ties only could lead to over-concentration on local resources, and thus confine firms' access to market information and alternative financial resources. This indicates that the optimal relational embedded case refers to the network composed of both embedded ties and arm's-length ties, which can moderate the shortcomings of each type of tie while preserving their strengths, optimizing the firm's range of available action (Uzzi, 1999; Uzzi & Lancaster, 2004).

To test the aforementioned ideas, we constructed network measures based on a social network module in the survey. The survey adopted two network instruments. The first was the "New Year greeting network" instrument (Bian & Li, 2001), which is essentially a variant of name generators

(Marsden, 1990). The idea behind this instrument is that it is often diffi-cult to ask the respondent to define the boundary of their social networks. The number of people they can recall depends on the questions, events, and other contextual information. To reduce this ambiguity, scholars paid careful attention to choosing the proper questions, and tried to determine the most appropriate events during which one's network is fully mobilized. The New Year Greeting network instrument presumes that the spring fes-tival is the most important Chinese holiday and a major networking event during which people visit or call their family members, relatives, friends, colleagues, or business partners. The purpose of the greeting can be both expressive and instrumental, and the person one contacts may be a close friend or a significant acquaintance. The first question that interviewers asked is how many people a household contacted during the last spring fes-tival. The contact method could be house visits, phone calls, emails, or text messages. The number of people contacted was used as a proxy of network size. The respondents were then asked to recall how many of the people they contacted were acquaintances, as opposed to relatives or close friends. The share of weak ties was calculated as the ratio of number of acquaintances to the total number of contacts.

The data shows that, in general, the networks of Chinese entrepreneurs are highly cohesive, consisting mainly of their friends and relatives. The aver-age proportion of such strong ties is 82 percent. In addition, in 90 percent of the respondents' networks, at least 50 percent of their network contacts are their friends and relatives. In Model 1 (see Table 4.1), we incorporated several network measures. The variable relational embeddedness was opera-tionalized using the proportion of weak ties in one's network; we logged this variable to correct its skewed distribution. The coefficient of this variable is positive and statistically significant, indicating that financial ambidexterity is positively associated with the proportion of weak ties in entrepreneurs' social networks.

These results only partially support our prediction. In a separate analy-sis (not shown), we tried to determine whether the share of weak ties has an inverse U shape relationship with financial ambidexterity. That is, as the proportion of weak ties increased to a certain level, entrepreneurs may have fewer strong ties that allow them to make use of informal sources of finance. But this insignificant curve-linear effect can be attributed to the way we measured the tie strength. As Kotha and George (2012) argued, an ideal measure of tie strength would require a 7-point Likert-scale. Because such information is not available, we have to seek alternative ways and use the types of ties as proxy of tie strength or closeness. Bruderl and Preisend-orfer (1998) also encountered a similar problem. They solved this issue by classifying the types of ties into strong (including spouse, parents, friends, and relatives) and weak (including business partners, acquaintances, former employers, former coworkers). Kotha and George further developed this classification by dividing the weak tie category into professional ties and ties

Table 4.1 Heckman's Models Predicting SMFs' Financial Ambidexterity

DV: Financial Ambidexterity	Model 1		Model 2		Model 3	
	β	(SE)	β	(SE)	β	(SE)
Independent Variables						
Relational embeddedness	0.004***	0.001			0.004***	0.001
Resource embeddedness	0.003*	0.001			0.002*	0.001
Institutional embeddedness	0.003*	0.001			0.002	0.001
Entrepreneurs' education			0.002	0.001	0.002	0.002
Total household income			0.012***	0.002	0.012***	0.003
Total liquid asset			0.004*	0.002	0.007*	0.002
Control variables						
Starting debt position	−0.005***	0.001	−0.004***	0.001	−0.004***	0.001
Ethnic Han Chinese	0.004	0.007	0.008	0.008	0.016*	0.008
Recall time	−0.009***	0.002	−0.009***	0.002	−0.009***	0.002
Firm age	0.002*	0.001	0.001*	0.001	0.002*	0.001
Firm size	−0.001	0.002	−0.002	0.002	−0.002	0.002
Generalized trust	0.011†	0.006	0.010†	0.006	0.010†	0.006
Inverse mill ratio	−0.113***	0.017	−0.143***	0.027	−0.199***	0.030
Constant	0.367***	0.034	0.242***	0.039	0.326***	0.047
N	5021		5800		5021	
BIC	−961		−972		−1023	

Notes: † p < 0.1, * p < 0.05, ** p < 0.01, *** p < 0.001 (two-tailed tests). Cluster robust standard errors reported.

with strangers. We find Kotha and George's classification is more informative. However, because the questionnaire of this survey does not make a distinction between family members and close friends, we therefore relied on the strong tie notion from Bruderl and Preisendorfer's study to denote contacts who are focal entrepreneurs' family members, relatives, or friends and used Kotha and George's professional ties to denote acquaintances, former employers, and former coworkers. That being said, we suggest future studies to further explore this issue by using the Likert-scale-based tie strength measures.

Resource Embeddedness

Resource embeddedness is the third type of network feature that affects entrepreneurial outcomes. It is defined as the degree to which network contacts possess valuable resources. Therefore it is a function of the resource attributes of individual alters. Some argue that the quality of resources embedded in one's network is even more important for entrepreneurial success than structural or relational embeddedness (Batjargal, 2003; Burt, 1992). When it comes to financial resource mobilization, two types of embedded resources are of great importance: the first is the wealth a social contact possesses, and the second is the contact's social status or power, which determines his or her social influence. In this section, we make a distinction between these two forms of resources, and use resource embeddedness to indicate the amount of available financial resources. In the next section, we will discuss the influence of social power and social influence and use that as proxy of institutional embeddedness.

The proportion of resource-rich contacts in one's network is an important factor that affects the abundance of embedded financial resources. We are fully aware that there are many ways to quantify the economic resources in one's network. The survey data we used only gives us limited information on this issue. In addition to the measurement of entrepreneur's structural and relational network properties, the researchers asked the respondent to answer how many contacts in one's New Year Greeting network were urban residents. We argue that this information can be utilized to measure the quantity of economic resources that are embedded in one's network. This is because the rural–urban divide has long been regarded as an important source of social economic inequality in China. The persistent rural–urban divide and the recent increase in social and economic disparities can be attributed to urban-biased policies and institutions, such as labor mobility restrictions, the residence permit system, the welfare system, and financial policies of inflation subsidies and investment credits to the urban sector (Yang, 1999).

Data from the National Bureau of Statistics shows that during the first decade of the twenty-first century, the ratio of urban residents' income to rural residents' income ranges from 2.90 (year 2001) to 3.33 (year 2007,

2009) (NBS, 2010). Compared to income inequality, asset inequality between rural and urban residents is even more striking. Data from the China Financial Study Association shows that the average bank deposit of urban residents is six times more than the average deposit of rural residents (CFSA, 2006). These data suggest that when an entrepreneur has more urban contacts, he or she can mobilize more within-network financial resources. In addition to convenient access to more embedded financial resources, urban contacts can benefit entrepreneurs by providing them with more financial information or knowledge that is necessary to mobilize resources from the formal financial sector. Therefore, we expect that the proportion of urban ties in one's network is positively associated with the financial ambidexterity of SMFs.

In this study, we constructed the measure based on respondents' answers to the question of how many people they contacted during the spring festival hold an urban resident permit. The variable was calculated as the share of urban contacts in the contacts list. Model 1 in Table 4.1 reports the estimated effects of urban ties. The positive and significant coefficient shows that as the share of urban contacts increases, firms are more likely to achieve a better balance between informal and formal financial resources, in other words, a higher level of financial ambidexterity.

Institutional Embeddedness

A fourth type of embeddedness is institutional embeddedness, which refers to the institutional resources embedded in entrepreneurs' networks. In transitional economies where bureaucratic power can still exert influence on the distribution of economic resources, access to contacts who hold positions in the bureaucratic system is an advantage in mobilizing formal sector resources (Batjargal, 2003). In the Chinese context, local states often have close relations with local banks or credit unions. It is common practice for officials to use their administrative power to influence credit decisions that favor certain individuals or organizations (Ong, 2006; Shih, 2004). Besides bank loans, the state itself often provides various development loans, agriculture subsidies, and food-for-work programs to rural residents (Rozelle, Park, Benziger, & Ren, 1998). Although the resources can come from both central and local governments and may be distributed by local bank branches, allocation decisions are still heavily influenced by the local states. Local officials have considerable discretion in determining the eligibility and allocation of certain types of funds (Wu, 1997; Zhang, 2005). Knowing someone who works inside local government agencies can thus increase entrepreneurs' likelihood of acquiring quality financial resources from formal financial institutions.

In addition, the connections to the state sector also turn out to be beneficial to entrepreneurs. Just like other valuable resources, these resources are unevenly distributed across economic sectors, and the state sectors enjoy preferential treatment from the state banks. Therefore, having contacts who are high in the state sector helps entrepreneurs get ahead in the marketplace because first, these people tend to have extensive knowledge or expertise that is vital for entrepreneurs to acquire financial resources, and second, business professionals, such as executives who manage large corporations and banks, usually have greater discretion in allocating material resources and lucrative contracts (Batjargal, 2003). Studies show that low-wealth entrepreneurs who have upward-reaching connections to those that possess greater social resources do obtain a higher level of formal financial resources (Casey, 2012). Therefore, we expect that having institutional ties enables entrepreneurs to mobilize financial resources from formal sectors, which complement their own resource endowment and lead to higher financial ambidexterity.

We tested this idea using the second social network instrument included in the survey. The position generator instrument (Lin & Dumin, 1986) differs from the name generator in that the former views the society as having a pyramidal structure, in which resources, status, and power are skewed toward the top. In order to measure an actors access to positions at various levels of this pyramid, scholars first sampled a number of different positions from a given society's occupational structure. The sampled positions must represent people at different levels, and they should not be the rare positions that are difficult to access. However, the original position generator method does not provide much information on the content of social resources. It measures the general social resources (or social capital) and falls short in quantifying the specific types of social resources that really matter for households' economic wellbeing. Therefore, in the subsequent analysis we borrowed insights from the resource generator method and classified the positions sampled into different categories. In the survey, the researchers included twenty-two different occupations. Several occupations on this list have close connections to the state sector, for example, the village cadre, local party leader, government official, leader of public service units or state-owned firms, and administrative staff. We counted the number of such positions that a respondent had connections with and then calculated the percentage of such positions in his/her total number of positions accessed. This ratio was used to measure the institutional embeddedness of entrepreneurs.

Descriptive data shows that 95 percent of the respondents have less than 40 percent of institutional ties in their network. And almost no one has a network that is composed of institutional ties only. It is therefore difficult to say whether the marginal effects of institutional embeddedness on firms' financial ambidexterity will decline at a certain point. What the data shows is a linear relationship between these two factors. Model 1 in Table 4.1 shows that the coefficient of institutional embeddedness is positive and significant, indicating that institutional embeddedness is positively associated with firms' financial ambidexterity. It facilitates SMFs to overcome their resource constraints by utilizing the expertise and institutional influence of their social contacts, and thus increase firms' capability to effectively use both informal and formal sector financial resources.

Network Compensation Hypothesis

As proposed in the previous section, the degree of network embeddedness can influence the entrepreneurs' likelihood of gaining resources from formal or informal financial intermediaries by serving as important information channels, connecting entrepreneurs and investors, and providing direct financial assistance. Entrepreneurs with a broad and diverse network will have more opportunities to mobilize market resources, whereas those with a more confined network will have to rely more on the informal financial intermediaries that are relatively easy to access (Bruderl & Preisendorfer, 1998). In addition to the influence of various types of network embeddedness, previous studies also imply that the extent to which the entrepreneurs rely on the resources possessed by their direct social contacts, i.e., informal resources, is also contingent on entrepreneurs' own resource endowment, i.e., the human capital and financial capital they possess (Bates, 1997; Bruderl & Preisendorfer, 1998; Waldinger, Aldrich, & Ward, 1990).

Scholars argue that compared with the better-off entrepreneurs, those with low financial capital or human capital are more successful in mobilizing the resources possessed by their close network contacts, such as families, relatives, and friends. This "network compensation hypothesis" postulates that entrepreneurs with a low stock of endowment try harder to mobilize informal resources as a way to compensate for the unfavorable position by referring to their personal ties (Bruderl & Preisendorfer, 1998). Studies show that people with little formal education tend to have less extensive financial knowledge, or have a lower chance of accessing professional financial knowledge (Chang, 2005; Cornwell & Cornwell, 2008). This knowledge deficiency negatively influences their probability of engaging in corresponding credit, saving, and investment practices (Hilgert, Hogarth, & Beverly, 2003). In addition, entrepreneurs with poor financial endowment, e.g., low income or financial assets, are less likely to obtain formal sector loans due to their inability to provide acceptable collateral and their low ability to repay the loans (Mohieldin & Wright, 2000). As a result, entrepreneurs who wish to start, maintain, or expand their businesses need to overcome these limitations by mobilizing resources through informal intermediaries.

It is also argued that the effects of embeddedness tend to be confounded with the socioeconomic status of the respondents. Studies show that people with higher socioeconomic status (SES) tend to have resource-rich networks. Moreover, because social networks tend to be economically and educationally homogenous, the higher one's SES, the more resources are embedded in one's network. In other words, high-SES people not only have more financial knowledge but also tend to have more extensive financial networks that allow them to mobilize both formal and informal financial resources. It is therefore necessary to clarify whether the embeddedness effects can be attributed to the effects of one's SES.

To test this network compensation thesis, we incorporated the SES variables into our study. We first estimated the independent effects of respondents' SES through three proxies, i.e., entrepreneurs' educational background, their household income, and their liquid assets. The model results show that income and liquid assets have positive and significant relationships with firms' financial ambidexterity. In the next model (Model 3), we incorporated both embeddedness measures and SES measures. If the network compensation thesis is valid, then we expect the effects of the embeddedness measures will be mediated by the SES variables. The results of Model 3 (Table 4.1) show that, except for institutional embeddedness, the effects of the other two embeddedness measures still hold, indicating that the effects of embeddedness measures cannot be fully mediated by the SES measures. This does not fully support the network compensation thesis and thus confirms that the network embeddedness influence is not a confounding effect.

Although the focus of this study is the effect of network embeddedness, there are other factors in the model that deserve a general discussion. The level of generalized trust in a given region is such a factor. Studies have shown that this factor is systematically associated with the development of the local financial market and with the financial behaviors of local residents because financing is "an exchange of a sum of money today for a promise to return the money in the future" (Guiso, Sapienza, & Zingales, 2004: pg. 527). Some further argue that trust is crucial for enhancing social exchange and communication, and trust toward a generalized other or toward institutions can lead to increased efficiency and productivity by reducing the need for monitoring time and associated costs (Doh & Acs, 2010; Fukuyama, 1995; Putnam, 1995; Thoni, Tyran, & Wengstrom, 2012). High generalized trust can effectively reduce the perceived risks associated with transactions with extra-community actors (Rotter, 1980). Trust is also a significant predictor of cooperative behavior and is the basis for reciprocity, acting to reduce the inevitable frictions of social life. Moreover, in certain societies trust toward organizations or institutions reflects people's confidence in organizations or institutions and proxies the quality of local governance (Guiso et al., 2004; Lee, Jeong, & Chae, 2011). In this sense, a high level of trust can thus translate directly into high levels of economic development and set conditions for entrepreneurial behaviors (Doh & McNeely, 2011).

To test this idea, we constructed a measure of generalized trust based on the survey data. The survey asked the respondents how much trust they had in a variety of people and organizations, such as village leaders, the local government, local police, doctors, or judges. The respondents could choose a number from one (no trust at all) to four (a great deal of trust). The Cronbach's Alpha values across these five items (alpha = 0.86 across five items) were then averaged by country to reflect overall levels of generalized trust in a county. We chose counties rather than townships or prefectures as the basic unit for community-level trust because most small businesses operate within the range of counties, and most local economic and social management functions are carried out by county-level government. The coefficients of the generalized trust in all three models are positive and significant, indicating that a high level of generalized trust increased the financial ambidexterity of SMFs.

Conclusion

Policy makers and researchers have long been interested in the importance of entrepreneurship as a tool or strategy for improving economic opportunity or fostering the inclusion of low-wealth minority groups and communities in the economic mainstream (Wimborg & Landstrom, 2000). However, to determine the potential of entrepreneurial strategies, a greater understanding is needed as to the microsocial processes that influence the quality and quantity of resources that an individual can mobilize toward the exploitation of an entrepreneurial opportunity (Casey, 2012; Kotha & George, 2012). Past studies have focused on the effects of structural and relational properties of entrepreneurs' social networks on their resource-seeking behavior; however, much less attention has been paid to the effects of the resource properties of such networks.

This study fills the first gap by employing new measurements to simultaneously explore the effects of three types of network embeddedness on entrepreneurs' financial ambidexterity. We found that relational embeddedness, measured as the strength of social ties, significantly affects SMFs' resource seeking behavior. When entrepreneurs have more weak ties, they are more likely to access heterogeneous information, which allows entrepreneurs to go beyond their immediate social circle, which in many cases are their primary sources of finance. We also find that firms' resource embeddedness, measured by the proportion of urban ties, affects firms' financial ambidexterity through two means. For one thing, because urban residents tend to be more affluent than rural residents, when entrepreneurs have more urban contacts, they have a greater pool of financial resources, which they can utilize to meet their urgent financial needs. For another, urban residents are more likely to have more financial knowledge, which can help entrepreneurs apply for formal financial resources. In addition, our results show that upward-reaching connections can help entrepreneurs overcome constraints in accessing formal sector resources. Entrepreneurs are more likely to receive financial support from banks and other formal financial institutions when they have connections to those that hold important positions in the state bureaucratic system.

In addition, this analysis further explores the perplexing relationship between network effects and socioeconomic status effects. We explicitly test the network compensation theory, which argues that disadvantaged social groups make more effort and are more successful in activating their private-network resources. Similarly, the higher ambidexterity of some entrepreneurs may be attributed to their higher socioeconomic status, which is often regarded as creditworthiness by formal financial institutions rather than the effects of network embeddedness. We incorporated both explanations into the same model and the results indicate that the effects of network embeddedness cannot be fully mediated by entrepreneurs' socioeconomic status. This indicates that although these two factors are often closely associated, their effects are largely independent and function through different mechanisms.

Appendix
Variables

Financial ambidexterity. We drew the main research question from the economy module of the survey. The respondents were asked to report whether they had borrowed money for business in the past twelve months. If they received an affirmative answer to this question, the interviewer continued to collect information on the single most significant loan acquired during this timeframe. In terms of the types of financial sources the respondents had used, the questionnaire provided twelve choices that fell into three basic categories. The first was informal sources, including extended family members, relatives, close friends, and acquaintances. The survey did not include professional moneylenders as a separate choice because they could overlap with the former four types of social contacts. The second category was formal sources, consisting mainly of banks and credit unions. The third category included other financial sources, such as government agencies, village committees, work units, religious or charity organizations, international organizations, and nongovernmental organizations. The notion of financial ambidexterity refers to the extent to which firms can effectively explore new financial sources and meanwhile exploit the benefits of the existing financial sources. We therefore used the Herfindahl-Hirschman index of SMFs' sources of finance. We excluded those firms with only one loan in the previous year. We then calculated the proportions of loans from formal, informal, and other sources and then calculated the HHI index. To make the results more interpretable, we subtracted the HHI index from one. The variables thus generated have higher values when firms maintain a balance among these three types of financial sources, and lower values when they only focus on one of the three possible sources.

Several control variables were included in the main and selection models. Entrepreneurs' education refers to the years of education received by the entrepreneur who takes charge of the firm. Total household income was calculated as total household income from both agricultural and nonagricultural sources in the past year. This includes incomes from selling agricultural products, land or property leasing, business income, wages and salary, bonuses, subsidies, and gift money. Total liquid assets were measured as the total market value of all liquid assets, including savings in bank accounts, cash held at home, and cash stored in other places (Spilerman, 2000). To reduce recall bias, the researchers asked respondents to report the amount of their total assets they had on May 1, China's Labor Day. Household ethnic type is a dichotomous variable with one indicating households in which all members are Han Chinese and zero indicating households with members from minority groups. In addition, per capita loan was included to control for regional variations in the overall availability of financial resources. This variable was calculated as provincial bank loan residues divided by total population of a province. It is true that a city- or county-level per capita deposit or loan would be a more accurate indicator than the provincial average in accounting for the effect of financial resource availability, but due to data limitations, provincial-level data was the most reliable and complete data available to researchers. Resident type was used to proxy the extent to which a household was integrated into urban society. Its value equals one if there is at least one household member (but not all) who holds an urban resident permit (*hukou*) and zero if all household members hold rural resident permits. Table 4.1 presents descriptive statistics of the variables and Pearson's correlations.

Method

In this study, the dependent variable is SMFs' financial ambidexterity, which is based on the financial information of the SMFs in the previous year. This only applies to those who have borrowed money in the past year. Sample selection bias is a common problem that should be properly handled in such analysis, because the observations are selected in ways that are not independent of the outcome variables in the study. The potential source of bias in this study is that entrepreneurs who did not borrow are excluded from the analysis. Heckman's selection model is an appropriate solution for this problem. The model assumes that the likelihood of borrowing in the last year is a function of both the independent variables in the model and the likelihood that an entrepreneur borrows money. The method first estimates the selection model to predict whether an entrepreneur borrows or not, then calculates the inverse mill ratio, and then incorporates the inverse mill ratio in the analyses that predict the degree of financial ambidexterity. We used the OLS model to estimate how independent variables affect entrepreneurs' choice between formal and informal financial sources. The selection criterion was whether or not an entrepreneur borrowed money in the past year.

In order to account for the within-cluster correlation, we used the robust cluster estimator to calculate standard errors.

Selection Model: The first-stage Heckman's model addresses the selection question by modeling the effects of a series of covariates on whether an entrepreneur seeks external financial resources. The results show that among the three indicators of entrepreneurs' own human and economic capital endowments, education and their income did not significantly influence borrowing decisions, whereas the shortage of liquid assets was a significant factor that leads entrepreneurs to seek external financial resources. Moreover, entrepreneurs who experienced adverse economic change in the past year are also likely to need external financial assistance. In contrast, entrepreneurial households with members who hold an urban resident permit tend to have better economic conditions and a lower need to borrow. Moreover, the estimates of rho and its standard error indicate that the correlation coefficient between error terms of the main equation and the selection equation is significant, suggesting that the use of Heckman's method is appropriate.

References

Adler, P. S., & Kwon, S.-W. (2002). Social capital: Prospects for a new concept. *Academy of Management Review, 27*(1), 17–40.

Ahlstrom, D., & Bruton, G. D. (2006). Venture capital in emerging economies: Networks and institutional change. *Entrepreneurship Theory and Practice, 30*(2), 299–320.

Aldrich, H. E., & Zimmer, C. (1986). Entrepreneurship through social networks. In H. E. Aldrich (Ed.), *Population Perspectives on Organizations* (pp. 13–28). Uppsala: Acta Universitatis Upsaliensis.

Ayyagari, M., Demirguc-Kunt, A., & Maksimovic, V. (2008). Formal versus informal finance: Evidence from China. *World Bank Policy Research Working Paper,* 4465.

Ba, S. (2013). *Report on Small and Micro Business Financing: Chinese Experience and Asian Paths.* Beijing: The Development Research Center of the State Council of China.

Bates, T. (1997). Financing small business creation: The case of Chinese and Korean immigrant entrepreneurs. *Journal of Business Venturing, 12,* 109–124.

Batjargal, B. (2003). Social capital and entrepreneurial performance in Russia: A longitudinal study. *Organization Studies, 24*(4), 535–556.

Batjargal, B., & Liu, M. (2004). Entrepreneurs' access to private equity in China: The role of social capital. *Organization Science, 15*(2), 159–172.

Besley, T., & Coate, S. (1995). Group lending, repayment incentives and social collateral. *Journal of Development Economics, 46*(1), 1–18.

Bian, Y. (1997). Bringing strong ties back in: Indirect ties, network bridges, and job searches in China. *American Sociological Review, 62*(3), 366–385.

Bian, Y., & Li, Y. (2001). The social capital of Chinese urban families. *Qinghua Sociological Review, 2,* 1–18.

Birley, S. (1985). The role of networks in the entrepreneurial process. *Journal of Business Venturing, 1*(1), 107–117.

Blau, P. M. (1964). *Exchange and Power in Social Life.* New York: Wiley.

Bruderl, J., & Preisendorfer, P. (1998). Network support and the success of newly founded business. *Small Business Economics, 10,* 213–225.

Burt, R. S. (1992). *Structural Holes: The Social Structure of Competition.* Cambridge, MA: Harvard University Press.

Casey, C. (2012). Low-wealth minority enterprises and access to financial resources for start-up activities: Do connections matter? *Economic Development Quarterly, 26*(3), 252–266.

CFSA, C. F. S. A. (2006). *Almanac of China's Financial and Banking.* Beijing: Almanac of China's Financial and Banking Publishing House.

Chang, M. L. (2005). With a little help from my friends (and my financial planner). *Social Forces, 83*(4), 1469–1497.

Chow, C. K.-W., & Fung, M. K. Y. (2000). Small business and liquidity constraints in financing business investment: Evidence from Shanghai's manufacturing sector. *Journal of Business Venturing, 15,* 363–383.

Christensen, G. (1993). The limits to informal financial intermediation. *World Development, 21*(5), 721–731.

Cornwell, E. Y., & Cornwell, B. (2008). Access to expertise as a form of social capital: An examination of race and class based disparities in network ties to experts. *Sociological Perspectives, 51*(4), 853–876.

Davidsson, P., & Honig, B. (2003). The role of social and human capital among nascent entrepreneurs. *Journal of Business Venturing, 18,* 301–331.

De Graaf, N. D., & Flap, H. D. (1988). "With a Little Help from My Friends": Social resources as an explanation of occupational status and income in West Germany, The Netherlands, and the United States. *Social Forces, 67*(2), 452–472.

DiMaggio, P. J., & Louch, H. (1998). Socially embedded consumer transactions: For what kinds of purchases do people most often use networks? *American Sociological Review, 63,* 619–637.

Doh, S., & Acs, Z. (2010). Innovation and social capital: A cross-country investigation. *Industry and Innovation, 17*(3), 241–262.

Doh, S., & McNeely, C. L. (2012). A multi-dimensional perspective on social capital and economic development: An exploratory analysis. *Annals of Regional Science, 49,* 821–843. doi:10.1007/s00168-011-0449-1

Dubini, P., & Aldrich, H. (1991). Personal and extended networks are central to the entrepreneurial process. *Journal of Business Venturing, 6,* 305–313.

Ferrary, M. (2003). Trust and social capital in the regulation of lending activities. *Journal of Social-Economics, 31*(6), 672–699.

Fukuyama, F. (1995). *Trust: The Social Virtues and the Creation of Prosperity.* New York: Free Press.

Ghate, P. (1992). *Informal Finance: Some Findings from Asia.* New York: Oxford University Press.

Granovetter, M. S. (1973). The strength of weak ties. *The American Journal of Sociology, 78*(6), 1360–1380.

Granovetter, M. (1990). The old and the new economic sociology: A history and an agenda. In R. Friedland & A. Robertson (Eds.), *Rethinking Economy and Society* (pp. 89–112). New York: Walter de Gruyter.

Granovetter, M. (2005). The impact of social structure on economic outcomes. *The Journal of Economic Perspectives, 19*(1), 33–50.

Guiso, L., Jappelli, T., & Terlizzese, D. (1996). Income risk, borrowing constraints, and portfolio choice. *American Economic Review, 86*(1), 158–172.

Guiso, L., Sapienza, P., & Zingales, L. (2004). The role of social capital in financial development. *The American Economic Review, 94*(3), 526–556.

He, G. (1999). A perspective of rural residents' credit activity: Financial restraint and financial deepening in rural areas. *China Rural Economy, 10*, 42–48.

He, Z., & Wong, P.-K. (2004). Exploration vs. exploitation: An empirical test of the ambidexterity hypothesis. *Organization Science, 15*(4), 481–494.

Hilgert, M. A., Hogarth, J. M., & Beverly, S. G. (2003). Household financial management: The connection between knowledge and behavior. *Federal Reserve Bulletin, 89*(7), 309–322.

Hoang, H., & Antoncic, B. (2003). Network-based research in entrepreneurship: A critical review. *Journal of Business Venturing, 18*, 165–187.

Hustedde, R. J., & Pulver, G. C. (1992). Factors affecting equity capital acquisition: The demand side. *Journal of Business Venturing, 7*, 363–374.

Jiang, S. (2009). The evolution of informal finance in China and its prospects. In J. Li & S. Hsu (Eds.), *Informal Finance in China: American and Chinese Perspectives* (pp. 12–38). New York: Oxford University Press.

Kotha, R., & George, G. (2012). Friends, family, or fools: Entrepreneur experience and its implications for equity distribution and resource mobilization. *Journal of Business Venturing, 27*, 525–543.

Laurenceson, J., & Chai, J. C. H. (2003). *Financial Reform and Economic Development in China*. Northampton, MA: Edward Elgar Publishing.

Lee, D., Jeong, K.-Y., & Chae, S. (2011). Measuring social capital in East Asia and other world regions: Index of social capital for 72 countries. *Global Economic Review, 40*(4), 385–407.

Li, J., & Hsu, S. (2009). *Informal Finance in China: American and Chinese Perspectives*. New York: Oxford University Press.

Lin, N. (1999). Social networks and status attainment. *Annual Review of Sociology, 25*, 467–487.

Lin, N. (2001). *Social Capital: A Theory of Social Structure and Action*. New York: Cambridge University Press.

Lin, N., & Dumin, M. (1986). Access to occupations through social ties. *Social Networks, 8*, 365–385.

March, J. G. (1991). Exploration and exploitation in organizational learning. *Organization Science, 2*(1), 71–87.

Marsden, P. V. (1987). Core discussion networks of Americans. *American Sociological Review, 52*(1), 122–131.

Marsden, P. V. (1990). Network data and measurement. *Annual Review of Sociology, 16*, 435–463.

Mizruchi, M. S., & Stearns, L. B. (1994). Money, banking, and financial markets. In N. J. Smelser & R. Swedberg (Eds.), *Handbook of Economic Sociology* (pp. 313–341). Princeton, NJ: Princeton University Press.

Mohieldin, M. S., & Wright, P. W. (2000). Formal and informal credit markets in Egypt. *Economic Development and Cultural Change, 48*(3), 657–670.

NBS, N. B. O. S. (2010). *China Statistical Yearbook*. Beijing: China Statistical Yearbook Publishing House.

Ong, L. (2006). The political economy of township government debt, township enterprises and rural financial institutions in China. *The China Quarterly, 186*, 377–400.

Peng, M. W. (2003). Institutional transitions and strategic choices. *The Academy of Management Review, 28*(2), 275–296.

Petersen, M. A., & Rajan, R. G. (1994). The benefits of lending relationships: Evidence from small business data. *Journal of Finance, 49*(1), 3–37.

Portes, A., & Sensenbrenner, J. (1993). Embeddedness and immigration: Notes on the social determinants of economic action. *American Journal of Sociology, 98*(6), 1320–1350.

Putnam, R. D. (1995). Bowling alone: America's declining social capital. *Journal of Democracy, 6*(1), 65–78.

Rotter, J. B. (1980). Interpersonal trust, trustworthiness, and gullibility. *American Psychologist, 35*, 1–7.

Rozelle, S., Park, A., Benziger, V., & Ren, C. (1998). Targeted poverty investments and economic growth in China. *World Development, 26*(12), 2137–2151.

Shane, S., & Cable, D. (2002). Network ties, reputation, and the financing of new ventures. *Management Science, 48*(3), 364–381.

Shanmugam, B. (1991). Socio-economic development through the informal credit market. *Modern Asian Studies, 25*(2), 209–225.

Shih, V. (2004). Factions matter: Personal networks and the distribution of bank loans in China. *Journal of Contemporary China, 13*(38), 3–19.

Shirai, S. (2002). Banks' lending behavior and firms' corporate financing pattern in the people's republic of China. *ADB Institute Research Paper, 43*.

Spilerman, S. (2000). Wealth and stratification processes. *Annual Review of Sociology, 26*, 497–524.

Tang, S.-Y. (1995). Informal credit markets and economic development in Taiwan. *World Development, 23*(5), 845–855.

Thoni, C., Tyran, J.-R., & Wengstrom, E. (2012). Microfoundations of social capital. *Journal of Public Economics, 96*, 635–643.

Tushman, M. L., & O'Reilly, C. (1996). Ambidextrous organizations: Managing evolutionary and revolutionary change. *California Management Review, 38*, 8–30.

Uzzi, B. (1997). Social structure and competition in interfirm networks: The paradox of embeddedness. *Administrative Science Quarterly, 42*(1), 35–67.

Uzzi, B. (1999). Embeddedness in the making of financial capital: How social relations and networks benefit firms seeking financing. *American Sociological Review, 64*(4), 481–505.

Uzzi, B., & Lancaster, R. (2004). Embeddedness and price formation in the corporate law market. *American Sociological Review, 69*(3), 319–344.

Waldinger, R., Aldrich, H. E., & Ward, R. (1990). *Ethnic Entrepreneurs*. Newbury Park, CA: Sage.

Wimborg, J., & Landstrom, H. (2000). Financial bootstrapping in small businesses: Examining small business managers' resource acquisition behaviors. *Journal of Business Venturing, 16*, 235–254.

World Bank. (1989). *World Development Report*. New York: Oxford University Press.

Wu, G. (1997). Discussion on poverty alleviation subsidized-loan policy. *China Rural Survey, 4*, 7–13.

Xin, K. K., & Pearce, J. L. (1996). Guanxi: Connections as substitutes for formal institutional support. *Academy of Management Journal, 39*(6), 1641–1658.

Yang, D. T. (1999). Urban-biased policies and rising income inequality in China. *American Economic Review, 89*(2), 306–310.

Zelizer, V. A. (2005). *The Purchase of Intimacy*. Princeton, NJ: Princeton University Press.

Zhang, J. (2005). Farmer, state and rural credit system. *Journal of Finance, 296*, 1–12.

5 Adaptation and Innovation in the Early Stages of Transition

To understand managerial behavior and organizational strategy in China today, it is useful to isolate and study managerial response to the opportunities, constraints, and challenges that faced enterprises in the very early years of reform. Research on organizations makes clear that an ability to adapt to radical change is an important indicator of competitive advantage, organizational legitimacy, and survival; and research on western countries has shown that the strategies firms use during times of dramatic change can also shape the long-term structure of both the organization and the environment in which the organization is located (D'Aveni, 1994; Hannan & Freeman, 1989; Volberda, 1996). The environment in the first decade of China's reform was, indeed, characterized by rapid change and severe shocks that threatened firm survival and, at the very least, had the potential to hinder performance; managerial response to that environment provided the foundation on which cotemporary Chinese firms were created and established many of the strategies that organizational decision makers use today.

In this chapter, we examine the adoption of two managerial practices that began to emerge in the early years of reform (1979–1989) and that were an integral part of the formation of China's market economy: the adoption of piece wages and buying/selling producer goods on markets. We focus on these behaviors because they are important indicators of firm strategy in their own right but also because they provide a window into managerial innovation in that critical era more generally. The first strategy that we study—paying piece rate wages—is a quintessential market-oriented labor practice. As such, piece wages were not permitted during the socialist era; however, officials granted state-owned firms permission to use this form of compensation in the first years of China's reform. State officials monitored and directed many firm activities during transition, but piece rate use was largely left to manager discretion from early in the reform era. Piece rates accounted for a lower percentage of total employee compensation in China than in other transition economies and not all firms used piece rates; however, their use grew considerably after 1979, and more than 40 percent of formerly state-owned firms used them by 1989 (Keister, 2002).

The second strategy we study—the use of markets rather than state redistributors to buy and sell producer goods—is fundamental to a transition away from a planned economy, and a willingness to participate in market activity early in reform is an important indicator of managerial response to changing environmental conditions. Market exchange of producer goods occurred in China prior to reform, but it usually involved only small, rural firms and affected a trivial fraction of total producer good purchases (Wong, 1986). During reform, a growing number of firms, including many large SOEs, began to engage in market exchange of producer goods for the first time (Naughton, 1996). During the 1980s, the state continued to control a large portion of industrial output, but authorities increasingly allowed firms to buy inputs and sell output with contacts identified by the firm on terms negotiated by the partners to the exchange. Because enterprises were able to retain profits from direct sales, market exchange also increased revenues, promoted firm growth, and contributed to aggregate economic expansion (Wu & Zhao, 1987). Although the use of markets for producer goods grew rapidly, there was considerable variation among firms in participation in these markets, particularly in the first decade of reform (Keister, 2000); this suggests that there are lessons to be learned from adoption of market practices that might inform understanding of managerial decision-making during China's transition.

Managerial decisions regarding piece wages and engagement with markets also provide a unique opportunity to explore the relative role of organizational and environmental influences on firm behavior, a tension that pervades organization theory. Research on western firms suggests that either internal organizational incentives and preferences (Dess & Beard, 1984; Keats & Hitt, 1988; Pfeffer & Salancik, 1978) or external pressures (Buchko, 1994; DiMaggio & Powell, 1983; Meyer & Rowan, 1977) determine innovative organizational responses. In reality, both internal and external processes are likely important, but the relative weight of these influences is unclear. We integrate ideas from strategic choice and institutional theory to propose that different combinations of influences are salient at different stages in the spread of a new practice; we also propose that the relevant influences are different for the adoption of piece wages compared to engagement on markets. Because the decision to use piece wages was largely left to the discretion of managers in the early stages of reform, is it likely that strategic choice was particularly salient in those years. Over time, however, mimetic processes are likely to have become more relevant. In contrast, the decision to engage with markets was a practice that involved the state, a factor that is typically overlooked in western studies but that is critical to understanding managerial behavior in China. We propose that state intervention shaped the degree to which internal and external influences were salient in managerial decision-making, and that this was evident in firm sales of products on markets. We propose that access to non-state financial resources allowed firms to reduce dependence on the state and engage product markets, but we also stress that the specific source of a firm's financing would affect use of product markets in meaningful ways.

To study these ideas empirically, we used longitudinal (1979–89) data on 769 former firms in four provinces (Sichuan, Jiangsu, Jilin, and Shanxi). The dataset is particularly unique among data on Chinese firms during transition because it contains information on firm-level decision-making. Such detail is critical to understanding the process by which firms adapted to reform. This data was collected by the Institute of Economics of the Chinese Academy of Social Science (CASS); the Chinese Provincial System Reform Commission (the agencies responsible for implementing and evaluating reform measures) sent questionnaires to 800 enterprises, and 769 were returned. The response rate was high because the System Reform Commission was a government agency with which the enterprises have regular contact, although it did not directly oversee enterprise activity. The questionnaire had two parts. The first was a set of 70 questions regarding the enterprise structure, manager appointment, contracts, bonus and motivation systems, relations with governmental offices, and enterprise strategy. The second part included 321 quantitative questions, designed to be answered by the enterprise's accountant, covering many aspects of enterprise operations between 1980 and 1989 (Groves, Hong, McMillan, & Naughton, 1994, 1995; Keister, 2001, 2002). All firms included in this sample were SOEs, and the sample appears to reasonably represent the state-run industry during the time the data was collected on all dimensions except for firm size. The sample does appear to over-represent large SOEs, enterprises for which progress in reform had been modest relative to small enterprises and those in the non-state sector.

Innovation 1: Piece Rate Adoption

Linking pay to output was somewhat common in earlier historical periods, but the use of incentive-based compensation schemes was prohibited following China's 1949 communist takeover (Naughton, 1996). However, things began to change following the 1978 start of reform. The state continued to regulate labor practices, but as managerial authority over the operation of firms expanded, reformers gradually transferred responsibility for many of these practices to the firm (Naughton, 1996). In particular, reformers pushed for the development of a socialist market economy, and managers correspondingly began to adopt capitalist practices while retaining socialist methods of hiring, firing, and compensating workers (often because the state required it). Most firms continued to employ permanent workers through the end of the 1980s, but in 1984, all new employees were considered contract workers (those who had been hired previously as permanent employees were still guaranteed lifetime employment). Likewise, most organizations continued to accept workers allocated by state agencies even while beginning to acquire workers from newly developing markets (Dong & Hu, 1995). An important part of these changing labor practices was the reintroduction of piece wages; firms continued to use socialist compensation practices as well, but as early as 1981, many firms paid up to 20 percent of their workers as piece wage laborers. The transition to capitalist forms of compensation was gradual in China, particularly compared to European transition economies, but many Chinese managers enthusiastically embraced many practices, including piece wages. Yet given that managers had discretion in decisions to adopt these practices, there was variation across firms in adoption rates (Keister, 2000).

Ideas from strategic choice and institutional theory are both useful for understanding the conditions under which a Chinese SOE would adopt an innovative labor practice, such as paying piece wages, in the first decade of reform. Strategic choice refers to the role that influences internal to the firm play in determining the nature and timing of innovative actions. Managerial training and experience, organizational routines, and related capabilities all affect whether a firm adopts an innovation (Dutton & Duncan, 1987; Ginsberg, 1988; Tichy, 1983). From this perspective, firms' unique knowledge and capabilities allow managers to undertake new activities that, under the right set of internal and external conditions, can improve performance and the firm's long-term competitive position. A central concern is the nature of the capabilities that are relevant and how these develop and change over time (Ginsberg, 1988). Managerial innovation occurs when the firm has the necessary internal resources and capabilities to change and the change is to the firm's advantage given available information (Kelly & Amburgey, 1991).

Institutional theory highlights the external environmental factors that create incentives for altering organizational structures and strategic orientation (DiMaggio & Powell, 1983; Meyer & Rowan, 1977). Institutional ideas are more commonly used to study similarities among organizations than as a lens for understanding structural change in organizations; however, institutionalization is both a *process* and a *property* variable that is usefully extended to discuss change; this work suggests that innovation may result from external normative pressure, a need for legitimacy, or simply exposure (DiMaggio & Powell, 1983; Zucker, 1977). Tolbert and Zucker (1996) usefully proposed that the adoption of new practices begins with innovation and flows through habituation, objectification, and sedimentation. Although they do not explicitly identify internal, strategic factors as relevant in the early stages, the factors that lead to early experimentation are, indeed, internal and consistent with strategic choice arguments. Moreover, institutional arguments suggest that environmental factors become more salient over time and interact with internal factors to create a combination of influences on change. Incorporating organizational and environmental factors at different points in the change process suggests that a dual system is likely to develop within the organization as the old strategy is slowly abandoned and replaced by the new strategy.

Although research from these two perspectives often attempts to explain similar behaviors, the theories are seldom used together. In reading previous literature, it is possible to deduce that either strategic choice factors or institutional factors dominate firm behavior. In reality, both strategic choice and institutional factors are likely to shape firm behavior in all contexts. The importance of both strategic and institutional influences is likely to be particularly evident when firms are adapting to radical change because stagnant managerial decision-making is impossible. Indeed it is possible that drawing on ideas from both perspectives will provide a deeper understanding of managerial decision-making.

The Role of Managers in Piece Wage Adoption

In the early stages of change, organizations tend to act independently in response to specific problems, and as a result, manager and firm traits tend to be particularly salient determinants of adoption of new practices (Kelly & Amburgey, 1991; Tolbert & Zucker, 1996). In the early days of China's reform, the degree to which workers supported management and the manager's orientation toward markets were particularly salient. The factory manager responsibility system gave managers control over many decisions, but for decades workers had participated in running enterprises and making critical decisions (Naughton, 1996). This practice did not change immediately given the group orientation that was pervasive in Chinese firms (Child, 1972). Managers who had worker support were more able to adopt and implement innovative practices than those who were at odds with workers. Support was particularly important in the early stages of reform because pre-reform norms of the importance of workers were still recent, manager confidence was relatively low given the move to markets, and firm action was largely independent of the actions of other firms (Naughton, 1994). Workers supported the use of piece rates, in particular, because such a pay scheme had the potential to dramatically increase their wages. The importance of worker support declined as boards of directors increasingly played a role in manager appointment, but it was an important indicator of managers' abilities to institute change in the early stages of reform. Similarly, managers' orientations toward markets affected adoption of innovative practices: managers who were market-oriented were more likely to use piece rates given the meritocratic nature of the practice. Reforming the economic system forced managers to begin relying less on strategies such as cultivating bargaining position with superiors and more on profit maximization and improving competitive advantage, but naturally, this tendency varied across organizations.

Consistent with these ideas, Table 5.1 shows that worker support did, indeed, correlate positively with the adoption of piece wages in the early stages of reform, other potential factors controlled, but that worker support had no effect as reform progressed. This table includes results from logistic regression models of piece wage adoption in three time periods in the first decade of reform (see the Appendix at the end of this chapter for model

Table 5.1 Adoption of Piece Wages: Logistic Regression, 1979–1989

	1979–83	1984–86	1987–89
Manager traits			
Manager elected	.463=	.005	.316
	(.250)	(.278)	(.396)
Party secretary	−.400**	−.246=	−.166
	(.146)	(.148)	(.170)
Market-oriented	.054=	.124***	.192***
	(.034)	(.036)	(.042)
Market development			
Poor labor markets	.241*	−.103	−.071
	(.126)	(.128)	(.148)
Poor other markets	.140*	.035	−.071
	(.124)	(.131)	(.152)
Exposure			
Exposure	4.243***	–	–
	(.992)		
Exposure*profits	–	.008***	.003**
		(.002)	(.002)
Control variables			
Mining	2.039***	1.700***	.862***
	(.223)	(.249)	(.306)
Textiles	2.038***	1.975***	.012***
	(.150)	(.157)	(.197)
Manufacturing	.997***	.686***	.832***
	(.145)	(.159)	(.183)
Utilities	−.796**	−.339	−.334
	(.305)	(.273)	(.289)
Municipal owner	.376**	.066	.319*
	(.134)	(.135)	(.156)
College graduate	−.207	−.380**	−.436*
	(.120)	(.125)	(.148)
Airport	1.212***	.639***	.203***
	(.179)	(.173)	(.205)
Railroad	−.686***	−.782***	−.426***
	(.156)	(.155)	(.185)
n	4,216	2,153	2,150
Log likelihood	2,713***	2,377***	2,106***

Notes: = p < .10 * p < .05 ** p < .01 *** p < .001. Also controlled but not displayed are measures of age, workforce size, cumulative profits over the time period, and firm age.

details). The models show that worker support of managers was associated with a higher likelihood of piece wage use between 1979 and 1983 (Model 1); however, there is no effect of manager elections in the 1984 to 1986 time period (Model 2). This change continues through 1989 (Model 3), suggesting that the relevance of managerial elections expired by early in the reform period. In other words, innovative firms adopted market-oriented practices relatively quickly, and those managers that had worker support were better able to effectively attempt new practices. However, as time passed, other processes became salient and worker support was no longer a crucial influence on innovative behavior. It is important to note that the weak significance of this variable suggests that other processes were clearly more important than the model suggests from the beginning of the change process. This does not exclude the importance of firm traits; it just highlights the importance of the social. We also controlled for whether the manager was a party secretary, an important manager trait in the early stages of reform; our results suggest that holding this position was associated with a lower likelihood of using piece wages in the first years of reform but that this effect also disappeared by the mid-1980s.

The results included in Table 5.1 also show that managers with a generally positive orientation toward markets used piece rates more than their counterparts who were less positively inclined in the early stages of reform; moreover, our findings show that the effect of a market orientation became more important over time. Literature on the effect of China's reform on social processes, including literature that has explored both individual and organization level impacts, has emphasized that both market and political processes continued to shape the nature of China's economy in the early stages of reform. Our findings suggest that both economic and political influences were salient throughout the early stages of reform in the formation of organizational strategy. The continued importance of these influences through the end of the decade underscores the importance of political connections and ease at adjusting to emerging markets and contrasts these with the fleeting significance of worker support.

Market Development and Piece Wage Adoption

Markets for labor and other inputs were developing rapidly in the first decade of China's reform, and organization theory suggests that these changes would also affect the adoption of piece wages. In retrospect, we know that market development was very successful in China; however, in the first decade of reform, the movement to market forms of exchange created enormous amounts of uncertainty (Keister, 2001). Even transactions that seem basic and that are largely taken-for-granted in established market economies, such as how to compensate workers, created considerable amounts of uncertainty for managers in China's reforming economy. Labor surpluses and shortages alternately plagued firms, and at the same time, there was growing pressure to increase production and efficiency (often measured as output per worker). The need to hire workers and ensure that they were productive became extremely important, but the way managers attempted to meet these goals varied. In times of high uncertainty, managers strive to reduce both the uncertainty itself and the perception of uncertainty;

they are also likely to imitate others and to innovate when uncertainty is high (DiMaggio & Powell, 1983; O'Neill, Pouder, & Buchholtz, 1998). In particular, the use of piece rates was likely greater where markets were poorly developed, as it is a particularly innovative strategy that was perceived as necessary under highly uncertain conditions. As markets became more developed and economic conditions became more certain over time, uncertainty declined.

It follows that poorly developed labor markets would increase the use of piece rates in the early stages of China's reform, but that this effect would have declined over time as market uncertainty declined or disappeared. The models shown in Table 5.1 suggest that this is exactly what happened in China. All three models included in this table control for the degree to which labor and other markets were developed in the region (see Appendix for details). The coefficients for these market development variables are positive and significant in Model 1; that is, our findings suggest that market development was an important correlate of innovation in the early stages of reform when uncertainty was at its peak. However, the effect of market development disappears in Models 2 and 3, the models for the later time periods in which markets were more developed and uncertainty had started to wane. Because our sample size is constant over the time periods, these changing effects do not reflect statistical power or other issues related to sample size or composition; indeed, the continued significance of the control variables (e.g., the industry controls) suggests that the changing relationship between our key independent variables reflects changing economic and social conditions.

Social Processes and Piece Wage Adoption

There are also social processes that affect managerial response to dramatic change and the adoption of innovative strategies. For instance, exposure to the practices used in other firms has the potential to affect managers' decisions on a range of issues, including decisions about whether to adopt innovative practices. It is well documented that the diffusion of innovative practices results from a variety of pressures, including regulatory agencies, government agencies, laws, courts, professions, interest groups, and public opinion (Maanen, 1983; Meyer & Rowan, 1977; Scott, 1987; Zucker, 1987). Uncertainty has also been shown to affect diffusion (Haunschild & Miner, 1997; O'Neill, Pouder, & Buchholtz, 1998). When a practice is new, it is likely that imitation is frequency-based: organizations imitate the actions that have been taken by large numbers of other organizations because the legitimacy of the practice is enhanced (Tolbert & Zucker, 1996). Imitative behavior occurs both actively (Meyer & Rowan, 1977) and less deliberately as the practice becomes taken for granted (Zucker, 1977). There is also evidence that frequency of use of a practice by other organizations may serve as an indicator of the technical value of a practice (Abrahamson & Rosenkopf, 1993).

In the early stages of China's reform, simple exposure to other firms using the practice was what was relevant for motivating change. Because piece rates and other capitalist practices were both unheard of and taboo in China in the decades preceding reform, managers may not have thought to try such a practice in the early stages unless they witnessed their colleagues using the strategy. Simply being exposed to others using the new strategy was likely sufficient to lead to use of the strategy in the focal firm. Model 1 in Table 5.1 includes a measure of exposure to other firms using piece wages; this model shows that exposure was, indeed, an important correlate of adoption (i.e., the coefficient for exposure is positive and significant). It is possible that this indicates there was a smaller number of possible converts over time. Whereas this might be true in later time periods, in the time period on which we are focused, at most 40 percent of sampled firms used piece rates, suggesting that there were still plenty of potential converts. This finding also suggests that the exposure results are not simply an artifact of reformers allowing firms located in certain areas to use certain strategies at the same time. Historically, piece rates were not regulated in this way. Even if use of the strategy had been controlled geographically, the fact that firms were more likely to adopt a strategy that was consistent with that used by their profitable peers (rather than just any nearby firm) suggests social influence.

As time passed, however, simple imitation was replaced by active imitation of successful (i.e., profitable) others and acquiescence to other external pressures. Researchers have shown that under such conditions, the exposure effect will be greatest when the focal organization is exposed to use by successful or large others (DiMaggio & Powell, 1983; Haunschild, 1993). Specifically, organizations modeled themselves after others they perceived to be more legitimate or successful, such as those that were more profitable (DiMaggio & Powell, 1983). Such targeted mimetic behavior is more likely after a practice has been tried for some time and managers have recognized that others are using it. Moreover, if the use of the practice is responsible for the firm's profits, imitation is even more likely. In China, managerial efforts to improve, combined with exposure to the behavior and resulting success or failure of other firms, likely increased the nature of mimetic processes. Time increased the likelihood that firms would have had contact with others using different practices, and labor reforms, such as those that took effect in 1984, increasingly made firms aware of practices that had not been apparent before. Over time, managers became aware of the impact that early adoption appeared to have on the financial success of innovative firms, and pressure to adopt market-oriented practices used by successful firms in order to maintain or increase legitimacy also increased. As Table 5.1, Model 2 shows, exposure to other organizations using piece rates profitably was the relevant metric as reform progressed. This model includes the exposure measure weighted by profits (for later time periods when firms could have turned profits), and the model shows that the profit-weighted exposure measure is also positive and highly significant, suggesting that firms did, indeed, begin to mimic other, more profitable firms as reform progressed.

Innovation 2: Buying and Selling on Producer Markets

Ideas from strategic choice and institutional theory are also useful for understanding manager decisions to begin using producer markets to buy and sell goods in the early days of reform. However, this decision involved notably different processes than those underlying the adoption of piece wages. Prior to economic and industrial reform, local governments in China controlled a large proportion of standardized producer goods, such as coal, cement, and iron. Government agencies engaged in market-like sales and barter of goods across regions. Because firms were required to use government sponsors to operate outside their regions, however, these transactions were largely limited to local exchange. Small scale and rural firms were often able to operate independently on markets because competent government sponsors were rare and administrative control was relatively relaxed. As a result, these firms dominated early market transactions for producer goods. In provinces such as Jiangsu, where a significant number of rural industries were located or headquartered, market-like transactions already accounted for about 25 percent of the supply of key raw materials in 1978 (Naughton, 1996).

In contrast, the state regulated exchange and prevented market exchange for the majority of China's medium and large-scale SOEs. State ownership of firms created conflicting incentives for state administrators and firm managers, softened budget constraints, and lead to interdependence between the state and firms (Wong, 1986). Moreover, because they were owners of the enterprises, governments had objectives other than efficiency or profitability: they relied on firms to provide scarce inputs to other firms, maintain full employment, fund employee pension plans, and provide medical care, housing, and various other social welfare services (Kornai, 1992; Walder, 1995). These non-financial preferences ultimately outweighed state interest in the financial performance of the firms. Loss-making firms were able to survive as the government constantly reallocated funds obtained from profitable firms to less efficient enterprises. As neither firm survival nor growth was constrained by firms' budgets or financial performance, managers responded by hoarding resources and continuously bargaining with state officials for favorable treatment in much the same way eastern European firms responded (Kornai, 1979, 1986). The state was hesitant to discipline public enterprises because it relied on them for revenues and the provision of social welfare.

The financial system was intimately connected to the system of SOEs prior to reform; at that point, there was no financial market, although banks did exist as state agencies responsible for enacting and enforcing government monetary policy (Lardy, 1998). SOEs and banks operated on a transfer system of credit controlled by government bureaus, a system that was nearly completely separate from the currency system used by households and other (usually smaller) enterprises. The funds transferred among banks and SOEs were not convertible to cash, but the credit and currency systems did influence each other. Yet there was no central bank, and banks were not required to maintain reserves (Holz, 1992). Moreover, although the state began to experiment with monetary policy prior to reform, these policies were subordinate to the procedures that guided the determination and enforcement of output targets (Xu, 1998; Yi, 1994).

Previous research and policy prescriptions assumed that only by replacing state ownership completely could bargaining be eliminated and firms become viable economic entities (Kornai, 1992). However, instead of shifting the state ownership of enterprises to private hands immediately, China's reformers first focused on improving firm autonomy and developing incentive mechanisms for managers and workers in state enterprises. Firms gained the right to retain profits and obtained unprecedented control over output beyond mandatory plan targets (Jefferson & Rawski, 1994). Market transactions, previously only tolerated, were now encouraged to promote efficiency, independence, and ultimately financial performance. Firms, particularly those in the coastal areas, had increasing contact with foreign firms and products as international trade and investment expanded.

In order to differentiate supplies of industrial goods into plan and market components, the state introduced a dual pricing system in 1984. This change shaped firm adoption of market exchange practices in important ways. Under this system, firms were able to exchange marginal quantities of industrial inputs and output on markets where supply and demand determined prices. Reformers first implemented the dual pricing system in a limited number of regions and allowed only certain firms to participate, but before long, most firms in nearly all regions were able to participate. Because the same good could now be sold at very different prices depending on the allocation mechanism that regulated its sale, shortages developed and significant disparities between prices on markets and within the plan emerged during the early stages of this reform. Of course, this increased the incentives firms faced to move to markets, particularly given that state administrators had begun applauding market-oriented behavior.

Simultaneously, banking reform changed the way managers financed the firm. In 1983, direct grants to SOEs were replaced by interest-bearing loans in order to harden budget constraints. The People's Bank of China (PBOC) was separated from the Ministry of Finance and became the central bank in

1984. The PBOC gradually assumed control of the money supply and began to set monetary policy, regulate exchange rates, and oversee the financial system. Under the central bank, four specialized banks emerged as financial intermediaries. The Industrial and Commercial Bank, the Agricultural Bank, the People's Bank, and the Construction Bank remained government agencies but they gradually began to accept deposits and to lend capital independent of government intervention. Although their names identified the specialized banks with particular segments of the economy, the banks were free to lend to firms in all industries. Firms applied for funds, and their requests were increasingly evaluated on the merit of the firm and the application, with decreasing regard for government policy. Yet these banks remained government agencies, and their lending at times reflected state policy more than the financial objectives of the bank (Goldie-Scott, 1995; Yi, 1994).

As a result of these changes, a growing number of firms started to actively seek access to markets for both productive inputs and industrial output (Wong, 1986). The first decade of China's economic reform witnessed a visible shift from planning to the market for most state enterprises and rapid industry growth led by the state sectors. China's real output increased almost fivefold from 1980 to 1992, with the majority contributed by state sector enterprises (Jefferson & Rawski, 1994). Many state enterprises adapted quickly to markets, and most began to buy and sell to some extent on markets; however, there was naturally some variation in the extent to which firms began to buy and sell products on markets, creating a unique opportunity to study the degree to which firms embraced this new form of conducting business.

Financial Market Development and Use of Product Markets

Strategic choice and institutional theories suggest that firm capacity to transition to markets depends on both a firm's internal incentives to alter its behavior and external opportunities to change the way business is done. During economic transition in China, fiscal constraints shaped a great deal about organizational decision-making because they affected both willingness and opportunities (Guthrie, 1997; Keister, 2000). The degree to which financial markets were developed, in particular, affected both manager preferences and the availability of opportunities to engage in market exchange. When managers encounter uncertainty, they nearly universally seek ways to reduce risk (DiMaggio & Powell, 1983; O'Neill, Pouder, & Buchholtz, 1998). In transition economies where uncertainty associated with poorly developed markets is particularly salient, managers are especially attuned to the need to protect their interests (Guthrie, 1999; Keister, 2001; Peng, 2004). In China, in areas where financial markets were more developed, financing was relatively easy to obtain. As a result, managers were more certain that they would have funds to continue operating in the future, they were more certain that their potential trade partners would have funds to pay for goods, and they were more confident that markets would be stable enough to sustain repeated exchange.

Consistent with strategic choice arguments, managers experimented because they perceived that they had the capability to change. They were able to withstand the additional risk that accompanied experimentation with a new form of exchange. Consistent with institutional arguments, firms perceived lower risk associated with market experimentation in areas with developed markets: where financial markets were relatively well developed, managers experienced an environment in which confidence in finance was high, regardless of the type of funding the firm itself received. Moreover, in areas with relatively well-developed financial markets, normative pressure to use markets began to expand and further compelled managers to experiment with product markets. As a result, firms located in areas with relatively well-developed financial markets were more likely to experiment with product markets, regardless of the type of funding they received, than their counterparts located in areas with less developed financial markets.

Table 5.2 includes generalized least squares models of the degree to which firms relied on markets for the acquisition of material inputs and output sales. The dependent variables in these models are the ratio of market inputs to planned inputs (Model 1) and the ratio of market sales to planned sales (Model 2). Because most firms used markets to some extent, we opted to model the extent of market participation (i.e., the two ratios) rather than modeling use (i.e., a zero-one measure). Table 5.2 shows that both ratios are positively related to financial market development, all other factors held constant (see Appendix for model details and variable descriptions). This suggests that managers located in areas with relatively well-developed financial markets made bigger commitments to using product markets. There are likely both direct and indirect reasons for these findings. The direct explanation is that managers in areas with developed financial markets had better access to capital to fund expansion and experimentation. They also likely encountered potential exchange partners who had the same freedom. This suggests that strategically, the managers were more certain than their counterparts in less developed areas of the likely benefits and long-term potential of such exchange. That is, consistent with strategic choice arguments, they likely perceived that given the conditions they experienced, their firms had the capability to be competitive in market exchange. These findings also suggest that managers were more confident in the stability of markets because they were exposed to developing markets of various sorts. This measure does not indicate that product markets were stable, but rather that a related market was developed. In areas where markets are stable, the contextual conditions encourage experimentation and may even produce

Table 5.2 Use of Markets for Inputs and Sales: Linear Regression, 1979–1989

	Market inputs/ planned inputs	Market sales/ planned sales
Financial resources		
Financial market development	.320***	.578***
	(.060)	(.081)
Central government funds (log)	−.130***	−.140
	(.003)	(.08)
Bank funds 1980–1984 (log)	.160**	.410*
	(.060)	(.180)
Bank funds 1985–1989 (log)	−.029*	−.031*
	(.015)	(.012)
Local government funds (log)	.049**	.046*
	(.017)	(.020)
Bonds issued by firm (log)	−.067*	−.094**
	(.032)	(.022)
Control variables		
Competition from non-state firms	−.049***	−.033*
	(.009)	(.014)
Retained earnings (log)	−.020	.036
	(.014)	(.023)
Total assets (log)	−.169***	−.140**
	(.030)	(.044)
Chemical industry	−.169	.623***
	(.078)	(.131)
Building materials industry	−.063	.625***
	(.105)	(.156)
Machinery industry	−.810***	.449***
	(.071)	(.105)
Electronics industry	.045	.918
	(.119)	(.176)
Temporary workers (log)	−.004	−.019
	(.011)	(.018)
Party member (1 = yes)	.536*	.631*
	(.212)	(.300)
Technical school graduate (1 = yes)	−.036	−.030
	(.106)	(.157)
College graduate (1 = yes)	.094	.098
	(.071)	(.104)
Year	.123***	.179***
	(.010)	(.015)
n = 6,320		
R^2	.066	.062

Notes: * $p < .05$ ** $p < .01$ *** $p < .001$. Models are general linear models; standard errors are in parentheses. Also controlled but not displayed are measures of workforce size, cumulative profits over the time period, and firm age.

normative pressures to use markets. Our findings do not demonstrate these arguments, but they are consistent with both the direct and indirect explanations.

Central Government Funds and the Use of Product Markets

Although market context was clearly important, the strong state in China continued to shape a great deal of economic behavior during transition. Indeed, many of China's SOEs continued to receive large amounts of funding from the central government. These firms were usually high priorities for the state because they were dominant firms in vital industries (e.g., defense, telecommunications), provided essential jobs, contributed important resources to the state, or were otherwise deemed critical. Firms that were high priorities did not face the same uncertainties that other firms faced and were either not permitted to or did not need to experiment with product markets. For these firms, both internal incentives and external institutional pressures advocated avoiding markets. This suggests neither that managers were not behaving strategically nor that they were not affected by institutional pressure. Rather, the strong relationship these firms continued to have with the state meant that a particular type of institutional pressure—market uncertainty—was largely irrelevant. Strategic decision-making dictated not experimenting with markets but rather continuing to foster a relationship with the strongest institutional force in the economy: the state. As the models in Table 5.2 show, the amount of central government funds that a firm received was negatively and significantly associated with both using market inputs and market sales. This does not imply that firms were not strategic actors nor does it suggest that they were immune to institutional pressure. In contrast, the results provide support for the argument that firms that continued to have a strong relationship with the state were less concerned than their counterparts with weaker ties to the central government about market uncertainty.

Bank Loans and the Use of Product Markets

As reform progressed, various forms of funding that did not originate with the central government began to affect a range of managerial decisions, including decisions about how to approach markets. In 1983, for example, the central government passed the grants-for-loans act, which allowed large enterprises to experiment with non-state funding sources; at the same time, the central government was reducing its overall patronage of firms. As a result, non-state funds became more appealing. In many cases, non-state funds were more certain, involved less political maneuvering and bargaining to maintain, and had the potential to eliminate problems related to supply shortages. In addition, non-state capital allowed managers to reduce their dependence on the state, which reduced uncertainties about

levels of state funding and decreased the risk of having profits redirected
to loss making firms (Keister, 2001). As a result, many enterprises started
to actively seek external funding, including bank loans, loans from other
companies, investment from other companies, and equity and bond issues
to raise capital.

Despite the increasing number of options, bank loans were the most
common form of external finance in the early 1980s for at least two reasons. First, bank loans were relatively easy to obtain, and second, these
loans were fairly low risk because they were backed by the state. Because
receiving bank loans was an important indicator of firm position in the
state hierarchy and because these loans reflected firm strategy more broadly,
receiving loans is an important indicator of a firm's willingness to experiment with product markets. In particular, in the first few years of reform,
firms that received bank loans were more likely to experiment with markets because these firms were relatively low state priorities. Firms seeking
external funds in the early stages of reform may have been released from
government control early and thus faced external pressure to find new ways
to replace other functions that the state used to fill, including obtaining
productive inputs and marketing output. Firms that received bank loans,
as opposed to those who had not been able to secure loans, however, also
likely felt a degree of security. Because bank loans often involved relatively
little risk, they could be regarded as a sort of intermediate form of finance
for managers who were reluctant to assume the risk of borrowing from
wholly non-state sources (Goldie-Scott, 1995). The amount of bank loans a
firm was able to obtain directly affected its ability to conceive of or implement strategies that were instrumental to improving their efficiency and
effectiveness during the reform. Consistent with this, the results shown in
Table 5.2 indicate that between 1980 and 1984, receiving more bank loans
increased the proportion of resources committed to markets both in inputs
and sales.

Following the financial reforms of 1983, however, the meaning of bank loans
changed because the state replaced direct grants to SOEs with interest-bearing
loans. At that point, bank loans became higher risk because they had interest
associated with them. Enterprises that were still receiving bank loans after 1984
may not have had other alternatives because they were not adapting to financial markets yet. Similarly, after 1983, there was normative pressure to begin
using forms of finance that were entirely non-state. Thus state action in 1983
changed the meaning of both internal strengths and external pressures, and
firms that were still receiving bank loans after 1984 were less likely than their
counterparts to adapt to developing product markets. As a result, the empirical relationship between bank funds and the use of product markets changed
in about 1984, as the models in Table 5.2 demonstrate: the variable indicating
bank loans received between 1980 and 1984 is positive and significant, but the
variable indicating bank loans received between 1985 and 1989 is negative and
significant.

The changing relationship between bank loans and market participation suggests that government action produced a very important change in firm behavior regardless of whether it was intended to produce this change. In the early 1980s, as markets developed and budget constraints hardened, managers may have applied for bank loans because they were independent. Thus receiving these loans may indicate that these were firms that were not controlled by the state and that were free to experiment. Following the 1983 financial reforms, however, our findings suggest that firms that were still receiving loans were a different type of enterprise. In particular, those still receiving bank loans at that point probably did not have alternatives because they were not adapting well. Likewise, normative pressure after 1983's legislation was to use non-bank forms of capital, and those still using bank loans were less likely to behave consistently with other pressures to marketize. In short, these results suggest that state action changed the meaning of both internal strengths and external pressures.

Local Government Funds and the Use of Product Markets

Yet another way that China's central state affected firms was by increasingly transferring control of firms to lower levels of government. China's economy was characterized by significant regional differences even in the pre-reform era: prior to reform, planning was done not only at the central government level, but also at various local levels, including province, city, county, and even townships (Wong, 1987). Local governments controlled most physical and financial resources and played an important role in shaping the institutional environment in which firms were embedded. Although development of the product market following reform allowed firms to be less dependent on administrative allocations, local governments remained important, primarily because of their control of financial resources (Wong, 1987). In the early stages of reform, local governments received funds from firm profits and taxes as a result of fiscal decentralization. They also influenced the bank lending process via their administrative power over local banking systems. The allocative power of local governments was further expanded, as they were granted the authority to set profit-retention rates for local enterprises. As markets were liberalized, local control of product prices and levels of both income and industrial–commercial taxes was strengthened.

The level of local government control of investment decisions and resource flows directly influenced the evolution of local markets. Local governments with smaller industrial bases often had stronger incentives to encourage firms to rely on markets (Walder, 1995). Compared with governments at higher administrative levels, local governments often had clearer financial incentives and constraints. Governments with larger industrial bases had to ensure that firms provided reliable sources of products, particularly industrial inputs, for other firms in the jurisdiction. The governments thus tended to care more about maintaining a stable supply of inputs rather than minimizing the marginal cost of production (Walder, 1992, 1995). However, local governments at lower administrative levels had fewer non-financial interests in firms, and their revenues were more closely linked to firms' financial performance. Because they had fewer entities to monitor and because there were fewer bureaucratic barriers to information flow, local governments were more aware of firms' decision-making as well and were more active in encouraging firms under their supervision to make pro-market decisions. This allowed them to make faster and more effective decisions concerning their operations.

The models in Table 5.2 underscore that local governments played a critical role in permitting or even encouraging firms to begin to rely on markets for buying productive inputs and selling industrial output. That is, receiving local government funds is positively and significantly associated with use of both market inputs and selling products on product markets. This finding is consistent with strategic choice arguments that managers assess their capabilities and strengths and draw on those. Yet this is also consistent with institutional arguments that suggest that external pressures determine much about where and how firms innovate. In this case, the relevant contextual influence appears to be the local government. What is perhaps most interesting is the role that the central state played in determining which influences were most salient for these firms. Because the central government transferred control of many firms to lower level governments, the incentives and pressures these firms felt encouraged them to behave in direct opposition to the firms over which the state maintained control. In particular, those firms that were released by the central state entered markets more rapidly and with greater force than those that stayed under the control of the central state. The long-term implications of this are uncertain, of course, but the implication is that firms that were not protected by the central government are likely to become more adept at dealing with market exchange and the activities that implies (i.e., raising capital, innovation, competition). This finding also highlights the fact that only firms under central government control were slow to adapt to markets, and those under municipal governments are being reformed.

Bonds and the Use of Product Markets

Although it was rare, some firms did begin to use other external finance sources during the 1980s. Issuing bonds, in particular, gradually became more popular beginning in the 1980s. By the end of 1986, a total of 10 billion yuan worth of firm bonds had been issued (Gao & Zhuang, 1999). Relative to obtaining bank loans, issuing bonds was risky because it required a serious repayment commitment from the firm, whereas the central state could forgive grants or loans if it deemed forgiveness necessary. Yet central state authorities regulated bond issues more closely than they did other non-state sources of funds, and the state did occasionally rescue firms that encountered capital emergencies as a result of bad bond issues. Thus issuing bonds was more similar to receiving funds from the central government than to obtaining non-state capital, and firms that issued bonds may not have faced the same uncertainties that other firms faced. As a result, the internal incentives and external pressures these firms faced would have discouraged experimentation with markets. As the results shown in Table 5.2 demonstrate, firms that issued bonds were less likely to use markets for obtaining and selling products than firms that did not issue bonds.

Our findings also show that competition from non-state firms is negatively related to a firm's reliance on markets for both input purchases and output sales. The degree to which local markets were developed shaped firm adaptation in ways that may seem counterintuitive but that are perfectly consistent with managerial efforts to reduce risk. In transition economies, where uncertainty associated with poorly developed markets was particularly salient, managers were particularly attuned to the need to protect their interests (Guthrie, 1997; Keister, 2001; Peng, 2000). Yet local, and to some degree national incentives encouraged experimentation with market practices. In areas where markets were poorly developed, it is likely that firms perceived less competition or less risk associated with competition. Thus the perceived risk associated with market transactions was likely lessened. As a result, firms located in areas with relatively poorly developed product markets were more likely to experiment with this new form of exchange than their counterparts in areas with more developed markets. In contrast, retained earnings were positively related to market experimentation. This finding is consistent with research that shows that retained earnings affected firm-level decision-making and market adaptation during transition. It is likely that firms with greater retained earnings felt more confident about taking risks, such as experimenting with markets.

Conclusion

Understanding managerial strategy in the early days of reform can provide important insight into how managers behave today and how the organizations they run are structured. In this chapter, we explored how managers adopted two important innovative behaviors in the first decade of reform: piece wages and buying/selling producer goods on markets. We showed that worker support of managers, a market-orientation for managers, and market development all influenced the adoption of piece wages in the early stages of reform. We also showed that managers imitated others using this innovative strategy. An important theme that was evident in our results, however, was that the relative importance of various processes changed over time. As reform progressed, worker support of managers and market development became less salient and simple imitation gave way to imitation of specific, usually profitable others. Similarly, we found that both strategic choices and institutional factors affected firm decisions to buy and sell products on markets in the first decade of reform. We found that the source of funds to which firms had access was an important, albeit changing, influence on their use of product markets.

Understanding these important changes is instructive for understanding the way managers behave in contemporary China, and these patterns also offer insight into the importance of change and organizational traits that improve responsiveness more generally. For instance, research on innovative firm behavior in the west has largely been restricted to explanations that emphasize internal, strategic factors or external, institutional factors. Our results suggest that, in reality, firms make strategic decisions that take firm capabilities into account and also react to external institutional constraints. Few organization theorists would dispute our central contention that both internal and external processes are important, but the relative weight of these influences has not been clear in the past. Our findings suggest that an important factor determining the relative salience of internal and external influences is the state. The state seldom enters strategic choice analyses and it enters most institutional analyses as an afterthought. Yet our results suggest that the state can—and in some contexts does—determine which factors will be relevant and when they will matter. In the specific case of China's transition, the state determined which firms it would continue to control and which it would release to local government control or to the market. This act determined the relative mix of internal and external constraints that firms faced in the short run. In the long run, the central state's decisions about which firms to protect initially is likely to influence which firms are adept at negotiating market exchange and which remain weak dinosaurs. Of course, there are some industries that are protected in nearly all economies (e.g., defense), and the mere presence of state control does not necessarily imply reduced competition. This does suggest, however, that future research might explore cross-national differences in state intervention in the economy and how this affects the incentives to which managers respond.

Appendix
Research Methods

To test our ideas, we used two sets of analyses. First, we used logistic regression models to examine piece rate adoption; second, we used general linear models to study market entry. For the logistic models, the dependent variable was a dichotomous indicator of whether the firm used piece wages in a given year. To estimate the models, we broke the data into three time periods to compare patterns in early through late reform: we estimated separate equations for 1978–1983, 1984–1986, and 1987–1989. Specifying a single spline function or a full interaction of time with the independent variables produced results that are substantively equivalent to those we report. We used 1984 as the first cut point because enough time had elapsed since the start of reform to see some adoptions and because reformers instituted major labor reforms in that year. Similarly, by 1987, sufficient time had passed for firms to have been exposed to the practices of their peers, to internalize the information they had gathered, and to revise their own practices in response. We used a standard two-model strategy to account for diffusion. The first equation determines the effect of use of the strategy by each organization on each other organization (called exposure). The equation takes the form:

$$E_i = \beta_0 + \Sigma\beta_k X_{ki} + \varepsilon_i \qquad\qquad (1)$$

where E_i = the proportion of total wages paid as piece wages by each organization (i); β_0 = the intercept; X_{ki} = the set of k independent variables that describe organization i and the region in which it is located (e.g., economic conditions); β_k = the estimated effect of the k independent variables on the use of piece wages; and ε_i = the disturbance term for (1). Using equation (1), we then obtained predicted values (E_i^*) for each organization that indicate the expected use of piece rates, given characteristics of the organization, and the region in which the organization was located. For each pair of firms, we then divided the predicted value by the geographic distance between the two organizations. The potential for exposure for each organization i to practices used by all other organizations is:

$$\text{Exp}_i = \Sigma(E_j^*/D_{ij}) \qquad\qquad (2)$$

where Exp_i = the exposure for organization i; E_j^* = the predicted use of piece rates for organization j, based on parameter estimates in equation (1); and D_{ij} = the (greater circular) geographic distance between the headquarters for organizations i and j. This measure uses the latitude and longitude for each firm and takes the curve of the earth into account in calculating the distance between the two points. Finally, we used Exp_i as a predictor variable in addition to the original set of social and economic characteristics used in equation (1) in the final logistic regression equation. The logistic regression equation was estimated by maximizing a likelihood equation that does not assume non-autocorrelation.

The second set of analyses explored the factors that were associated with the proportion of inputs that firms obtained through markets and the proportion of sales conducted over markets. Dependent variables in the second set of analyses included: (1) the ratio of total raw material inputs purchased at market prices to total raw material inputs purchased at state planned prices, and (2) the ratio of total sales at market prices to total sales at state planned prices. We logged both ratios to reduce skewness; the unit of analysis is the firm-year between 1980 and 1989, and both independent and dependent variables can change each year. We used Generalized Least Squares (GLS) regression to estimate the models because the error terms were both heteroskedastic and correlated over time. GLS is a technique that allows us to produce more accurate statistical tests by correcting estimates of the errors of the coefficients when the data violate ordinary least squares assumptions. Practically, GLS coefficients are interpreted identically to Ordinary Least Squares coefficients.

Our independent variables are lagged one year and vary across models to best approximate our theoretical interests and the processes that contribute to each dependent variable. In our logistic models of piece wage adoption (Table 5.1), we included a dummy variable indicating whether the general manager was elected by the organization's workers and whether s/he was a party secretary. We also used a series of market-related questions to create a scale indicating a positive orientation toward markets. We included two indicators of market development based on manager reports of development of labor, and other (production, consumer, and financial) markets were established in the local area. We included dichotomous indicators of whether the organization was in mining, textiles, manufacturing, or utilities industries. We controlled for manager's education to capture the effect of human capital. We also included controls for access to an airport or a commercial train station (dummy variables developed using municipal-level data).

In our market entry models (Table 5.2), we included several measures of financial conditions and resources. We included a (logged) indicator of total funds received in the previous year from the central government, and we included separate (logged) indicators of total bank loans received from 1980–1984 (giving firms a year to react to the 1983 legislation) and from 1985–1989. We measured (logged) local government funds in the previous year as total state funds that were not distributed by the central government, including provincial, prefectural, county, and municipal funds. Bonds were the (logged) total value of public bonds issued by the enterprise in the previous year. We controlled for firm traits that may have affected adaptation to markets, including competition from non-state firms, using the ratio of non-state firms to state firms in the province that may have deterred SOEs from entering markets. We also controlled for (logged) retained earnings, profits, and total assets.

We also controlled for the number of temporary workers (logged) as an indicator of progressivity. Firms that employed more temporary workers were more progressive because temporary employment is a quintessential market practice. Progressive firms may move to markets sooner than their more cautious counterparts. Finally, we controlled for age, as older firms may be more secure about engaging in innovative behaviors. Age squared controls for the likelihood that the effect of age diminishes at larger values.

To control for the possibility that the manager's traits shaped firm behavior, we included measures of the manager's communist party affiliation and education using three dummy variables: whether the manager was a party member, graduated from technical school, or graduated from college. Finally, we represented time with a continuous indicator of year ranging from 1980 to 1989 to capture changes in firm behavior as China's transition progressed.

References

Abrahamson, E., & Rosenkopf, L. (1993). Institutional and competitive bandwagons: Using mathematical modeling as a tool to explore innovation of diffusion. *Academy of Management Review*, 18,487–517.

Buchko, A. A. (1994). Barriers to strategic transformation. In P. Shrivastava, A. Huff, & J. Dutton (Eds.), *Advances in Strategic Management* (Vol. 10, pp. 81–106). Greenwich, CT: JAI Press.

Child, J. (1972). Organizational structure, environment and performance: The role of strategic choice. *Sociology*, 6, 1–22.

D'Aveni, R. A. (1994). *Hypercompetition: Managing the Dynamics of Strategic Maneuvering*. New York: Free Press.

Dess, G. G., & Beard, D. W. (1984). Dimensions of organizational task environments. *Administrative Science Quarterly*, 29, 52–73.

DiMaggio, P. J., & Powell, W. W. (1983). The iron cage revisited: Institutional isomorphism and collective rationality in organizational fields. *American Sociological Review*, 48, 147–160.

Dong, J. L., & Hu, J. (1995). Mergers and acquisitions in China. *Federal Reserve Bank of Atlanta Economic Review*, 80, 15–29.

Dutton, J. E., & Duncan, R. B. (1987). The creation of momentum for change through the process of strategic issue diagnosis. *Strategic Management Journal*, 8, 279–295.

Gao, P., & Zhuang, Y. (1999). *Zhongguo Zhaiquan Shichang Toushi (China's Bond Market)*. Beijing: Zhongguo Caizheng Jinrong Chubanshe.

Ginsberg, A. (1988). Measuring and modelling changes in strategy: Theoretical foundations and empirical directions. *Strategic Management Journal*, 9, 559–575.

Goldie-Scott, D. (1995). *Banking in China*. London: Financial Times Publishing.

Groves, T., Hong, Y., McMillan, J., & Naughton, B. (1994). Autonomy and incentives in Chinese state enterprises. *Quarterly Journal of Economics*, 109, 183–209.

Groves, T., Hong, Y., McMillan, J., & Naughton, B. (1995). China's evolving managerial labor market. *Journal of Political Economy*, 103, 873–891.

Guthrie, D. (1997). Between markets and politics: Organizational responses to reform in China. *American Journal of Sociology*, 102, 1258–1304.

Guthrie, D. (1999). *Dragon in a Three-Piece Suit: The Emergence of Capitalism in China*. Princeton, NJ: Princeton University Press.

Hannan, M. T., & Freeman, J. (1989). *Organizational Ecology*. New York: Oxford University Press.

Haunschild, P. R. (1993). Interorganizational imitation: The impact of interlocks on corporate acquisition activity. *Administrative Science Quarterly*, 38, 564–592.

Haunschild, P. R., & Miner, A. S. (1997). Modes of interorganizational imitation: The effects of outcome salience and uncertainty. *Administrative Science Quarterly*, 42, 472–500.

Holz, C. (1992). *The Role of Central Banking in China's Economic Reforms*. Ithaca, NY: Cornell University East Asia Program.

Jefferson, G. H., & Rawski, T. G. (1994). Enterprise reform in Chinese industry. *Journal of Economic Perspectives, 8,* 47–70.

Keats, B. W., & Hitt, M. A. (1988). A causal model of linkages among environmental dimensions, macro organizational characteristics, and performance. *Academy of Management Journal, 31,* 570–598.

Keister, L. A. (2000). *Chinese Business Groups: The Structure and Impact of Interfirm Relations During Economic Development*. New York: Oxford University Press.

Keister, L. A. (2001). Exchange structures in transition: A longitudinal analysis of lending and trade relations in Chinese business groups. *American Sociological Review, 66,* 336–60.

Keister, L. A. (2002). Adapting to radical change: Strategy and environment in piece-rate adoption during China's transition. *Organization Science, 13,* 459–474.

Kelly, D., & Amburgey, T. L. (1991). Organizational inertia and momentum: A dynamic model of strategic change. *Academy of Management Journal, 34,* 591–612.

Kornai, J. (1979). Resource-constrained versus demand-constrained systems. *Econometrica, 47,* 801–820.

Kornai, J. (1986). *Contradictions and Dilemmas: Studies on the Socialist Economy and Society*. Cambridge, MA: MIT Press.

Kornai, J. (1992). *The Socialist System: The Political Economy of Communism*. Princeton, NJ: Princeton University Press.

Lardy, N. R. (1998). *China's Unfinished Economic Revolution*. Washington, DC: The Brookings Institution Press.

Maanen, J. V. (1983). *Qualitative Methods*. Beverly Hills, CA: Sage.

Meyer, J. W., Rowan, B. (1977). Institutionalized organizations: Formal structure as myth and ceremony. *American Journal of Sociology, 83,* 340–363.

Naughton, B. (1994). China's reforms: Structural and welfare aspects; Chinese innovation and privatization from below. *American Economic Review, 84,* 266–270.

Naughton, B. (1996). *Growing Out of The Plan: Chinese Economic Reform, 1978–1993*. New York: Cambridge University Press.

O'Neill, H. M., Pouder, R. W., & Buchholtz, A. K. (1998). Patterns in the diffusion of strategies across organizations: Insights from the innovation of diffusion literature. *Academy of Management Review, 23,* 98–114.

Peng, M. W. (2000). Controlling the foreign agent: How governments deal with multinationals in a transition economy. MIR: *Management International Review, 40,* 141–165.

Peng, M. W. (2004). Outside directors and firm performance during institutional transitions. *Strategic Management Journal, 25,* 453–471.

Pfeffer, J., & Salancik, G. R. (1978). *The External Control of Organizations: A Resource Dependence Perspective*. New York: Harper and Row.

Scott, W. R. (1987). The adolescence of institutional theory. *Administrative Science Quarterly, 32,* 493–511.

Tichy, N. M. (1983). *Managing Strategic Change*. New York: Wiley.

Tolbert, P. S., & Zucker, L. G. (1996). The institutionalization of institutional theory. In S. R. Clegg, C. Hardy, & W. R. Nord (Eds.), *Handbook of Organization Studies* (pp. 175–190). Thousand Oaks, CA: Sage.

Volberda, H. W. (1996). Toward the flexible form: How to remain vital in hypercompetitive environments. *Organization Science, 7,* 359–374.

Walder, A. G. (1992). Property rights and stratification in socialist redistributive economies. *American Sociological Review, 57,* 524–539.

Walder, A. G. (1995). Local governments as industrial corporations: An organizational analysis of China's transitional economy. *American Journal of Sociology*, *101*, 263–301.

Wong, C. (1986). The economics of shortage and problems of reform in Chinese industry. *Journal of Comparative Economics*, *10*, 363–387.

Wong, C. (1987). Between plan and market: The role of the local sector in post-mao China. *Journal of Comparative Economics*, *11*, 385–398.

Wu, J., & Zhao, R. (1987). The dual pricing system in China's industry. *Journal of Comparative Economics*, *11*, 309–318.

Xu, X. (1998). *China's Financial System under Transition*. New York: St. Martin's Press.

Yi, G. (1994). *Money, Banking, and Financial Market Emergence in China*. New York: Westview.

Zucker, L. G. (1977). The role of institutionalization in cultural persistence. *American Sociological Review*, *42*, 726–743.

Zucker, L. G. (1987). Institutional theories of organization. *Annual Review of Sociology*, *13*, 443–464.

6 The Spillover of Liberalization Policies Among Chinese Cities

Introduction

The quantity and quality of infrastructures have significant impacts on both local economic development and the welfare of urban residents. As China moves toward a more industrialized and urbanized economy, the demand for better infrastructures and utility services also grows dramatically. Because the old state-dominated infrastructure investment system cannot satisfy the huge capital needs in these sectors, local governments are forced to find alternative financial resources for expanding service capacities or improving service quality. During this process, governments at both central and local levels made institutional reforms and allowed foreign and private investors to enter these once highly restricted areas to own or operate facilities. The liberalization of the infrastructure and urban utility sectors through the introduction of various types of public and private partnerships thus has become a popular policy choice for many local governments. However, there is huge variation among cities in their efforts to form public and private partnerships in managing their existing infrastructure or building new infrastructure or urban utility projects. In this chapter, we borrow insights from neoinstitutional theory and policy diffusion studies to explore the driving forces that underlie the liberalization process.

Since the early 1990s, a few coastal Chinese cities, such as Qingdao, Ningbo, and Shanghai, have begun to introduce new urban development policies that have been adopted by cities in North America, Europe, Australia, and Asia (Brenner, 2004; Harvey, 1989; Jessop & Sum, 2000; Owen, 2002). In these cities, public sector resources and powers are utilized to promote economic growth. Traditional regulatory and welfare functions of local governments are marginalized. Market criteria are used to evaluate the goals and efficiency of government practices, and there is a new emphasis upon improving municipal finances through revenue enhancement in addition to conservative budgetary practices. Many entrepreneurial cities have identified publicly sponsored land, real estate, and infrastructure development as the main vehicle for both increasing revenues and promoting local economic growth. Despite the considerable social, economic, and political differences that existed among these cities, efforts to stimulate economic growth have been remarkably similar in their concentration on the retention and attraction of leading economic sectors (Harvey, 1989; Leitner, 1990; Leitner & Sheppard, 1998).

Like their international counterparts, Chinese cities try to mobilize internal as well as external financial resources and increase investments in urban infrastructure sectors, culture, tourism, and recreation projects so as to enhance the cities' images and create a "good business climate" to lure domestic and foreign capital. As these practices gradually disseminated across the country, more cities began to emulate the policies that were proven to be effective in model cities. During this process, new content was added to the so-called "capitalizing on cities" strategy. Thanks to the great theorizing efforts from the policy research communities and policy making professionals, this strategy has evolved into a well-defined policy paradigm.

In 2004 the Sichuan province launched a legislative effort toward adding the idea of capitalizing on cities into provincial law. Although the bill was unable to gain support at the provincial people's congress, the text of this document provides us an opportunity to see how local legislators understand and define the new paradigm. The major contents of this bill are as follows:[1]

> *Section 1 (Goal): [This act is] to strengthen the management and business operation of urban public assets, to promote the capitalization of urban resources, to properly use resources, and to improve the value of urban assets.*
>
> *Section 3 (Definition): Capitalizing on cities refers to the process that governments at county level and above use market mechanisms to construct urban infrastructure, develop urban utility industries, allow different market entities to operate urban public assets. Local governments should supervise the business operation of urban public assets, promote the efficient and sustainable use of urban resources, promote urban construction and development, and improve the quality of management.*
>
> *Section 7 (Leadership): Counties and cities at both county and prefecture levels are responsible for coordination of the activities that facilitate the marketization of urban assets.*
>
> *Section 13 (Means): Local governments at county and city levels should explore the new function of cities, improve the quality of urban environment and the cultural taste, improve cities' value; and optimize the utilization of urban land and space, improve regional environment conditions, promote the formation of differential land rent, improve the value of urban land assets.*
>
> *Section 17 (Means Cont.): Local governments can use Build-Operate-Transfer (BOT) or Transfer-Operate-Transfer (TOT) contracts to promote the construction of new urban district and infrastructures. Governments can use the revenue from differential land rent to subsidize firms/*

*individuals to encourage them to invest in urban infrastructures, con-
struct and operate urban utility and industries.*

*Section 19 (Means Cont.): Local government should adopt a con-
cessionary management system for the following utility sectors: urban
roads, bridges, tunnels, sewerage, waste management, heat supply,
power, water, and gas distribution, and public transportation.*

*Section 20 (Means Cont.): Local government can transfer the mana-
gerial rights to market entities through means such as public bidding
and auction. These means apply to the management of urban public
facilities, city parks, public sanitation, and so forth.*

This document in fact summarized the major policy measures that Chinese cities adopted in promoting local economic growth in the new era:
first, local governments seek to capitalize their assets by identifying publicly sponsored land and real estate development as the main vehicle for
both increasing revenues and promoting local economic growth. Second,
local governments not only directly invest heavily in infrastructure, but also
actively liberalize the infrastructure sector (e.g. subways, water supply, and
waste management) to private investors (Henisz, Zelner, & Guillen, 2005).
Third, local governments compete to lower the entry barriers for foreign
direct investment, and try their best to cultivate a good business climate
to attract investors. Fourth, market criteria are used to evaluate the goals
and efficiency of government practices, and there is a new emphasis upon
improving municipal finance through revenue enhancement in addition to
conservative budgetary practices (Harvey, 1989; Leitner, 1990).

These policies embody the principles in the Washington Consensus,
which advocates for privatizing state controlled enterprises and assets,
abolishing regulations that impede market entry or restrict competition,
prioritizing public spending toward provisions of key pro-growth services
like infrastructure investments, and facilitating the inflow of foreign direct
investment (Williamson, 1990, 1993). So the policies that aim to capitalize
on the cities are in fact a clear manifestation of neoliberal doctrines at the
sub-national level.

The rise of neoliberal policies over the past three decades has been
regarded as one of the most significant events in modern history. Almost
all states have embraced some version of neoliberal theory and adjusted at
least some policies and practices, either voluntarily or in response to institutional pressures (Harvey, 2005a). The election of conservative governments
in North America and western Europe, the pursuit of austere stabilization
policies in Latin America, and the regime change in eastern Europe and the
Soviet Union, as well as the market reform in the formerly socialist countries, have all marked this period as one during which neoliberalist doctrines
gradually replaced Keynesianism principles (Campbell & Pedersen, 2001).

Neoliberalism is a multifaceted notion. In the first place, it refers to a set of
institutionalized normative principles and "proposes that human well-being

can best be advanced by liberating individual entrepreneurial freedoms and skills within an institutional framework characterized by strong private property rights, free markets and free trade" (Campbell & Pedersen, 2001; Harvey, 2005a: 2). Moreover, neoliberalism is also expressed in state policies: liberalization, deregulation, privatization, and depoliticization. These policies aim to promote unfettered competition by getting the state out of the business of ownership and getting politicians out of the business of direct intervention into economic management. By the 1990s, this family of policies was fairly clearly defined as a now-famous concept, "the Washington Consensus," which advocates trade liberalization, tax reform, fiscal discipline, deregulation, utilizing foreign direct investment, and so forth (Mudge, 2008; Savas, 2005; Williamson, 1990, 1993).

Under the neoliberalist paradigm, the role of the state is limited in creating and preserving an institutional framework appropriate to such practices. The state has to guarantee the quality and integrity of money. It must establish defensive forces to protect the legal structure and secure private property rights. The state should also provide public goods, such as education, social security, and environmental protection when markets fail to do so. However, beyond these tasks, state intervention should be kept at a minimum (Harvey, 2005a). All these aspects share a common and distinctive ideological core: the elevation of the market over all other forms of organization (Mudge, 2008).

The transition to neoliberalism is highly uneven in its timing, scope, and nature. Global transformations and local institutional conditions and dynamics shaped perceptions and the perceived necessity of economic liberalization, and also shaped the channels through which the ideas and policies diffuse (Fourcade-Gourinchas & Babb, 2002). The rationale for adopting neoliberal polices relied on different perceptions and assessments of adopters' own economic problems and what the shift to the market was meant to accomplish. In institutionalist terms, the emergence and path of the neoliberal policy regime was socially constructed through the mediation of national institutions and culture (Dobbin, 1994; Hall, 1989).

Whereas neoliberalism is often considered to have been invented in the Anglo-Saxon world, its contemporary origin is as much Chinese as western. The reform and opening-up policy adopted in late 1978 is regarded as one of the milestone events of neoliberalist expansion. It occurred even before the election of Margaret Thatcher as British Prime Minister, Paul Volcker's selection as the chairman of the Federal Reserve, and Ronald Regan's election as the U.S. president (Harvey, 2005a). The rise of neoliberalism in China was driven by the party's need to improve the country's economic performance, which had been seriously affected by the Cultural Revolution and tight state regulations over market forces. In this historical context, the party fully embraced the market-oriented ideology, and made neoliberalism a useful policy tool for the authoritarian state to promote economic growth and strengthen its legitimacy for political dominance (Gao, 2009).

Unlike its western counterparts, China follows a distinct trajectory of neo-liberalist expansion. A striking feature of Chinese neoliberalism is a vibrant neoliberal economy coexisting with a powerful authoritarian state. This contradicts the prevailing neoliberal model in two ways. First, economic liberalization does not go hand in hand with political democratization. Whereas the country's economy is increasingly open to the global market, its political system has not changed much in the past three decades. Second, although the market power has substantially increased during the reform era, the state has not relinquished its control over the economy; instead, state intervention is still active and influential and can be easily identified in many economic sectors (Blanchard & Shleifer, 2001; Fligstein & Zhang, 2011; Hall & Soskice, 2001; Yeung, 2003). Third, compared with the local governments in some developing or transitional economies, the Chinese local governments play the role of a "helping hand" and promote market development in the local economy (Jin, Qian, & Weingast, 2005).

As Campbell and Pedersen (2001) argue, neoliberalism, at the empirical level, is less coherent than it is assumed to be. It is often a loose conglomeration of institutions, ideas, and policy prescriptions from which actors pick and choose depending on prevailing political, economic, social, historical, and institutional conditions. As a result, the specific policy structure is far from uniform, and varies greatly across countries. When it comes to China, one of its unique characteristics is the coexistence of neoliberal institutions with the authoritarian state. Unlike other developing countries, which adopt neoliberal economic policies as prescribed in the Washington Consensus and also carry out political democratization, China adopts similar neoliberal economic policies but resists the democratic political change. However, this does not mean that the authoritarian state will be in conflict with neoliberal doctrines. In most cases, the authoritarian state actively uses its political power and institutional resources to implement neoliberal policies. At the same time, the authoritarian state has been very cautious in expanding neo-liberal policies to new fields; it tries to ensure that neoliberalism is nothing more than a policy tool for the state (Gao, 2009: 425).

This coexistence leads to a series of questions: (1) what are the key factors that make policy makers at various levels choose to adopt seemingly "capitalist" economic policies? (2) what are the mechanisms that have facilitated the diffusion of neoliberal policies across the country? (3) how do intergovernmental relationships, both horizontal and vertical, affect the local government's behavior toward market development?, and (4) to what extent does the Chinese experience confirm, challenge, or enrich our knowledge on policy changes?

Private Participation in Infrastructure Sectors

To empirically address the aforementioned issues, in this chapter we focus on the policy that encourages private participation in infrastructure sectors.

Private investments in infrastructure sectors can take many different forms and participate in different sectors. When choosing which sector to liberalize and through what means, local governments have to consider their own capacities and characteristics specific to each sector. In terms of investment arrangements, a PPI project can take the form of a management and lease contract, concessions, greenfield projects, or divestiture. These arrangements differ in the demand for administrative and regulatory resources, as well as in their degree of dependence on private sector participation.

The choice between concessions and divestitures depends largely on whether it is more desirable to regulate private sector involvement through contractual arrangements or through a regulatory agency. In most developing countries and transitional economies, the institutional environment is uncertain and constantly evolving; therefore the local governments find it relatively easier to regulate private partners through contracts, because the contract terms can be detailed in advance and the ownership does not change (Bellier & Zhou, 2003; World Bank, 1994). For a given city, the choice of arrangement types reflects its social and political considerations, investment needs, and more importantly its openness to private participation. For example, in many countries the constitution prohibits private ownership of public goods. Officials in these countries sometimes have to choose concessions or BOT methods to avoid legal barriers (Bellier & Zhou, 2003).

For private investors, choosing from different arrangements is also driven by their perception of investment risks or profitability associated with a certain project. They can choose to provide expertise or technology and bear no management or investment risks, to be more actively involved by being responsible for certain operation or management risks, or to be fully involved through privatizing the entire project and taking various risks.

Among these four types of arrangements, the most conservative type is management and lease contracts (MLC). Under such contracts, governments still maintain their ownership and investment stake. For management contracts, the government pays a private operator a fee. The private operator takes on the operational risk. For leasing contracts, the government leases the assets to a private operator for a fee. The private operator takes on the operational risk. This model is usually adopted when governments need the private management experience and technology, but are reluctant to relinquish ownership due to their desire to maintain control or unwillingness to implement needed reforms.

The next higher level of the private participation model is concession. In this model, a private entity manages a public service for a given period, during which it assumes significant investment risks and some commercial risks. The private entity is responsible for delivering services to users according to terms and conditions specified in the concession contract. The public entity still owns the assets. This model is popular in water and transportation sectors.

Greenfield contracts give private investors partial ownership rights for a given period and allow private investors to play a larger role in management and operation of the projects. Under such contracts, a private entity or a public–private joint venture builds and operates a new facility for the period specified in the project contract; at the end of the contract, the private entity will transfer the ownership of the facility to the government. For these contracts, a government usually provides minimum revenue guarantee. Most greenfield projects in China take the build-operate-transfer (BOT) scheme.

The highest level of private participation is divestitures. In this model, a private entity buys an equity stake in a state-owned enterprise through an asset sale, public offering, or mass privatization. In this model, the participants can involve both foreign and domestic funding. This model was most frequently used during the state sector reform in the late 1990s, when the central government adopted the "grasp big and let the small go" strategy. Local governments at various levels followed this guideline and sold their money-losing state enterprises to various non-state investors.

Among these four types of arrangements, the most common private participation models in China are concession and greenfield projects. The major advantage of these two models is that they are neither too conservative nor too radical. They give private entrepreneurs considerable incentives, while allowing the state to maintain its control over the ownership of state assets. During the late 1990s, the three major models—concession, greenfield project, and divestitures—were competing models. Although the former two models have slightly more applications, their overwhelming advantage over divestiture had not been established until China entered the World Trade Organization in 2001. After 2001, the former two types of projects increased dramatically. This trend suggests that, after a long period of experiment and comparison, the state has eventually found the ideal arrangement type that can balance market power and authoritarian control over the strategic economic sectors.

In this chapter, we used a compiled panel dataset, which incorporates information on the implementation of PPP programs among Chinese cities and the basic city level statistics. Data on the PPP projects were drawn from the Private Participation in Infrastructure Database managed by the PPI project team at the World Bank.[2] The team annually collects basic information on privately participated infrastructure projects implemented in mainland China. The team acquired the project information from public sources such as (1) Factiva; (2) specialized publications such as Project Finance International, Project Finance, reports of rating agencies, Global Power reports, Power in Asia, or the Privatization barometer; (3) sponsor websites or public agencies granting the contracts; and (4) multilateral agencies' websites, including press releases and annual reports. The researchers supplemented the public information by requesting further information from public companies, developers and sponsors, government agencies, and regulatory agencies. Project information collected includes the year of financial closure, sponsor, share of private capital, sector, project location, project type, project status, and so forth. Infrastructure projects were included in the database if they met several criteria. Table 6.1 shows the distribution

Table 6.1 Total Projects and Investments by Sectors, 1990–2008

Sector	Sub-sector	Number of Projects	Total Investment (in USD million)
Energy	Electricity	174	33,062
	Natural Gas	182	4,277
Telecom	Telecom	4	14,518
Transport	Airports	17	2,766
	Railroads	8	6,084
	Roads	133	25,397
	Seaports	62	13,202
Water and Sewerage	Treatment Plant	273	5,543
	Utility	31	2,884
Total		884	107,732

Source: The World Bank PPI Database.

of the PPI projects across infrastructure sectors and the cumulative investments in each sector.

Due to data availability constraints, we focused on cities with a rank higher than or equal to the prefecture level, because urban infrastructure liberalization is typically carried out at these levels. By the end of 2008, there were 333 prefecture level (and above) cities in China (National Bureau of Statistics, 2009). The earliest data go back to 1992, when Deng Xiaoping made his southern tour and the party held its fourteenth congress. These two events mark the beginning of the second phase of transition of the Chinese economy, during which the establishment of a market oriented market system was set as the goal of the reform (Naughton, 2007).

The data on city-level social economic information was drawn from the China City Statistical Yearbook (1992–2009) published by China Statistics Press. This data was merged with data on the adoption of the land banking system and infrastructure liberalization by different cities. The primary data on adoption time of the land banking systems was drawn from several secondary sources and was collected during 2007 and 2008. The primary data sources were business and public-units registration records and official land banking documents from the Chinese local law information database. To supplement and cross-validate the adoption information, we also drew data from other sources, such as the China economic news dataset provided by China Info Bank Corporation, local newspapers, and government websites.

The Effects of Internal Determinants

Local Economic Development

The first factor that drives the diffusion of liberalization policies is the level of local economic development. Scholars argue that the factors causing an organization, usually countries or states, to adopt a new program or policy are the political, economic, and social characteristics of the organization

(Berry & Berry, 2007). The explanations thus formulated contend that state policy makers respond to internal characteristics of their state environments when crafting policies (Daley & Garand, 2005). This is because the characteristics of an organization may substantially influence the perception of an innovation's costs and benefits, as well as affect the timing and the probability that an organization will innovate. It is argued that the organization's probability for innovation is negatively related to the strength of obstacles to innovation and positively related to the motivation to innovate and the availability of resources for overcoming the obstacles (Mohr, 1969).

The motivation to innovate is the perceived severity of a practical problem. Problem severity can influence the motivation of officials to adopt a policy by clarifying the need for the policy, or by stimulating the demand for the policy by societal groups. When political leaders perceive that a social or political problem has become serious enough to endanger the effectiveness of their management or local interests, they tend to adopt the policy initiatives (Berry & Berry, 1990; Daley & Garand, 2005).

The federalist governance structure of the Chinese political system makes such indigenous reform possible. Such a decentralized structure enabled government, from the provincial to the prefecture and county levels, to set specific local rules for their jurisdiction that were not hierarchically prescribed. These rules defined crucial procedures for privatization, such as the level of private shares or asset prices. Such autonomy can be summarized as "adapting (macro) policies to local conditions" (Krug & Hendrischke, 2008). This governance structure makes the prompt adjustment to new ideas or new policies possible for local governments.

Since the late 1990s, urban infrastructure improvements have become major problems for many Chinese cities, especially for those experiencing fast urbanization and industrialization processes. The privatization of local urban infrastructure and utility firms provides a new way to attract and utilize external resources to improve the condition of infrastructures and quality of utility services. Economically advanced cities are more willing to adopt such a system because rapid industrialization, urbanization, and rising living standards lead to higher demands for new infrastructure and utility service capacity.

To empirically test these explanations, in Table 6.2 we incorporated several measures that indicate the level of local economic development. GDP per capita is a conventional measure indicating the level of economic development of a city. The industrialization rate refers to the ratio of the local secondary industry GDP to the total local GDP. It indicates the demand for infrastructure services that originated from industrial growth. The urbanization rate refers to the proportion of residents who hold urban resident permits in a given city. It captures the demand that originated from the increase in the urban population.

The Cox's proportional hazards models (see Appendix for details) presented in Table 6.2 lend support to our argument. Model 1 shows that the

Table 6.2 Models Predicting Infrastructure Privatization

Variable	M1		M2		M3		M4		M5		M6		M7		M8	
Independent Variables																
Per Capita GDP	0.10	***	0.10	***	0.03	*	0.02	†	0.10	***	0.10	***	0.10	***	0.11	*
Industrialization	-0.01		-0.01		0.01		-0.01		-0.01		0.01		-0.01		0.05	
Industrialization (square)	-0.01	***	-0.01	**	-0.01	**	-0.01	**	-0.01	*	-0.01	**	-0.01	**	-0.01	**
Urbanization	-0.01		-0.01		-0.01		-0.01		-0.01		-0.01		-0.01		0.01	
Transfer Dep. Ratio	—		-1.70		—		-1.80	***	—		—		-1.66	**	-2.02	†
Political Status	—		—		1.51	***	0.93	*	—		—		0.73	†	3.39	*
Provincial Pressure	—		—		—		0.22	*	—		—		0.10		-0.06	
Prov. Press * TDR	—		—		—		0.56	*	—		—		0.59	*	-0.34	
Prov. Press * Political Status	—		—		—		-0.28	*	—		—		-0.09		0.06	
Innovation Exposure	—		—		—		—		0.79	*	—		0.62	†	0.15	*
Peer Pressure	—		—		—		—		—		0.01	**	0.01	**	0.06	***
Normative pressure	—		—		—		—		—		—		—		0.36	**
Control Variables																
Fixed Asset Investment	0.17	***	0.16	**	0.05	**	0.10	*	0.16	***	0.18	***	0.19	***	0.64	***
Wage	0.03		0.00		-0.01		-0.02		0.05		0.03		0.02		-0.12	
Population	0.03		0.02		0.03		0.01		0.03		0.03		-0.01		0.14	
Passenger Transportation	0.01		0.01	***	0.01		0.01		0.01		0.01		0.01	*	0.01	
Cargo Transportation	0.01		0.01		0.00		0.00		0.00		0.00		0.00		0.01	
Time Varying Covariates																
Per Capita GDP	-0.01	***	-0.01	***	—		—		-0.01	***	-0.01	***	-0.01	***	—	
Passenger Transportation	-0.01	**	-0.01	***	—		—		-0.01	***	-0.01	***	-0.01	**	—	
Log Likelihood	-997		-992		-1,005		-995		-995		-993		-966		-709	
AIC	2,017		2,008		2,030		2,019		2,014		2,011		1,967		1,457	
Wald Chi2	145		145		89		104		151		174		215		629	
Degree of Freedom	11		12		10		14		12		12		18		19	
N	3,142		3,142		3,142		3,142		3,142		3,142		3,142		3,142	

Notes: † $p < 0.1$, * $p < 0.05$, ** $p < 0.01$, *** $p < 0.001$ (two-tailed tests); Huber-White robust standard errors were used but not reported. Models 1–7 are Cox's proportional hazards models, and Model 8 is a random-effects probit model.

per capita GDP is positive, significantly suggesting that economically more advanced cities are more likely to carry out liberalization policies. The industrialization rate has a curvilinear relationship with the adoption rate, indicating that cities that have lower- to middle-level industrialization levels are more likely to have high adoption rates than cities with high industrialization rates. Therefore we can say that local leaders who face the challenges from rapid urbanization and industrialization processes are more likely to adopt these new urban policies.

After fitting Cox's proportional hazards model, we performed a test to see whether proportional hazard assumptions still hold for the model. The global test rejects the proportionality assumption, and variable-specific tests show that the effects of per capita GDP and passenger transportation may not be constant over time. When the tests on individual covariates were rejected, we included the covariates as time varying covariates and let them interact with log time, which is a standard remedy for the non-proportionality problem. In addition, we also used a link test to check the model specification and the robustness of the estimates. To account for possible heteroskedasticity problems, we used Huber-White standard error estimators, which are robust when heteroskedasticity problems are present. The newly estimated model show that the effects of these two variables change significantly over time. Per capita GDP and passenger transportation are more influential in the early stage of the diffusion, and their effects become weaker in the late diffusion phase.

Fiscal Resources

Previous literature on policy diffusion also emphasizes the importance of financial resources and political resources on innovation (Berry & Berry, 2007). Regarding financial resources, their availability is a prerequisite for many policy innovations, because new policy programs often require additional fiscal expenditures. Reforms in the public finance system have profound impacts on the evolution of the infrastructure investment regime. The observed diversification of the infrastructure financing structure and the increasing marketization of the urban utility and infrastructure industries are closely related to the reforms in the state fiscal management system. In many developing countries, the fiscal pressure is more intense and the prospect of shifting investment responsibility to private infrastructure providers plays a more significant role in the increasing acceptance of private sector involvement in infrastructure (Annez, 2007).

Prior to economic reform, China adopted a Soviet type, centrally managed fiscal system, in which all revenues were remitted to the central government, and then various transfers from the upper level were given to provinces and cities according to the central government's fiscal plan. The main revenue sources in this period were levies and surcharges from SOEs at various levels. There were no special taxes, user charges, or funds collected for urban construction purposes. In such as system, municipal governments virtually retained no extra fiscal resources that could be used to construct or maintain urban infrastructures. As a result there was no steady flow of investments to the urban infrastructure sector in many years (Chan, 1997; Wu, 1999).

In the early 1980s, a fiscal contract system, together with other decentralized economic management regulations, were implemented nationwide. Urban governments in this era acted as both urban public goods providers and the actual owners of municipal SOEs. Under this system, urban governments' revenue heavily relied on profits and taxes remitted by local SOEs, which were also the main sources of urban infrastructure investment. In addition, local states often delegated much of the infrastructure and other social service responsibilities to the SOEs. When the economic transition greatly accelerated the pace of industrialization and urbanization, although urban governments tried, they still could not supply infrastructure and social services to their growing economy and population (Chan, 1997; Wong, 1992; Wong, Heady, & Woo, 1995). Similar to many developing countries, shortfalls in urban infrastructure could easily be found in transportation, water supply, electricity supply, and communications (Bahl, 1999; OECD, 2005).

When fiscal contract systems effectively boosted local economic growth, it also generated strong localism and led to a huge regional disparity in terms of economic development and public service quality (Wong, 1992). In 1994, the fiscal contract system was replaced by the Tax Sharing System (TSS), which fundamentally changed the intergovernmental fiscal relations. The immediate goal of this new system was to increase two ratios. The first ratio was the proportion of fiscal revenue in the total national GDP. It intended to increase the state's revenue collection capacity. And the second ratio was the central government's share in the total fiscal revenue. The reform designed new taxes and tax sharing schemes, in which the major, easily collected taxes were designated as either central taxes or central–local sharing taxes. Local governments maintained the bulk of corporate income taxes and some other minor taxes. Among these local taxes, an urban land use tax, a real estate tax, and an urban maintenance and construction tax were collected for local infrastructure construction and maintenance (see Table 6.3).

However, when TSS significantly changed the revenue sharing scheme, the expenditure division between central and local governments remained largely unchanged. Compared with other developing countries, Chinese local governments had heavier expenditure responsibilities: they were expected to finance public utilities and transportation, maintain urban infrastructure, and provide other costly social services, such as education, health care, and so forth (Bahl, 1999). This gave rise to a huge fiscal gap that needed to be filled by various general or earmarked fiscal transfers. The allocation of these transfers was controlled by the central government or, alternately, the provincial governments. Therefore, local governments were forced to find alternative revenue sources or financial arrangements to construct new

Table 6.3 Revenue Assignments Between the Central and Local Governments

---

I. Taxes exclusively assigned to the central government

---

1. Excise taxes
2. Taxes collected from the Ministry of Railroads and from the headquarters of banks and insurance companies
3. Income taxes, sales taxes, and royalties from offshore oil activities of foreign companies and joint ventures
4. Energy and transportation fund contributions
5. Seventy percent of the three sales taxes collected from enterprises owned by the Ministry of Industry, the Ministry of Power, SINOPEC (petrochemicals), and the China nonferrous metals companies
6. All customs duty, Value-added Tax (VAT), and excise taxes on imports
7. Enterprise income tax collected from banks and other financial institutions

---

II. Taxes shared between the central and local governments

---

8. Value-added tax (75 percent central, 25 percent provincial)
9. Natural resource taxes (coal, gas, oil, and other minerals if the enterprises are fully Chinese owned)
10. Construction tax on the cost of construction of buildings that are outside the plan and financed from retained earnings
11. Salt tax
12. Industrial and commercial tax, and income tax levied on foreign and joint venture enterprises
13. Security and exchange tax (50 percent central, 50 percent provincial)—added in late 1990s
14. Income tax of all enterprises—added in 2002
15. Personal income taxes—added in 2002

III. Taxes exclusively assigned to local governments

---

16. Business (gross receipts) tax falling on sectors not covered by VAT (transportation and communications, construction, finance and insurance, post and telecommunications, culture and sports, entertainment, hotels and restaurants, and other)
17. Rural market (stall rental) trading tax
18. The urban maintenance and construction tax (a surcharge on the tax liability of enterprises for business tax, consumption tax, and VAT)
19. The urban land use tax
20. Vehicle and vessel utilization tax
21. Thirty percent of the product and VAT revenues collected from enterprises owned by the Ministry of Industry, Ministry of Power, SINOPEC, and the China nonferrous metals companies
22. Value-added tax on land
23. Education surtax
24. Entertainment and slaughter taxes
25. Property tax
26. Surtax on collective enterprises
27. Resources tax
28. Fixed asset investment tax (discontinued in 1999)
29. Fines for delinquent taxes

---

infrastructure in order to meet the needs of rapid urbanization and industrialization (Wong, 2000).

Currently, urban infrastructure development relies on four primary sources. The first is budgetary allocation from central and local governments, which consists of about 15 percent of the entire investment (Wu, 2010). As mentioned above, local governments have been placed in a fiscal squeeze due to a downward shift of expenditure and an upward shift of revenue. This diminishes the share of the local budgets available to finance infrastructure construction and leads to a steady decline in the proportion of urban infrastructure investment that is financed from the budgetary sources (Su & Zhao, 2007). The proportion of total urban infrastructure investment from budgetary sources declined from 50 percent in 1991 to 29 percent in 2001, and this decline continued thereafter and reached 27 percent in 2005 (Su & Zhao, 2007; Wu, 2010).

Extra-budgetary sources, such as fees and user charges, are the second channel of urban infrastructure financing. These funds used to be an important financial source for local governments. However, the fiscal reforms in the mid-1990s have imposed more restrictions in terms of collecting and managing these funds. The central government even passed new accounting regulations to put some of the major fees into the newly established fund budget category and put it under their supervision. The proportion of this source in the total infrastructure financing declined sharply from 50 percent in the mid-1990s to 10 percent in the early 2000s (Su & Zhao, 2007).

The financing gap left by the declining government fiscal input has been filled primarily by various bank loans. Starting from the mid-1990s, the share of investment financed by loans increased dramatically. National policy has identified the urban infrastructure sectors as a top priority for bank lending. By 2001, more than 60 percent of Chinese cities have infrastructure loans from banks, and the total outstanding loans for urban infrastructures amount to 74.2 billion yuan (Su & Zhao, 2007). The proportion of total urban infrastructure investment from this source increased from 5 percent in 1990 to more than 30 percent in 2005 (Wu, 2010).

In addition to these financial sources, foreign capital and private capital (including foreign direct investment, domestic private funds, and international bonds) has begun to play an important role in urban infrastructure finance. Foreign companies responded enthusiastically when China opened the door for foreign investment in urban infrastructure sectors. As a result, joint ventures were formed to build and operate roads, bridges, and urban utilities. Various types of public–private partnerships were adopted to attract more non-state investments in the infrastructure sector while allowing foreign and domestic private investors to benefit from the urban infrastructure industry.

The marketization[3] of the infrastructure sometimes requires local governments to have a substantial fiscal power to subsidize private sector investors. In order to attract private entities to invest in the local infrastructure sector, local governments often provide fiscal support to the investors to reduce the financial risks of a project or to make it financially viable. They need to provide credible assurance to investors that sensible binding obligations will be honored (Dailami & Klein, 1998). Local governments can provide a cash subsidy to a project or agree to fulfill the obligations of a purchaser (typically a SOE) with respect to the private entity in the case of non-performance by the purchaser (e.g., power purchase agreement, water purchase agreement). In other circumstances, local governments need to provide a debt guarantee, according to which the local state will guarantee repayment to creditors in the case of a default by a private entity. When a project's revenue is in the form of user fee payment by the end use customers (e.g., toll road, subway), the local state often sets a minimum revenue level for the private operator.

In certain circumstances, local governments may be required to reimburse the private entity for losses on debt services due to fluctuations in the value of the local currency (Ehrhardt & Irwin, 2004; Farquharson, Mastle, Yescombe, & Encinas, 2011). Therefore, in order to implement a private participated project, local governments need to have substantial fiscal power, which enables them to buffer the risks of the private sector investors. The results in Table 6.1 also provide evidence to support our argument. We used a city's transfer dependency ratio to measure the local fiscal health. The dependency ratio measures the extent to which a prefecture depends on its superiors for fiscal resources. Chinese budgetary law does not allow subprovincial governments to borrow or permit the emergence of fiscal deficits, so local fiscal gaps are usually filled by fiscal transfers from higher levels. A higher dependency ratio indicates a weaker fiscal capacity of the local government. We see that the coefficient of this measure is negative and significant, which indicates that when a city is fiscally better off, i.e., is less dependent on its superiors for fiscal resources, then it is more likely to liberalize its infrastructure markets early.

Political Resources

In addition to fiscal resources, political status is also a crucial factor for institutional changes. This is because a high political status is often associated with a high governance capacity, which is a prerequisite for policy innovations (Berry & Berry, 2007; Daley & Garand, 2005). Many studies confirm that the status of focal organization is crucial to the diffusion process (Cohen, 1972; Knoke, 1982; Strang & Soule, 1998). Organizations with a higher status usually adopt a change first and then may require lower status organizations to follow (Guthrie, 1999; Palmer, Jennings, & Zhou, 1993; Wejnert, 2002).

In China's hierarchical administrative system, local governments are divided into nine political statuses: municipalities, independent planning cities (*jihua danlieshi*, 计划单列市), deputy provincial cities, provincial capitals, prefecture cities, prefectures, county-level cities, counties, and urban districts under prefecture. Higher political status means greater socio-economic management power (Chan, 1997; Wong, Heady, Woo, & Asian Development Bank, 1995). For example, in terms of economic management power, independent planning cities are treated as equivalents of provincial governments; they report directly to the central government, can approve projects with larger investments, and remit revenue directly to the Ministry of Finance. The central government even gives them special quotas, a birth quota for example, with regard to certain socioeconomic affairs (Chan, 1997; Solinger, 1993; Wong et al., 1995). In the Chinese context, having a higher administrative status not only means the city has greater social–economic management power but also indicates that the city's leadership is more likely to enjoy higher political rank and therefore have more autonomy in formulating local socioeconomic policies (Chan, 1997; Wong et al., 1995).

When it comes to the infrastructure privatization issue, a city's political autonomy is important for the successful implementation of projects with private participation. It is found that the failure of private participated projects is often closely associated with the limited authority of local governments. Local governments may be subject to various pressures or direct intervention from higher levels of government, and thus may be less predictable and less capable of making credible commitments than national governments (Gomez-Ibanez, 2003; Kessides, 2004). In addition, the costs of regulatory opportunism are lower for cities with lower status than for cities with higher status because the repercussions of arbitrary behavior, especially with foreign investors, are less costly to local governments than to a national government. Private investors are likely to view contracts with lower status cities as particularly risky for this reason (Annez, 2007: 327). In Model 3 of Table 6.2, we estimated the effects of political status. The positive and significant coefficient suggests that cities at higher administrative levels are more likely to liberalize their infrastructure markets early.

The Effects of Institutional Forces

In addition to local economic and political conditions, the diffusion of liberalization policies is also likely to be driven by institutional forces. The institutional theories posit that when organizations adopt an innovative practice, they not only consider the efficiency gains brought by the new practice: a new department and operating procedure may be adopted to improve legitimacy, to cope with environmental uncertainties by emulating successful adopters, to conform to the will of other organizations on which the adopters depend, or to respond to the persuasive cultural accounts (DiMaggio & Powell, 1983, 1991; Dobbin, Simmons, & Garrett, 2007; Knoke, 1982; Meyer & Rowan, 1991; Strang & Meyer, 1993).

Effect of Coercive Force and Its Contingencies

The first type of institutional force is the coercive pressure from the authorities or organizations that an actor depends on (DiMaggio & Powell, 1983; Dobbin et al., 2007; Meyer & Rowan, 1977). This mechanism focuses on the regulative effects of formal rules and enforcement mechanisms sanctioned by the state (North, 1990; Peng, 2003; Scott, 1995). As an important base of legitimacy, coercive pressure can either originate from the established legal framework or from the resource dependence relations between the focal organization and the organization that controls its resources (Blau, 1964; DiMaggio & Powell, 1983; Emerson, 1962; Mizruchi & Fein, 1999; Pfeffer & Salancik, 1978).

With regard to the diffusion of neoliberal policies among prefectures, we argue that the major source of coercion comes from the provincial governments. This is because first, although local institutional reform can be influenced by national politics when the central government uses national legislation and defines a national standard for certain sectors or issues, such interference is neither frequent nor direct. The central government usually guides local institutional development by setting up various "models." The role of this macrolevel interference is to provide an overarching institutional architecture, which sanctions local institutional differentiation and allows institutional competition (Krug & Hendrischke, 2008). Because such influence is equally present in all localities, it probably can shed light on the longitudinal variation of institutional developments, but cannot convincingly explain the regional differentiation in terms of institutional development.

Related to the first point, a second consideration is that since 1978, decentralization reform has allowed provinces to play a much more active role in economic and social management than the ministries at the central level (Huang, 1996; Li & Zhou, 2005; Qian & Xu, 1993). Reforms have granted the provincial governments with greater discretion in allocating economic resources and approving investment and construction plans. Correspondingly, they are also held accountable for the consequences of their decisions. Provincial governments are just like the middle-level managers in the Chinese bureaucratic system who are responsible for the social and economic development of their jurisdiction, and the political promotion of the provincial leaders is also significantly affected by local economic performance during their tenure (Li & Zhou, 2005; Whiting, 2001). That being said, an adequate understanding of the local policy making process has to take into account the influence of those in higher levels, especially the influence of the provincial governments.

To test the effects of provincial pressure, we systematically collected official documents on the infrastructure sector management promulgated by the provincial governments. To measure the magnitude of the provincial pressure, we identified key policy elements associated with the infrastructure liberalization process. We then calculated how many of these components were highlighted in the documents of a given year in a given province. We used the cumulative number of key components that had been mentioned in the provincial documents as the level of coercive pressure exerted by the provincial governments. In Table 6.1, Model 4 tests the effects of the coercive pressure variable. The coefficient is positive and significant, indicating that when provincial governments give clear orders to the subordinate prefecture level governments to promote liberalization reform, then the latter are more likely to adopt such a policy and begin to give green lights to PPP projects.

However, the effectiveness of such coercive power tends to be moderated by the inter-organizational resource dependence relations (DiMaggio & Powell, 1983; Mizruchi & Fein, 1999; Oliver, 1991; Peng, 2003; Zucker, 1987). This is because when an actor is required to adopt a new practice, the resource dependence relations with the actors who exert pressure are important factors in shaping organizational responses (DiMaggio & Powell, 1983; Oliver, 1991; Pfeffer & Salancik, 1978; Salancik, 1979). In the Chinese political system, two types of inter-governmental relationships can moderate the effectiveness of provincial orders, namely fiscal dependency and political dependency (Jin et al., 2005; Li & Zhou, 2005).

Regarding fiscal dependency, political scientists find that federal states often combine coercive order and financial incentives when promoting new programs. Those states that receive more financial support from the federal government are more likely to adopt the new policy (Daley & Garand, 2005). As mentioned above, the current Chinese financial system allows the higher-level government to centralize a larger proportion of fiscal resources in their hands and gives them control over the distribution of fiscal transfers. Under such a system, higher-level governments usually have a greater say regarding the sharing rule with their subordinates in terms of tax revenue and transfers. For those who depend heavily on transfers from above, the incentives for compliance and disincentives for resistance are obvious (Wong, 2000). We can therefore expect that when higher-level governments give no adoption requirements, fiscally weak cities will postpone the adoption because larger transfer or fiscal dependency usually indicates poor economic conditions.

However, when adoption is encouraged by the higher-level governments, then cities that depend heavily on transfers are more likely to respond earlier and adopt the system. Model 4 in Table 6.2 incorporated the interaction terms between coercive pressure and fiscal dependency. The coefficient is positive and significant, which suggests that if a city is more dependent on the provincial government for financial resources to cover its expenditure, the city tends to show more respect to the resource provider's, i.e., the provincial government's, opinion. In this case, they would be more likely to approve the PPP programs in their cities early.

A second intergovernmental relationship that moderates the effects of coercive pressure is the political dependency relations among governments, which originate from China's hierarchical administrative system. In this system cities are divided according to differing political status. Having a higher political status not only means having greater social–economic management power, but also indicates that the city's leadership is more likely to enjoy higher political rank and therefore have more autonomy in formulating local social–economic policies (Meyer, 2008; Wong et al., 1995). When the prospect and the effectiveness of a new system are still uncertain, higher-status cities can decide to adopt the system without suffering too many political constraints.

However, when they feel that the higher-level governments are advocating a reform plan that does not fit their situation, they are more likely to bargain with provincial governments to postpone or even suspend the reform in their jurisdiction. Given their high political and economic status, their opinions carry more weight with their superiors than the opinions of lower-status cities. We therefore argue that when the politically more powerful cities have more discretion on policy making, the provincial government's suggestions may be less effective for these cities because they have greater discretion to decide the extent to which and the timeline for responding to the provincial government's order. The interaction term between coercive pressure and the city's political status in Model 4 is negative and significant, which indicates that as the city's political status increases, the influence of the provincial governments' orders on these cities tends to decrease.

Effect of Geographic Proximity and Peer Competition

Besides the influence of higher-level governments, the reform decisions of the peer cities can also be a powerful force that drives the focal city to innovate. Walker (1969) finds that states often emulate innovative practices adopted by their neighboring states. This is because emulating is a way of "satisficing" and it can simplify the decision-making process. Two mechanisms are often quoted to support this argument: social learning and competition. Walker argues that state policy makers are often affected by the human cognitive bias of accepting familiar things and being reassured by those things close to them. The policy makers often closely monitor the policies of other states in order to search for solutions to similar problems they encountered. Among the many states, those geographically proximate states are more likely to be used as sources of innovation information because proximity can affect the frequency of communication and the nature of interactions between actors, which then facilitates imitative behaviors (Rogers, 1995).

In addition to the social learning explanation, scholars also argue that geographical proximity fuels the diffusion process because it encourages competition between neighboring states over scarce resources. Berry and Berry (1990) find that a state may adopt a lottery to avoid having its citizens cross the borders to buy tickets in a neighboring state's lottery. Peterson and

Rom (1989) show that a state sets its public assistance at the same level as its neighbors to avoid attracting poor immigrants from them.

Intensive regional economic competition among Chinese cities emerges as decentralization reform proceeds. China's decentralized economic management system gives local governments considerable autonomy in engineering local development strategies (Blanchard & Shleifer, 2001; Jin et al., 2005; Weingast, 1995; Zheng, 2007). This decentralized structure then leads to intense inter-city competition over capital, resources, and labor. For example, local governments design investment incentives that aim to attract investors from neighboring provinces or prefectures.

However, regional competition is not limited to the acquisition of investments and labor; some further argue that regional competition is also evident at the institutional level. Cities are induced to create hospitable investment environments through providing better infrastructure, utilities, greater security for factor owners, and fair access to resources and markets, so as to attract investors or resources from other regions (Harvey, 2005a; Montinola, Qian, & Weingast, 1995a). It is reported that local governments frequently organize study trips to other regions and learn new measures and policies from the more advanced places. Because capital and labor will move to the jurisdiction where the rate of return is highest, the local governments will be forced to imitate "good practices" in order to maintain their competitiveness (Krug & Hendrischke, 2008). Just as Tiebout (1956) argued, competition rewards local governments that are friendly to markets as factors of production move to their regions, whereas it punishes heavily interventionist local governments as they lose valuable factors of production. So we expect that such horizontal competition or imitation may be an important force that drives the diffusion of innovative institutions across different locations.

A similar explanation is competitive mimicry. Unlike the regional diffusion model, the institutional mimicry model emphasizes the influence from a given social group (either role equivalent or structural equivalent peer groups) rather than simple geographic clustering. The effects of these two mechanisms are additive rather than substitutive. Aside from this distinction, the underlying mechanisms assumed in both explanations are quite similar. When the outcomes of a practice are uncertain, then the trait-based imitation process becomes more salient then the proximity of geographic locations (Haunschild & Miner, 1997).

To study the trait-based imitation process, some researchers use the characteristics of individual firms and indicators of the general economic environment as indexes of similarity (Fligstein, 1985; Guler, Guillen, & Macpherson, 2002; Haveman, 1993; Mizruchi & Stearns, 1988); other researchers argue that structural equivalence of members in a network modulates the adoption of innovations because it affects the homogeneity of adopters' behavior (Aldrich, 1979; Burt, 1987; Davis, 1991; Galaskiewicz & Burt, 1991; Guler et al., 2002; Han, 1994). Structural equivalence emerges if ego and alter occupy the same position in the social structure and have the same relation with other actors in the same system. It is predicted that ego will quickly adopt any innovations that seem to make alters more successful (Abbott & DeViney, 1992; Burt, 1987; Davis, 1991; Galaskiewicz & Burt, 1991; Guler et al., 2002; Han, 1994).

China's administrative system is rich in structural equivalence relations. This system is analogous to a nested hierarchical structure in which multiple same-level units are affiliated with a common higher-level unit. The ties between lower- and higher-level units can be economic planning, fiscal, or political in nature, and the units at the lower levels share similar status and structural positions (Guthrie, 2005; Walder, 1992, 1995). Units are thus structurally equivalent if they are at the same level and affiliated to the same superior unit.

This de facto federalist structure gives local governments considerable autonomy in engineering local development strategies and also leads to intense interurban competition (Dougherty & McGuckin, 2008; Krug & Hendrischke, 2008). Interurban competition can be both political and economic. Politically speaking, same-level units are subject to similar evaluation standards, which higher-level officials use to evaluate the performance of lower-level leaders. Under this system, local leaders at the same level compete for rewards such as tenure, remuneration, and advancement opportunities (Whiting, 2001). Competitive relations among structurally equivalent cities influence the diffusion process significantly. Some cities may quickly imitate new practices that others have adopted because they fear the new practices will benefit their competitors, even when the real effects are still uncertain (Krug & Hendrischke, 2008).

To empirically test the imitation effects, we constructed two measures. The first measure was innovation exposure. The value of this variable indicates the level of innovation pressure from neighboring states. When constructing this variable, we also made the assumption that the influence tends to be weaker when the distance between two cities is greater. We therefore weighted the influence of a given city by its distance from the focal city. The second measure was peer pressure, which was operationalized as the cumulative number of adoptions within a trait-based social group (Haunschild & Miner, 1997). Following previous studies, we calculated this variable as the year-end cumulative number of adopters divided by the total number of units in the same peer group (Fligstein, 1985). Cities at the prefecture level and above in the same province were treated as a peer group. This is because they are affiliated with the same provincial government and occupy similar administrative positions in China's administrative system, even though their political status might differ.

Model 5 tests the effect of innovation exposure; the estimated coefficient of the innovation exposure shows that this effect is positive and statistically significant. This suggests that the intensity of the exposure to a new idea or an innovative policy can promote other cities' innovation decisions. Model

6 tests the effect of competitive mimicry. The model result supports our argument. The estimated coefficient is positive and significant. This suggests that by imitating the strategies of other cities, especially cities that are structurally equivalent, focal cities can reduce innovation risks and search costs. This process can be either blind imitation of the decisions of other cities or an active or targeted imitation that aims to learn successful experiences from others.

Effect of Normative Forces

The liberalization of infrastructure sectors is a complex policy project that needs the inputs of various policy making professionals. This process represents a collective struggle of members of an occupation to define the conditions and proper methods of their work (DiMaggio & Powell, 1983; Zucker, 1987). New policy norms advocated by experts often build on the experiences of early adopters, which later lead to innovations even when there are no particular examples in a given group.

Previous studies have focused on the theorization efforts of clearly defined professional associations, which have a clear hierarchical organizational structure. However, not all professional influence can be exerted through such a well-defined organization. Recent studies have shown that when a well-defined professional organization is in absence, loosely organized professional or social movement communities may also accomplish the theorization task (Haveman, Rao, & Paruchuri, 2007). When it comes to the theorization of the neoliberal urban policies in China, the theorization task is mainly accomplished by policy analysts and local officials who form a loosely connected epistemic community. These policy making professionals promote the diffusion of new ideas through: (1) introducing new policy ideas to a group of policy makers and articulating the institutional conditions under which a new policy could take effect, and (2) comparing and summarizing the experimental policy measures in different locations and specifying the advantages and limitations of the new policies.

In addition to the full time policy researchers in government-sponsored think tanks, some local officials also play an important role in the theorization process. These local officials usually have accumulated abundant local knowledge concerning how to establish and operate a new system in a given locality. These work experiences and expert knowledge eventually facilitated the implementation of various complex policy measures and contractual agreements. With their help, the advantages and working mechanisms of the neoliberal urban policies are gradually theorized and spread within the policy making communities, and eventually the neoliberal policies become normative solutions.

In this study, we operationalized this factor as the number of expert articles on infrastructure liberalization practices that appear in various professional journals. We drew data from the China National Knowledge

Infrastructure (CNKI) database, which covers all major journals published during the study period. We used "BOT, marketization of infrastructure, private participation in infrastructure" to search for articles on infrastructure liberalization. These articles were limited to the Political, Law, Social Science, Economics and Management fields. The estimation of the effect of normative pressure is more complicated. We used a random-effects probit model (see Appendix for more technical details) to explore the effect of normative pressures on the adoption of infrastructure privatization policies. The reason for using this method is twofold. For one thing, normative pressure measures the aggregate level of professional publications on infrastructure privatization policies. Therefore, this variable only varies over time but has no variation across cities. Cox's proportional hazards model cannot generate estimations for such variables, so the use of an alternative modeling strategy is needed. For another, although the interpretation of the statistical findings of random-effects probit models differs from the Cox's model results, they both explore the effects of the covariates on the adoption decisions. So the new models can be used as a robustness check of the substantive findings.

The probit model (Model 8 in Table 6.2) shows that the normative pressure measured by the number of published professional articles on infrastructure privatization policies and practices in a given year has a positive and significant impact on the propensity of adopting the corresponding policies. This suggests that as the theorization of infrastructure liberalization advances, its advantage and legitimacy are gradually known by other cities. When the liberalization of infrastructure and the urban utility sector is increasingly portrayed as a more plausible and effective way to mobilize financial resources to construct new facilities and to overcome management problems, it becomes a normative solution and affects the local government's innovation decisions.

Conclusion

Public–private partnership (PPP) has gained popularity during the liberalization reforms in infrastructure sectors around the world. As China is integrated into the world economy, China's private sector becomes a major force that redefines the landscape of the local infrastructure markets. Despite widespread adoption of pro-market policies, cities differ greatly in the extent to which they allow the private sector to participate in these sectors. Building on the literature of policy diffusion and innovations, we argue in this chapter that the internal characteristics of cities, pressure from neighboring and structurally equivalent peer cities, and influence from provincial governments as well as policy research communities strongly affect the extent of local liberalization reforms. We find generally robust support for our arguments, using an analysis of projects with private participation in 333 Chinese cities between 1992 and 2008.

Specifically, we argue that whether a city will liberalize its urban infrastructure and utility sector is significantly influenced by the local demand for better infrastructure. We find that cities with a stronger economy, higher industrialization rate, larger scale investment in fixed assets, and a bigger and floating population are more likely to require greater infrastructure service capacities. This high demand will positively affect a city's propensity for adopting the privatization policy. Moreover, we also find that the effects of some local socioeconomic characteristics are not linear. The effect of the industrialization rate shows a curvilinear relationship with the adoption rate, indicating that the marginal effects of the industrialization rate are declining. Infrastructure and utility service demand drives the industrialization process to a certain degree, and further increase is more likely to be associated with the improvement of the living standard and the development of service industries. In addition, this study suggests that the effects of local demand decline over time. The local economic characteristics are strongly associated with the adoption propensities in the early diffusion period. The late diffusion process is driven less forcefully by indigenous demand than by various institutional forces and competition pressure.

A local state's fiscal and political capacity is also crucial to the implementation of projects with private participation. Governments can attract private entities to invest in infrastructure sectors through two ways. First, they can offer financial support to investors, either in the form of subsidies or guarantees, in order to reduce the economic risks that may be caused by poor performance of the project or macroeconomic changes. Second, local governments can address the policy problems that underlie investors' concerns by ensuring policy stability, making the policy making process transparent, or establishing a sound regulatory framework (Dailami & Klein, 1998). Therefore, local governments' fiscal and political capacities are important for successful implementation of private participated projects.

This study also shows that the intergovernmental relations have significantly shaped the trajectory of policy diffusion in China. Along the vertical dimension, the central and provincial governments exert a strong influence on local policy making through the specification of macro policy guidelines or direct administrative order. However, the effectiveness of such pressure is not homogenous across cities, it is conditioned by resource dependence relations among different levels of governments. This dependence can take two basic forms, i.e., intergovernmental fiscal dependence and political dependence. Local governments can strategically choose compliance or resistance, depending on the degree to which the adoption of an innovation will rely on the resources from their superiors.

A second dimension is the horizontal intergovernmental relations. In this study, we further specify these kinds of relationships into two categories: competition or emulation among geographically proximate cities and competition or emulation among structurally equivalent cities. Geographic proximity facilitates the social learning process and promotes interjurisdictional competition for capital, labor, and other production factors. In highly competitive environments, local governments are keen to their neighbors' policy innovations and try to institute similar policies that may increase their competitor's competitiveness. In addition to this form of competition, local governments are also competing with peer cities that are subordinate to the same higher-level government. The leaders of these cities compete with each other for better local economic performance, which is closely related to their future promotion prospective. When a city liberalized its infrastructure sectors, other cities may also need to show their determination of reform by adopting similar if not more radical liberalization policies. On the one hand, this interjurisdictional competition may trigger the "bidding war," which decreases the average return brought by the new policies; on the other hand, this mechanism is also an effective way to eliminate the entry barriers for private and foreign capital and therefore promotes the establishment of a more market-friendly local institutional environment.

In addition, this study suggests that the professional policy communities have promoted the diffusion of infrastructure liberalization policies. For local governments, the adoption of such innovations is limited by both the lack of technical knowhow and by the ambiguity in the legitimacy of the privatization measures. The policy making and policy research professionals helped policy makers to overcome these limitations by systemically introducing the international experiences of various financing arrangements and by legitimizing private participation in the infrastructure sectors. The results of this study suggest that the theorization efforts of the policy research professionals are significant in promoting the marketization of the urban infrastructure and utility sectors.

Appendix
Research Methods

To tests the ideas developed in this chapter, we employed two different statistical methods to estimate the effects of the variables: (1) Cox's proportional hazards model, and (2) random-effects probit model predicting the adoption of PPP projects in the infrastructure sector.

Cox's Proportional Hazards Model

Event history analysis was the primary method of analysis used in this study. This approach is widely used to study the diffusion of various practices in a social system. The unit of analysis was city-year. The dependent variables of interest were the hazard rates, defined as the probability that officials in a city will adopt the policy innovations in a specific year, given that they have not already done so. Hazard rates are probabilities and cannot be directly observed. Event history models therefore use a dichotomous dependent variable to indicate whether local policy makers adopted the innovation in a given year (1 if yes, and 0 if no). Once the policy innovation was enacted in a city, there were no more city-year observations for that particular city because it was no longer in the risk set for policy adoption.

In particular, Cox's proportional hazards model was chosen for this analysis. This is because the model allows researchers to estimate the effects of parameters without specifying the baseline hazard function. The general form of this model is

$$h_i(t) = h_0(t) \exp \left(\beta_1 x_{i1} + \beta_2 x_{i2} + \cdots + \beta_k x_{ik} \right)$$

where $h_i(t)$ is the hazard function of observation i, $h_0(t)$ is the unspecified baseline hazard function, and βs are the regression coefficients of independent variables. The coefficient is interpreted as the multiplicative effects on the hazard, which means a unit increase of covariate x_j will cause $\exp(\beta_j)$ change of the hazard, holding other covariates constant (Fox, 2002).

Cox's regression model can also accommodate time-varying covariates, such as urbanization, industrialization rates, and local per capita GDP. In doing so, observations with time-varying covariates are transformed into multiple observations; in other words, the model treats each time period for an individual case as a separate observation (Fox, 2002).

Random-Effects Probit Models

The estimation of the effect of normative pressure involves more complication. Because this covariate only varies over time but is equal to all clusters in a given year, Cox's model does not yield estimates for effects as such. Therefore, we used a random-intercept probit model to explore the influence of normative pressure.

When expressed in the form of a latent-response model, the dependent variable y_{ik}^* can be viewed as an unobserved or latent continuous response, representing the propensity to adopt a new policy. More formally, the model for response on time point k (where $k = 1, 2 \ldots, n$) for city i ($i = 1, 2 \ldots$, N cities in the sample) is:

$$y_{ik}^* = \alpha_i + \beta_0 + \beta_1 t_{ik} + \beta_2 t_{2i} + \beta_3 t_{3ik} + \epsilon_{ik}$$

where
   t_{ik} = the time that corresponds to the kth measurement for city i;
   β_0 = the overall population intercept or response propensity at baseline $t = 0$;
   β_1 = the overall population trend coefficient describing rate of change in response propensity over time;

α_i = the random effect for subject i;
β_2 = the fixed effect of the subject level covariate x_2;
β_3 = the fixed effect of the time-specific covariate x_{3ik};
and ε_{ik} = an independent residual distributed N $(0, \sigma^2)$.

Innovation Exposure

To test the spatial diffusion hypothesis, the model used must take into account the following considerations: first, the model must consider the potential impact of policy adoptions in all cities on the adoption decisions in every other city. Second, it is highly likely that the potential impact of a policy innovation in one city on the adoption decisions of another city is weaker if the distance between these two cities is greater. Third, similarities in social and economic characteristics among cities may cause spurious inferences of spatial effects. Therefore, when estimating the spatial effect, the heterogeneity among cities must be controlled (Keister, 2002; Tolnay, Deane, & Beck, 1996). We constructed the innovation exposure measure to account for these complexities.

The innovation exposure measure was constructed by solving two equations. The first equation was used to determine the effect of policy adoptions by each city on all other cities. The equation takes the form:

$$O_i = \beta_0 + \Sigma\beta_k X_{ki} + \varepsilon_i$$

where

O_i = the odds of adopting the new policy by city i;
β_0 = the regression constant;
X_{ki} = a set of k variables that describe the social and economic features of city i;
β_k = the effect parameters that describe the effect of social and economic variables on the odds of adopting new policies;
and ε_i = the disturbance term for equation (2).

Using equation (2), we obtained a set of predicted values O_i^* for each city that describe the expected odds of adopting a certain policy, given the city's social and economic characteristics. For each pair of cities, the predicted value was then divided by the geographic distance between the two cities. The innovation exposure for each city i to the adoption decisions of all other cities was then calculated by the following equation:

$$IE_i = \Sigma\left(O_i^* / D_{ij}\right)$$

where

IE_i = the innovation exposure for city i;
O_i^* = the predicted odds of adopting a certain policy for city j;

and D_{ij} = the geographic distance between cities i and j, using the latitude and longitude for each city and taking the curve of the earth into consideration when calculating the distance between the two points.

The variable IE_i is then used as a predictor in addition to the original set of social and economic characteristics used in equation (2) in the final model (Cox's or probit model).

Notes

1 Zhongping He, 2004, "First legislation on 'capitalizing on cities' bottlenecked," People's Daily (4/26/2004), Retrieved on January 12, 2012 from http://unn. people.com.cn/GB/14748/2469322.html.
2 For an expended description of methodology used by the PPI team project, see ppi.worldbank.org/ . . . /methodology_expanded_May_2007.pdf
3 When a state-owned enterprises or government agency is forced to operate in a market environment, raise funds in the capital market, and sell its services to willing buyers as if they are market-oriented firms, then this process is called marketization. The aim of marketization is to achieve economic efficiency through exposure to market discipline. The marketization of the state sector can be achieved through reduction of subsidies from the state, deregulation, organizational restructuring, or privatization (Savas 2005).

References

Abbott, A., & DeViney, S. (1992). The welfare state as transnational event: Evidence from sequences of policy adoption. *Social Science History, 16*(2), 245–274.

Aldrich, H. (1979). *Organizations and Environments*. Englewood Cliffs, NJ: Prentice-Hall.

Annez, P. C. (2007). Urban infrastructure finance from private operators: What have we learned from recent experience? In G. E. Peterson & P. C. Annez (Eds.), *Financing Cities: Fiscal Responsibility and Urban Infrastructure in Brazil, China, India, Poland and South Africa* (pp. 307–338). Los Angeles, CA: Sage Publications Inc.

Bahl, R. W. (1999). *Fiscal Policy in China: Taxation and Intergovernmental Fiscal Relations*. San Francisco: The 1990 Institute.

Bellier, M., & Zhou, Y. M. (2003). *Private Participation in Infrastructure in China: Issues and Recommendations for the Road, Water, and Power Sectors*. New York: World Bank, International Finance Corporation.

Berry, F. S., & Berry, W. D. (1990). State lottery adoptions as policy innovations: An event history analysis. *American Political Science Review, 84*(2), 395–415.

Berry, F. S., & Berry, W. D. (2007). Innovation and diffusion in policy research. In P. A. Sabatier (Ed.), *Theories of the Policy Process* (pp. 307–362). Boulder, CO: Westview Press.

Blanchard, O., & Shleifer, A. (2001). Federalism with and without political centralization: China versus Russia. *IMF Staff Papers, 48*(4), 8.

Blau, P. M. (1964). *Exchange and Power in Social Life*. New York: J. Wiley.

Brenner, N. (2004). Urban governance and the production of new state spaces in western Europe, 1960–2000. *Review of International Political Economy, 11*(3), 447–488.

Burt, R. S. (1987). Social contagion and innovation: Cohesion versus structural equivalence. *American Journal of Sociology, 92*(6), 1287–1335.

Campbell, J. L., & Pedersen, O. K. (2001). The rise of neoliberalism and institutional analysis. In J. L. Campbell & O. K. Pedersen (Eds.), *The Rise of Neoliberalism and Institutional Analysis* (pp. 1–24). Princeton, NJ: Princeton University Press.

Chan, K. W. (1997). Urbanization and urban infrastructure services in the PRC. In C. Wong (Ed.), *Financing Local Government in the People's Republic of China* (pp. 83–126). New York: Oxford University Press.

Cohen, Y. S. (1972). *Diffusion of an Innovation in an Urban System; the Spread of Planned Regional Shopping Centers in the United States, 1949–1968.* Chicago: Department of Geography.

Dailami, M., & Klein, M. U. (1998). Government support to private infrastructure projects in emerging markets. *World Bank Policy Research Working Paper,* 1868.

Daley, D. M., & Garand, J. C. (2005). Horizontal diffusion, vertical diffusion, and internal pressure in state environmental policymaking. *American Politics Research, 33*(5), 615–644.

Davis, G. F. (1991). Agents without principles? The spread of the poison pill through the intercorporate network. *Administrative Science Quarterly, 36*(4), 583–613.

DiMaggio, P. J., & Powell, W. W. (1983). The iron cage revisited: Institutional isomorphism and collective rationality in organizational fields. *American Sociological Review, 48*(2), 147–160.

DiMaggio, P. J., & Powell, W. W. (1991). Introduction. In W. W. Powell & P. J. DiMaggio (Eds.), *The New Institutionalism in Organizational Analysis* (pp. 1–40). Chicago, IL: The University of Chicago Press.

Dobbin, F. (1994). *Forging Industrial Policy: The United States, Britain, and France in the Railway Age.* New York: Cambridge University Press.

Dobbin, F., Simmons, B., & Garrett, G. (2007). The global diffusion of public policies: social construction, coercion, competition, or learning? *Annual Review of Sociology, 33,* 449–472.

Dougherty, S. M., & McGuckin, R. H. (2008). The effects of federalism on productivity in Chinese firms. *Management and Organization Review, 4*(1), 39–61.

Ehrhardt, D., & Irwin, T. (2004). Avoiding customer and taxpayer bailouts in private infrastructure projects: Policy toward leverage, risk allocation, and bankruptcy. *World Bank Policy Research Working Paper,* 3274.

Emerson, R. M. (1962). Power-dependence relations. *American Sociological Review, 27*(1), 31–41.

Farquharson, E., Mastle, C. T. D., Yescombe, E. R., & Encinas, J. (2011). *How to Engage with the Private Sector in Public-Private Partnerships in Emerging Markets.* Washington, DC: The World Bank.

Fligstein, N. (1985). The spread of the multidivisional form among large firms, 1919–1979. *American Sociological Review, 50*(3), 377–391.

Fligstein, N., & Zhang, J. (2011). A new agenda for research on the trajectory of Chinese capitalism. *Management and Organziation Review, 7*(1), 39–62.

Fourcade-Gourinchas, M., & Babb, S. (2002). The rebirth of the liberal creed: Paths to neoliberalism in four countries. *American Journal of Sociology, 108,* 533–579.

Fox, J. (2002). *An R and S-Plus Companion to Applied Regression.* Thousand Oaks, CA: Sage Publications.

Galaskiewicz, J., & Burt, R. S. (1991). Interorganization contagion in corporate philanthropy. *Administrative Science Quarterly, 36*(1), 88–105.

Gao, B. (2009). The Rubik's cube state: A reconceptualization of political change in contemporary China. In L. A. Keister (Ed.), *Work and Organizations in China After Thirty Years of Transition* (Vol. 18, pp. 409–438). Bingley: Emerald.

Gomez-Ibanez, J. A. (2003). *Regulating Infrastructure: Monopoly, Contracts, and Discretion.* Cambridge, MA: Harvard University Press.

Guler, I., Guillen, M. F., & Macpherson, J. M. (2002). Global competition, institutions, and the diffusion of organizational practices: The international spread of ISO 9000 quality certificates. *Administrative Science Quarterly, 47*(2), 207–232.

Guthrie, D. (1999). *Dragon in a Three-Piece Suit: The Emergence of Capitalism in China*. Princeton, NJ: Princeton University Press.

Guthrie, D. (2005). Organizational learning and productivity: State structure and foreign investment in the rise of the Chinese corporation. *Management and Organization Review, 1*(2), 165–195.

Hall, P. (1989). *The Political Power of Economic Ideas: Keynesianism Across Nations*. Princeton, NJ: Princeton University Press.

Hall, P. A., & Soskice, D. W. (Eds.). (2001). *Varieties of Capitalism: The Institutional Foundations of Comparative Advantage*. New York: Oxford University Press.

Han, S.-K. (1994). Mimetic isomorphism and its effect on the audit services market. *Social Forces, 73*(2), 637–664.

Harvey, D. (1989). From managerialism to entrepreneurialism: The transformation in urban governance in late capitalism. *Geografiska Annaler: Series B. Human Geography, 71*(1), 3–17.

Harvey, D. (2005a). *A Brief History of Neoliberalism*. New York: Oxford University Press.

Harvey, D. (2005b). *A Brief History of Neoliberalism*. New York: Oxford University Press.

Haunschild, P. R., & Miner, A. S. (1997). Modes of interorganizational imitation: The effects of outcome salience and uncertainty. *Administrative Science Quarterly, 42*, 472–500.

Haveman, H. A. (1993). Follow the leader: Mimetic isomorphism and entry into new markets. *Administrative Science Quarterly, 38*(4), 593–627.

Haveman, H. A., Rao, H., & Paruchuri, S. (2007). The winds of change: The progressive movement and the bureaucratization of thrift. *American Sociological Review, 72*, 117–142.

Henisz, W. J., Zelner, B. A., & Guillén, M. F. (2005). The worldwide diffusion of market-oriented infrastructure reform, 1977–1999. *American Sociological Review, 70*(6), 871–897.

Huang, Y. (1996). *Inflation and Investment Controls in China*. Cambridge: Cambridge University Press.

Jessop, B., & Sum, N.-L. (2000). An entrepreneurial city in action: Hong Kong's emerging strategies in and for urban competition. *Urban Studies, 37*(12), 2287–2313.

Jin, H., Qian, Y., & Weingast, B. R. (2005). Regional decentralization and fiscal incentives: federalism, Chinese style. *Journal of Public Economics, 89*(9), 1719–1742.

Keister, L. A. (2002). Adapting to radical change: Strategy and environment in piecerate adoption during China's transition. *Organization Science, 13*(5), 459–474.

Kessides, I. (2004). *Reforming Infrastructure: Privatization, Regulation, and Competition*. Washington, DC: The World Bank and Oxford University Press.

Knoke, D. (1982). The spread of municipal reform: Temporal, spatial, and social dynamics. *The American Journal of Sociology, 87*(6), 1314–1339.

Krug, B., & Hendrischke, H. (2008). Framing China: Transformation and institutional change through co-evolution. *Management and Organziation Review, 4*(1), 81–108.

Leitner, H. (1990). Cities in pursuit of economic growth: The local states as entrepreneur. *Political Geography Quarterly, 9*(2), 146–170.

Leitner, H., & Sheppard, E. (1998). Economic uncertainty, interurban competition and the efficacy of entrepreneurialism. In T. Hall & P. Hubbard (Eds.), *The Entrepreneurial City: Geographies of Politics, Regime and Representation* (pp. 285–309). New York: John Wiley and Sons.

Li, H., & Zhou, L.-A. (2005). Political turnover and economic performance: The incentive role of personnel control in China. *Journal of Public Economics, 89*(9), 1743–1762.

Meyer, J. W., & Rowan, B. (1977). Institutionalized organizations: Formal structures as myth and ceremony. *American Journal of Sociology, 83*, 340–363.

Meyer, J. W., & Rowan, B. (1991). Institutionalized organizations: Formal structures as myth and ceremony. In W. W. Powell & P. J. DiMaggio (Eds.), *The New Institutionalism in Organizational Analysis* (pp. 41–62). Chicago: University of Chicago Press.

Meyer, M. W. (2008). China's second economic transition: Building national markets. *Management and Organziation Review, 4*(1), 3–15.

Mizruchi, M. S., & Fein, L. C. (1999). The social construction of organizational knowledge: A study of the use of coercive, mimetic, and normative isomorphism. *Administrative Science Quarterly, 44*(4), 653–683.

Mizruchi, M. S., & Stearns, L. B. (1988). A longitudinal study of the formation of interlocking directorates. *Administrative Science Quarterly, 33*(2), 194–210.

Mohr, L. (1969). Determinants of innovation in organizations. *American Political Science Review, 75*, 111–126.

Montinola, G., Qian, Y., & Weingast, B. R. (1995). Federalism, Chinese style: The political basis for economic success. *World Politics, 48*(1), 50–81.

Mudge, S. L. (2008). What is neo-liberalism? *Socio-Economic Review, 6*(4), 703–731.

National Bureau of Statistics. (2009). *China Statistical Yearbook.* Beijing: China Statistical Yearbook Press.

Naughton, B. (2007). *The Chinese Economy: Transitions and Growth.* Cambridge, MA: MIT Press.

North, D. (1990). *Institutions, Institutional Change, and Economic Performance.* New York: Cambridge University Press.

OECD. (2005). *Governance in China.* Paris: OECD Publishing.

Oliver, C. (1991). Strategic responses to institutional processes. *The Academy of Management Review, 16*(1), 145–179.

Owen, K. A. (2002). The Sydney 2000 Olympics and urban entrepreneurialism: Local variations in urban governance. *Australian Geographical Studies, 40*(3), 323–336.

Palmer, D. A., Jennings, P. D., & Zhou, X. (1993). Late adoption of the multidivisional form by large U.S. corporations: Institutional, political, and economic accounts. *Administrative Science Quarterly, 38*, 100–131.

Peng, M. W. (2003). Institutional transitions and strategic choices. *Academy of Management Review, 28*(2), 275–296.

Peterson, P. E., & Rom, M. (1989). American federalism, welfare policy, and residential choices. *American Political Science Review, 83*, 711–728.

Pfeffer, J., & Salancik, G. R. (1978). *The External Control of Organizations: A Resource Dependence Perspective.* New York: Harper and Row.

Qian, Y., & Xu, C. (1993). Why China's economic reforms differ: The M-form hierarchy and entry/expansion of the non-state sector. *Economics of Transition, 1*, 135–170.

Rogers, E. M. (1995). *Diffusion of Innovations* (4th ed.). New York: Free Press.

Salancik, G. R. (1979). Interorganizational dependence and responsiveness to affirmative action: The case of women and defense contractors. *The Academy of Management Journal, 22*(2), 375–394.

Savas, E. S. (2005). *Privatization in the City: Successes, Failures, Lessons.* Washington, DC: CQ Press.

Scott, W. R. (1995). *Institutions and Organizations.* Thousand Oaks, CA: Sage.

Solinger, D. J. (1993). *China's Transition from Socialism: Statist Legacies and Market Reforms, 1980–1990.* Armonk, NY: M. E. Sharpe.

Strang, D., & Meyer, J. W. (1993). Institutional conditions for diffusion. *Theory and Society, 22*(4), 487–511.

Strang, D., & Soule, S. A. (1998). Diffusion in organizations and social movements: From hybrid corn to poison pills. *Annual Review of Sociology, 24*, 265–290.

Su, M., & Zhao, Q. (2007). China: Fiscal framework and urban infrastructure finance. In G. E. Peterson & P. C. Annez (Eds.), *Financing Cities: Fiscal Responsibility and Urban Infrastructure in Brazil, China, India, Poland and South Africa* (pp. 74–107). Los Angeles: Sage Publications Inc.

Tiebout, C. (1956). A pure theory of local expenditures. *Journal of Political Economy, 64*, 416–424.

Tolnay, S. E., Deane, G., & Beck, E. M. (1996). Vicarious violence: Spatial effects on southern lynchings, 1890–1919. *American Journal of Sociology, 102*(3), 788–815.

Walder, A. G. (1992). Property rights and stratification in socialist redistributive economies. *American Sociological Review, 57*(4), 524–539.

Walder, A. G. (1995). Local governments as industrial firms: An organizational analysis of China's transitional economy. *American Journal of Sociology, 101*, 263–301.

Walker, J. L. (1969). The diffusion of innovations among the American states. *American Political Science Review, 63*(3), 880–899.

Weingast, B. R. (1995). The economic role of political institutions: Market preserving federalism and economic development. *Journal of Law, Economics, and Organization, 11*(1), 1–31.

Wejnert, B. (2002). Integrating models of diffusion of innovations: A conceptual framework. *Annual Review of Sociology, 28*, 297–326.

Whiting, S. H. (2001). *Power and Wealth in Rural China: The Political Economy of Institutional Change*. New York: Cambridge University Press.

Williamson, J. (1990). What Washington means by policy reform. In J. Williamson (Ed.), *Latin American Adjustment: How Much Has Happened?* (pp. 7–41). Washington, DC: Institute for International Economics.

Williamson, J. (1993). Democracy and the "Washington Consensus." *World Development, 21*, 1329–1326.

Wong, C. (1992). Fiscal reform and local industrialization: The problematic sequencing of reform in post Mao China. *Modern China, 18*(2), 197–227.

Wong, C. P. W. (2000). *Central-Local Relations Revisited: The 1994 Tax Sharing Reform and Public Expenditure Management in China*. Paper presented at the Central-Periphery Relations in China: Integration, Disintegration or Reshaping of an Empire, Hong Kong.

Wong, C. P. W., Heady, C. J., & Woo, W. T. (1995). *Fiscal Management and Economic Reform in the People's Republic of China*. New York: Oxford University Press.

Wong, C. P. W., Heady, C. J., Woo, W. T., & Asian Development Bank. (1995). *Fiscal Management and Economic Reform in the People's Republic of China*. Hong Kong; New York: Published for the Asian Development Bank by Oxford University Press.

World Bank. (1994). *World Development Report 1994: Infrastructure for Development*. New York: The International Bank for Reconstruction and Development/ The World Bank.

Wu, W. (1999). Reforming China's institutional environment for urban infrastructure provision. *Urban Studies, 36*(13), 2263–2282.

Wu, W. (2010). Urban infrastructure financing and economic performance in China. *Urban Geography, 51*(5), 648–667.

Yeung, W.-C. (2003). *Chinese Capitalism in a Global Era: Towards a Hybrid Capitalism*. New York: Routledge.

Zheng, Y. (2007). *De Facto Federalism in China: Reforms and Dynamics of Central-Local Relations*. Singapore: World Scientific Publishing.

Zucker, L. G. (1987). Institutional theories of organization. *Annual Review of Sociology, 13*, 443–464.

7 Changing Relational Patterns in Business Groups

The networks of interfirm relations that developed in business groups during the economic transition became an important part of China's emergent economic structure early in reform, and these early ties continue to provide structure to business and managerial decision-making today. In the mid-1980s, China's government began to encourage firms to form business groups (*qiye jituan*), coalitions of firms from multiple industries that interact over long periods of time and that are distinguished by elaborate interfirm networks of lending, trade, ownership, and social relations. The organizational structure of a business group is similar to that of a conglomerate, but relatively exclusive internal relations make the groups highly stable and resistant to reorganization. Shortly after the start of economic reform, Chinese reformers began to separate firms from state administrative bureaus, to reduce state support of firms, and to encourage the formation of business groups. Firms that joined business groups gained significant autonomy, and they also became responsible for finding inputs and marketing their products. As the firms sought sources of goods and capital, they quickly developed stable interfirm exchange ties similar to those found in Japan's *keiretsu* and Korea's *chaebol* (Keister, 2000). These business groups contributed in important ways to the economic structure that ultimately emerged in China. They also provided the context in which modern management practices came to China, and they may have contributed to selecting the firms and managers that survived the tumult that characterized the early years of reform by improving firm financial performance.

To better understand the formation and effects of early organizational changes, we devote this chapter to studying two issues related to the early business groups. First, we study the factors that encouraged firms to develop exchange relations (including personnel, financial, and commercial exchange) with each other in the business groups in the early stages of reform. It was these early ties that formed the basis of the groups' structures and that defined them as a unique organizational form. Specifically, we discuss the roles that firm traits (e.g., whether it was the core firm) and relational traits (e.g., the distance between firms, their prior relationships) played in the likelihood that a tie formed. We also look at the role that market development, administrative rank, and prior social relationships played in tie formation. The structure of these early interfirm relations also had the potential to affect the behaviors of individual firms and the benefits enjoyed by these firms both immediately and over time. Therefore, the second issue we study in this chapter is how business groups affected the firm financial performance of their member firms. Specifically, we study the relationship between business group structure and firm profitability in 1990, 1994, and 1999. By 1990, sufficient time had passed since the start of reform that some firms were potentially profitable, yet studying the groups in this year still gives us a glimpse into firm differences early in reform. By 1994 and 1999, the longer-term effects of group membership should be evident.

To explore these issues, we use data from two unique datasets. The first dataset includes 1988 and 1990 data on all business groups in non-sensitive industries that had registered with the state in 1985. We use this data to explore interfirm tie formation and firm performance early in reform. Keister collected this data by administering a questionnaire to the financial officer of each of the 40 core firms in face-to-face interviews (in Chinese without a translator). She was able to obtain the data from a single source for most business groups because core firms kept detailed records of member firm behaviors and practices (see Keister, 2000 for a detailed description of the data). To explore the effects of business group membership on firm performance later in reform, we used a second dataset, also collected by Keister but in collaboration with the Chinese Academy of Social Sciences. The firms in the second dataset are different from the firms in the first dataset because it was important to use a random sample to study firms as reform progressed, as firm births were frequent during China's transition. The second dataset is longitudinal, and we used information from 1994 and 1999 for 800 firms. The sample includes 433 state-owned enterprises (SOEs) and 367 collective enterprises, joint ventures, private firms, and other types of non-state companies (CNFs). The questionnaire had two parts. Part one was a set of 92 questions regarding the structure of the enterprise, manager appointment, participation in reform, organizational and management structure, manager incentives, firm strategy, relations with government offices, investment strategies, and related information. The firm's CEO (or the CEO's representative in a small number of cases) answered these questions. Part two was a series of 141 quantitative questions regarding enterprise operations. The firm's accountant answered these questions. These data include information about firm output, production expenses, wages and labor, investments, assets and liabilities, costs, profits, and related traits.

The Emergence of Chinese Business Groups

Although the notion of a business group is still unfamiliar to many western observers, these interfirm networks are common in many Asian economies (Lincoln, Gerlach, & Takahashi, 1992). Before the mid-1980s, business groups did not exist in China. However, as they dismantled the state administrative bureaus that oversaw firms prior to reform, reformers encouraged business groups to form and gradually transferred firm control to the groups (Keister, 2000). Reformers typically selected groups of firms from the same state bureau, designated a core (or central administrative) firm, and aided in developing the group's administrative component (People's Republic of China, 1980, 1984, 1986). Although it was rare early in reform, some firms also voluntarily formed business groups, and the state encouraged this outside of sensitive industries such as defense. All nascent groups (i.e., groups-in-formation) were required to register with the state and were considered a group once this process was complete. Most observers agreed that managers complied with the registration request because it was relatively simple and cost-free; moreover, managers were accustomed to being relatively compliant during the first years of transition (Dai & Li, 1988; Shanghai Association for the Study of Business Groups, 1995). The reformers targeted state-owned industrial firms because they accounted for 50 percent of total national output and 80 percent of exports and employed 102 million workers in the 1980s (Jefferson & Rawski, 1994). Yet collectives (*jiti*), joint ventures (*hezi* or *sanzi*), and private firms (*siren*) also joined business groups (Keister, 1999). Business groups became increasingly common starting in the late 1980s, and the 1990s saw an even more rapid expansion of this new organizational form. By 1985, 58 groups had formed, and by 1993, more than 7,000 existed (Reform, 1993). In 1993, 50 percent of firms were group members by some estimates, and group assets exceeded 135 billion U.S. dollars (Li, 1995).

China's business groups quickly became a viable organizational form similar to business groups in other countries. Historically, business groups have formed during transition or development when firms welcome the protection of stable relations, and the groups tend to persist if the state does not outlaw them as collusive (Amsden, 1989; Fields, 1995; Hamilton, 1991; Lincoln, Gerlach, & Takahashi, 1992). Because they were coalitions rather than independent legal entities, Chinese business groups typically did not pay taxes or issue stocks; however, they were stable structures with distinct boundaries distinguished by long-term lending and trade ties among member firms that were legally independent. Whereas *keiretsu* were either vertically or horizontally organized, China's early business groups tended to be related relatively vertically (Keister, 2000). The core firm was usually an industrial enterprise and typically owned a portion of most subsidiaries; the core firm also had some degree of control over member firms, usually reflecting the extent of the ownership relation. In most cases, the state relinquished control of the business groups, but it continued to observe and advise them and retained partial ownership in some member firms, particularly in protected industries.

Firms joined business groups for many reasons. They joined business groups in order to gain autonomy from state administrators who were increasingly seen as out of touch with developing markets. They also saw business groups as efficient: by joining forces with other firms, it was possible to create and take advantage of economies of scale. In addition, joining forces with a group allowed firms to compensate for market failures (Goto, 1982), gain a degree of control over their environments, and affect political change and develop joint products (Mascarenhas, 1989). For some firms, business group membership also carried some amount of prestige (Keister, 1998). Firms could join groups independently, and membership overlap between former bureaus and business groups faded quickly. Firms also independently established the stable lending and trade relations that came to define the groups. Cross-shareholding began in the 1990s after the opening of China's stock markets, but mergers were rare as property rights were not well defined until later in reform (Xie, 1996). Although the core firm often maintained detailed records of firm activities and aided in management, neither the core firm nor the state interceded in the formation of interfirm relations in the business groups because hundreds of ties quickly developed at all organizational levels. Like business groups in Asia, Latin America, and the Middle East, nearly all firms in China's business groups were connected to at least one other firm in the group through some form of lending, trade, ownership, joint production, or other stable formal relation. Member firms were also connected through social relations, although family ties and other social ties are less pervasive in Chinese business groups than they are in Korea's *chaebol* (Steers, Shin, & Ungson, 1989) or Taiwan's *guanxi qiye* (Numazaki, 1986). In addition to immense size, business group membership carried with it a degree of prestige within China. These groups resembled powerful foreign multinational corporations. To cash in on this additional advantage, firms of all sizes and in all industries had an added incentive to join groups, adding to the quantity and density of existing groups.

The Formation of Interfirm Ties in Chinese Business Groups

The factors that led firms to develop exchange relations with each other in China's business groups in the early years of reform provided the foundation on which the groups' structures formed. Of course, firms did not exchange randomly with each other, and the processes that led them to engage in different types of exchange (e.g., personnel versus financial versus commercial) varied. As a result, the process by which firms developed lending and trade ties under these conditions is relevant to understanding both China's transition and the ways firms behave more generally. Table 7.1 includes the results of logistic regression models of the presence of interfirm ties between pairs of companies in business groups in 1990; in these models, the interfirm tie is the unit of analysis. The four ties are board member, financial, commercial, and manager exchange. Exchanging members of the firms' boards of directors was a common practice early in reform and indicated social proximity and cooperation. Financial exchange is interfirm lending and borrowing of financial resources, a practice that filled the gap left by the declining activity of the central government in firm finance at a time when the financial market was in its infancy. Commercial exchange referred to buying or selling any productive inputs or finished products across firms, and manager exchange referred to the movement of directors, supervisors, or other administrators from one firm to another, another signal of interfirm cooperation. The Appendix at the end of this chapter includes additional details about the models and variables included in all tables.

An important first principle that is useful for understanding the formation of exchange relations is that rapid change during transition created informational asymmetries that made it difficult for firms to evaluate the needs, competencies, and reliability of potential trade partners. Buyers and sellers needed to determine whether particular ties were beneficial, but both were reluctant to reveal too much information about their own needs and competencies. The threat of opportunism made firms reluctant to be too forthcoming with information, but the joint hesitation to reveal information made it difficult for firms to assess the reliability of others and often prevented trust from developing. We know from research on organizations in other contexts that when uncertainty is high, managers turn to those with whom they have dealt successfully in the past in order to protect themselves from malfeasance and opportunism (Hagen & Choe, 1998; Powell, 1990). Consistent with these high levels of informational asymmetries, once a pair of firms in China's early business groups had established an exchange tie, they were likely to continue exchanging: the results in Table 7.1 show that the presence of a tie in 1988, the first time period for which we have data, is a very strong and positive predictor of the presence of a tie in 1990, the year in which we measured our dependent variable. That is, the lagged dependent variable is positive and significant in the models in Table 7.1. Stasis or consistency is common in all relationships, including relationships among firms; however, the speed at which China's firms and economy were changing in the late 1980s and early 1990s suggests that firms might have been searching for and finding new trade partners. Our findings suggest that the opposite is true; firms were staying in relationships that they had already established, at least in the relatively short period of 1988–1990. Our findings also suggest that the presence of prior exchange relations was highly correlated with the formation of each type of exchange that we study. In all four models in Table 7.1, the lagged dependent variable is positive and significant, suggesting that firms that exchanged in one period continued to exchange in later periods.

Differences in firm resources and power also affected the formation of exchange relations in the early business groups, and these patterns varied by the type of resource being exchanged. For example, board member exchanges tended to reflect imbalanced power and, therefore, tended to be unidirectional. That is, a less powerful firm (i.e., one that had some sort of dependence on another firm) was likely to be the receiver of a board member and

Table 7.1 Factors Influencing Tie Formation: Logistic Regression of Dyad Ties, 1990

	Board member exchange$_{ij1990}$	Financial exchange$_{ij1990}$	Commercial exchange$_{ij1990}$	Manager exchange$_{ij1990}$
Current ties				
Tie$_{ij1988}$ (lagged DV)	.746***	2.20***	2.23*	3.63**
	(7.94)	(1.43)	(1.37)	(2.43)
Reciprocity (tie$_{ji1990}$)	-1.11**	-.167***	1.46*	.970***
	(2.90)	(4.84)	(1.80)	(4.50)
Financial exchange$_{ij1988}$	1.51**	—	.929***	.533***
	(3.18)		(4.25)	(7.04)
Firm and dyad traits				
Core firm$_i$	.774*	.016**	.846**	.113**
	(1.92)	(2.90)	(2.45)	(1.96)
Core firm$_j$	-.247	-.518**	.138**	-.207***
	(1.00)	(2.00)	(2.23)	(8.51)
Finance company$_i$	.136**	.212***	.182	.352***
	(1.74)	(4.33)	(1.50)	(3.29)
Finance company$_j$	-.213	-.285***	-.255**	-.197***
	(1.04)	(.070)	(1.80)	(6.14)
Distance$_{ij}$	-.174*	-.345**	-.384***	-.295***
	(1.94)	(2.69)	(6.06)	(4.21)
Same city$_{ij}$	.557**	.445	.108**	.160***
	(2.63)	(.532)	(2.40)	(5.95)
Markets and power				
Market development$_i$	.396**	.707***	.419***	.558***
	(2.84)	(5.20)	(4.79)	(2.51)
Market development$_j$	-.425***	-.523**	-.458***	-1.10***
	(5.24)	(2.84)	(4.38)	(5.61)

(*Continued*)

Table 7.1 (Continued)

	Board member exchange$_{ij1990}$	Financial exchange$_{ij1990}$	Commercial exchange$_{ij1990}$	Manager exchange$_{ij1990}$
Social ties				
Same prior bureau$_{ij}$	.105***	.770***	.217**	.156***
	(3.75)	(6.51)	(1.76)	(4.84)
School ties$_{ij}$	.322***	.588*	.102***	.131***
	(3.44)	(1.87)	(3.43)	(4.33)
Two or more industries$_i$	.028**	.755**	.463***	1.70**
	(2.15)	(2.49)	(8.08)	(2.32)
Two or more industries$_j$	-.174*	.814	-.135**	-.136***
	(1.84)	(1.32)	(2.46)	(3.29)
Administrative rank$_i$	.136**	1.18***	.066	.279**
	(2.46)	(8.51)	(1.39)	(1.95)
Administrative rank$_j$	-.321	-.496***	-.596	-.557*
	(.811)	(7.04)	(1.53)	(2.42)
Dyad autoregressive term	.121***	.213**	.107***	.445***
	(4.50)	(2.32)	(8.15)	(4.76)
n	15,193	15,917	16,941	16,111
Pearson χ^2	648.90	843.22	445.82	557.60

Notes: * $p < .05$ ** $p < .01$ *** $p < .001$. Entries are coefficient estimates; absolute t-statistics are in parentheses. All market development, lagged dependent, and reciprocity variables are specified to correspond with the dependent variable (e.g., in models predicting the presence of a manager exchange in 1990, the market variables refer to labor market development and the lagged dependent variable is the presence of a manager exchange in 1988). Included in the regression (but not displayed) are dummy variables for each of the forty business groups, an indicator of whether each firm is in light (versus heavy) industry, the percent of profits remitted to the state, actual profits, and an indicator of each firm's total assets.

not a sender. As an example, if one firm had an ownership stake in another, it might "send" or assign a representative to the board of the firm in which it had a stake. The less powerful firm would be unlikely to reciprocate. For this reason, the results in Table 7.1 show that having a reciprocal tie (i.e. the reciprocity variable) has a negative sign in the board member exchange model: if firm *i* sent a board member to firm *j*, it was unlikely that firm *j* also sent a board member to firm *i*. These early ties are significant because they provided the foundation on which long-term power relations were established. Similarly, the sign on the reciprocity variable is also negative for financial exchange, indicating that financial transfers tended to be unidirectional as well. This pattern reflects resource differences in the early stages of reform that were holdovers from resource differences prior to transition and that may have contributed to ongoing resource differences even as firms became increasingly independent of the state. In contrast, commercial and managerial exchanges tended to be reciprocal in the early business groups: the coefficient for reciprocity is positive and significant in the third and fourth models of Table 7.1, indicating that firms that sent goods or managers to partners also received goods and managers from those partners. This is an important pattern that helped define the structure of the early business groups and that provided the foundation for early market activity as well.

Financial relationships were particularly important in the early years of reform, when independent commercial banks were just emerging and firms were only recently becoming financially independent of the state, and the presence of a financial relationship often correlated with the presence of other types of interfirm ties. For instance, a firm that loaned money to another firm had a financial interest in the borrower and would often send a representative to serve on the borrower's board as well. In Table 7.1, this pattern is evident in the positive association between the presence of an *ij* financial relationship and an *ij* board member exchange. The intuitive interpretation of this is: if firm *i* loaned to firm *j*, firm *i* was also likely to send a board member to firm *j* as well. The relationship between having a financial tie and having commercial or managerial ties was also positive in the early business groups. Unlike board member exchanges, however, commercial and managerial exchanges did not reflect power differentials. Rather, the positive relationship between having a financial tie and having either a commercial or a managerial tie reflects the fact that many interfirm relations were multiplex—or involved many types of exchange—in the early business groups. Having many types of connections with another firm was often useful as firms struggled to find information on the reliability, competencies, and needs of their trade partners (Keister, 2000, 2001); indeed research in other settings shows similar patterns and also demonstrates that multiplex relations can coalesce into relatively stable networks (Gulati, 1995), as the Chinese reformers intended for these early business groups.

Some firms occupied particularly important positions in the early business groups, and their positions in the group affected the likelihood that they were the sender or receiver in emergent exchange relations. The core firm and firms designated as the finance company were particularly important. The core firm (also called a head or parent company) was a central administrative firm but was also quite often most directly involved in the business or industry in which the business group primarily functioned (Keister, 2000). The finance company (*caiwu gongsi*) was a specialized firm that collected and redistributed funds within the group and that also obtained funds through state banks on behalf of member firms. The finance company was sometimes simply a lending organization, but often it was a firm that was more central and had above average resources enabling it to lend. As such, it was more common for the core firm and finance company to be the senders in an exchange relationship than the receivers. For example, the core firm and finance company were more likely to have an ownership stake in another membership firm and, therefore, they were more likely to be the senders of board members; likewise, the core firm and finance company typically had more financial resources and would be more likely to be the lenders than receivers in a financial exchange. In commercial and managerial exchange, again, the more central core firm and financial companies were more likely than other ordinary firms to send than to receive resources. These patterns are evident in the models shown in Table 7.1. In each model, if the firm is a core firm (designated core firm$_i$ in Table 7.1) or the finance company (designated finance company$_i$ in Table 7.1), the coefficient is positive and significant, indicating that this firm was likely to be the sender in the relationship. In contrast, if the firm is a core firm (designated core firm$_j$ in Table 7.1) or the finance company (designated finance company$_j$ in Table 7.1), the coefficient is negative and significant, indicating that this firm was likely to be the receiver in the relationship.

Geographic proximity often affects the structure of social relations, including relations among firms, because physical distance can determine the likelihood of interaction. Geography has become less salient in recent years as electronic communication bridges distances that once seemed insurmountable; however, in the early days of China's reform, geography was an enormous barrier that created challenges that are difficult to imagine today. China's vast size was certainly one challenge, but the lack of physical infrastructure was the more immediate deterrent to long-distance economic relations. Within cities and local areas, roads were relatively well maintained; however, between major municipalities, roads were often impassable by either ordinary or commercial vehicles. Between major municipalities and smaller cities, the conditions were even worse. The state of China's highway system made it extremely difficult to send shipments of goods across large areas, and it also made it very difficult for managers to travel to other areas to negotiate exchange with other firms. Airline service was also limited; there were few long-distance shipping companies, and insuring a shipment was almost impossible as private insurers did not exist. As a result, the early markets that developed were regional markets: firms located in one city tended to deal with others that were located in the same city or region. This reality is reflected in the likelihood that two firms in the early business groups established exchange relations. In all models in Table 7.1, the geographic distance between the cities in which the firms were located is negatively and significantly associated with the likelihood that they established any of the exchange relations we model. Likewise, if two firms were located in the same city, they were significantly more likely to establish exchange relations that two firms located in different cities. Although these geographic hurdles have largely been overcome in China in recent decades, it is useful to consider the role that geography played in shaping both the structure and influence of the early groups.

It has become taken-for-granted in the literature on China's transition that market development—and variations across regions in development— affected a good deal about how reform unfolded (Clarke, 2003; Guthrie, 1997; Peng, 2004; Walder, 2003). Accordingly, market development was an important correlate of early interfirm relations. Market development in China was gradual and uneven because reformers favored coastal and southern regions and because entrepreneurial firms in some areas quickly took advantage of new freedoms (Jefferson & Xu, 1991). Firms in developed regions had access to more resources and were better able to become suppliers, whereas firms in less developed areas were more likely to become borrowers and receivers. Yet access to resources had significance, for both buyers and sellers, beyond simple availability. High levels of uncertainty encouraged firms to find trade partners with whom they could form stable relations. Firms that needed resources valued suppliers that would be around in the future, and firms that had access to resources were able to take advantage of this position to cultivate dependence on their products that would persist in the future. To a potential buyer, firms in developed areas appeared to be more reliable, long-term partners because they were more likely to have access to resources in the future. There is even some evidence that managers were willing to pay a higher price to get resources from such firms because of the security the relation provided (Keister, 2001). Moreover, trading with a firm that was likely to be around in the future could reduce the cost of searching for new trade partners, which were particularly high in developing markets. To potential suppliers, the control of scarce resources created opportunities to reduce risk and to ensure future exchange by fostering dependence on their products (Cook, 1977; Pfeffer & Salancik, 1978). Resource access was particularly important in China given its legacy of supply shortages, and managers quickly learned to exploit resource advantages for security and long-term advantage by cultivating alliances with less advantaged firms. In the early stages of reform, relatively soft budget constraints partially assuaged concerns about compensation from firms with limited resources and further encouraged those in developed regions to exploit firms with limited access to resources. The patterns in Table 7.1 are consistent with these ideas; that is, firms located in developed areas were more likely to become suppliers and those in less developed regions were more likely to become buyers.

The role that social relations (*guanxi*) play in organizing economic activity in China has been well documented (Bian, 1997; Kipnis, 1997; Yan, 1996). During the highly uncertain early transition years, the influence of *guanxi* was particularly salient in the formation of economic relations (Bian, 1997; Kipnis, 1997). We already discussed the role that prior ties (i.e., ties in the prior year) and reciprocity played in early exchange relations in China's business groups, but other forms of social capital were also strongly associated with the formation of interfirm exchange ties. For example, managers who had personal social capital were likely to create ties because of the certainty that comes with such a relationship. In the models shown in Table 7.1, we measured social capital in two ways. First, we controlled for whether the firms were in the same administrative bureau prior to reform, a connection that would have generated social capital between managers of the firms. Second, we controlled for whether the managers had attended the same schools. The models show that both variables are strongly, positively associated with the presence of all four types of exchange ties. Notably, these and all the effects we show in Table 7.1 hold even when other important influences on exchange ties are held constant. These models are fixed effects models, thus they include dummy variables for each of the business groups. In addition, we control for whether each firm is in light or heavy industry and the percent of profits that the firms remitted to the state. Both of these variables indicate the degree of state involvement in the firm. We also controlled for firm size measures, including total profits and total assets. The strong significance of social capital despite these controls is consistent with what we know about the role of *guanxi* in China's reform and suggests that there was noticeable influence of pre-reform ties on the ties that emerged at the start of reform.

In sum, our findings underscore the unique processes that lead firms to establish lending and trade relations with each other inside business groups in the early stages of reform. Our evidence suggests that the rapid change that accompanied reform created informational asymmetries that affected how firms exchanged. We showed that once a pair of firms established an exchange tie, they were likely to continue exchanging, but that even with prior ties controlled, differences in firm resources and power also affected the formation of exchange relations. In addition, financial exchange was very important in the early years of reform, and having a financial relationship was associated with establishing other exchange relations. In addition, the core firm and the group's finance company were more often the senders in exchange ties, and geographic proximity encouraged exchange. Finally, our findings underscored the importance of market development and prior social relations in firm behaviors and processes early in reform. Although the transition context is unique, these results also speak to the process by which interfirm relations emerge, and thus to the general process by which social structures come into being. The somewhat unique transition context required some modifications of existing theory, but much of what we know of organizations from other contexts remained true.

Chinese Business Groups and Firm Profits

China's policy makers encouraged the formation of business groups, at least in part, to help firms adapt and thrive during and following transition. Certain group structures were supposed to protect firms from competition, create economies of scale, and enhance firm performance. The notion that similar business groups were instrumental in the economic successes of Japan and South Korea encouraged China's reformers, and early commentators provided anecdotal evidence that there were advantages to certain business group structures (Shanghai Association for the Study of Business Groups, 1995). In the remainder of this chapter, we consider two related questions. First, we discuss the relationship between business group structure and the financial performance of member firms in the early stages of reform. We studied all early business groups and look at whether variations in organization across groups was related to firm profits in the manner reformers imagined it would be. We focused on business group members in order to isolate the relative importance of various structural elements, and we excluded firms that were not business group members because there was no comparable structure to study. We were not selecting firms on the dependent variable because there was considerable variation in our outcome (profits) across firms. Additional detail on this sample is available in the introduction to this chapter and in other printed sources (Keister, 2000, 2001). Next, we used our second dataset to study whether the benefits of group membership were evident in the mid- and late-1990s as reform progressed. Using this data, we looked at whether group membership improved firm profits. In this portion of our discussion, we study SOEs and non-SOEs separately because by the mid-1990s there were sufficient numbers of enterprises conducting business outside traditional state boundaries, and it is likely that the processes whereby state- and non-state-controlled firms generated processes were different.

Business Group Traits and Firm Outcomes in the Early Transition Years

The interfirm ties that we studied in the previous section defined much about the groups, and some aspects of the structure of those relationships facilitated firm profitmaking early in reform. For example, the density of interfirm ties within the groups was positively associated with firm profits. Density is the proportion of the potential connections that are actual connections; a potential tie is one that could exist even if it does not (i.e., two firms could have a financial connection because they are in the same business group), and an actual tie is one that really exists (i.e., two firms have a financial connection). Thus, density is a trait of the group: if most firms were connected with most other firms, density would be very high. Conceptually, high network density implies a closely connected group of firms that potentially have the benefits that inter-actor connections can generate. For firms facing an emerging and rapidly changing economic environment, connections with other firms had the potential to be conduits for information about things like innovative managerial strategies and potential new markets; of course, these connections also carried tangible goods and resources, such as financial assistance, buyers for output, and suppliers of productive inputs.

Interlocking directorates were a particularly important type of interfirm tie in the early business groups. Interlocking directorates are not new to China; they existed in government ministries before reform when the same state representative was assigned to the boards of more than one firm. In the business groups, interlocks occurred when member firms acquired shares in each other and placed representatives on each other's boards. The interlocks had the same functional form as interlocks in other contexts (i.e., an individual occupies a seat on more than one board of directors); however, unlike in the U.S., where interlocks are both a source of information and a form of co-optation or monitoring, interlocks in China primarily function as an information source for the interlocked firms. The interlocks allowed information about technological advances, market opportunities, innovative strategies, and so on to pass among firms in the group. Empirical research on the relationship between interlocks and firm performance in the U.S., however, has been inconclusive largely because the most interlocked firms are those in financial decline (Palmer, 1983, 1986; Stearns & Mizruchi, 1987). In contrast, because the division of labor among financial institutions was different in China, interlocks were positively associated with firm performance in the early stages of reform. As Table 7.2, Model 1 shows, firms with interlocking directorates had higher profits early in reform (i.e., this is a firm-level variable). Similarly, as Model 2 shows, the higher the

Table 7.2 Business Group Structure and Firm Profits: GLS Regression, 1990

	Model 1	Model 2	Model 3
Profits (1988; lagged DV)	0.039	1.52	0.019*
	(1.64)	(1.14)	(1.89)
Group structure			
Financial exchange density	3.48***	3.80***	0.034***
	(8.75)	(5.92)	(3.14)
Commercial exchange density	0.002***	.034***	.0104***
	(8.13)	(4.98)	(4.30)

	Model 1	Model 2	Model 3
Manager exchange density	0.042*	0.053**	.011***
	(2.10)	(2.42)	(3.25)
Board exchange density	1.39	1.53	0.137**
	(0.980)	(.587)	(2.76)
Had interlocking directorates	1.14**	—	—
	(2.61)		
Percent of firms with interlocks	—	1.41***	—
		(3.22)	
Had a finance company	—	—	1.37**
			(1.96)
Had an R&D branch	0.380*	0.641*	.272**
	(1.44)	(1.89)	(2.35)
Group control variables			
Number of 2nd tier subsidiaries	5.29***	3.193***	3.50***
	(4.11)	(3.81)	(5.56)
Number of 3rd tier subsidiaries	0.014*	0.147	1.73***
	(1.75)	(1.49)	(3.55)
Firm control variables			
(log) total assets	0.002	0.053	0.305
	(0.68)	(0.89)	(0.93)
Thousands of workers	0.190	0.014	0.004
	(0.34)	(0.59)	(0.44)
Core firm	0.075***	4.46***	3.99***
	(4.11)	(4.79)	(3.92)
Total sales in the group	0.016***	0.844***	0.346***
	(2.55)	(7.42)	(3.13)
Adjusted R^2	0.243	0.248	0.219

Notes: * $p < .05$ ** $p < .01$ *** $p < .001$. Monetary values are in 100 million 1990 yuan ($12.5 million). Entries are GLS estimates of metric regression coefficients; absolute t-statistics are in parentheses. Included in the regression (but not displayed) are dummy variables for having a technology center (a state-supported research division), being in a protected industry, percent of profits remitted to the state, and location in same province as core firm. Table 7.2 contains generalized least squares (GLS) models of 1990 firm profits using 1988 measures of group structure and other variables as predictors; in these models, the firm is the unit of analysis. The first four variables shown in the table are measures of the density of financial, commercial, manager, and board member exchange density in the groups; in these models, density is calculated within a group because cross-group ties were rare early in reform and measuring potential ties outside of the groups would be extremely difficult. In addition, it is realistic to imagine that firms could have exchanged with others in their groups, whereas cross-group exchange was less likely in the late 1980s and early 1990s. The models in Table 7.2 vary by the type of interlock variable used (discussed below); these are not nested models. These models show that all forms of network density are positively and significantly associated with firm profits, other influences held constant. This important pattern underscores the significant role that some business groups played in China's early transition. Only two of the coefficients for our density variables are not significant: in Models 1 and 2, board member exchange density is not significant. However, in both models, the coefficients are positive and border on significant. The lack of significance in these models may reflect slightly smaller actual ties for board member exchange than for other forms of network density.

percentage of firms in the group with interlocks, the higher the profits of the focal firm (i.e., this is a group-level variable). We do not control for both the firm- and group-level interlock variables simultaneously because they are too highly correlated.

The finance company in China's business groups also facilitated firm performance at least in part because, in the late 1980s, financial markets were unable to distribute funds efficiently, leaving many firms without necessary capital. Firms that were members of some business groups had access to additional financing through the group's finance company. Reformers originally experimented with finance companies in the central industries and later in most other industries. Initially the activities of the finance companies were not monitored, but as their activity expanded regulations were implemented to control lending practices. The finance company enabled the member firms to engage in research and development, to better manage investments both within the group (i.e., investments in other firms that are members of the same group) and outside of the group, and, if necessary, to meet short-term operating expenses. As a result, firms in Chinese business groups with finance companies had advantages over firms in groups that did not have finance companies, and as Table 7.2 shows, these advantages were evident in higher firm profits. In Model 3, we control for a group-level indicator that the group had a finance company; this variable is positive and significant, indicating that firms in groups with a finance company did, indeed, have higher profits than firms in groups without a finance company. We use a separate model (Model 3) to demonstrate the effect of the finance company because there is a positive correlation between having interlocking directorates and having a finance company. Our models highlight the individual effects of these variables.

Finally, being a member of a business group with a research and development (R&D) branch was also positively associated with higher firm profits. As the name implies, the R&D branch was intended to provide forward-looking research and development services to member firms in order to encourage innovation and facilitate movement into new markets. The R&D branches were usually separate organizations that created economies of scale in the groups: individual firms did not have to engage in their own research, which would potentially have duplicated the R&D work occurring in other firms. Instead, each firm could focus on their core competencies and leave R&D to those with more expertise in the area. The advantages of this strategy are evident in the models shown in Table 7.2: the variable indicating that the firm was a member of a group with an R&D branch is positively and significantly associated with firm profits in all three models. Importantly, all of the findings shown in Table 7.2 are significant despite the various control variables we also included. In particular, all models controlled for size and vertical integration (group-level) by including indicators of the numbers of second- and third-tier subsidiaries; all models also include controls for firm traits, including total assets, number of workers, whether the firm was the core firm, and total sales in the groups. The strong associations between business group structure and firm profits despite these controls underscores the importance of the groups in shaping early firm outcomes that likely contributed to China's early growth and development.

In sum, our findings suggest that some structural traits in early business groups were correlated with higher profits for members of those groups. Network density—including financial, commercial, manager, and board member exchange density—was positively associated with firm profits. That is, in highly dense networks, firms were advantaged perhaps because these networks provided information about innovative managerial strategies and potential new markets that might otherwise have been lacking at this stage of reform. Similarly, in groups with interlocking directorates, firms had higher profits, a finding that is consistent with western organization theory but that has not been found in western research on firms. The difference in China's early reform years is that uncertainty was high enough and experience with market exchange was low enough that the connections created by interlocks may have had a more clear effect, as western research suggests they might. Similarly, in groups with a finance company and an R&D branch, firms were more profitable. In both cases, the group provided a service that would have been difficult to find outside the group, even in the early 1990s. Taken together, these results suggest that there were advantages to membership in some business groups, and these advantages may have undergirded the rapid growth that characterized China's early transition. Ideally, we would have data on these firms for multiple years after the reform, which would allow us to track their progress and change as reform progressed. Although we do have additional data on business groups—we discuss it in the next section—the rapid pace at which firms and business groups changed in the 1990s prevented us from following these firms.

Business Group Traits and Firm Outcomes in Later Transition Years

As China's transition progressed and the country's economic structure and participation in the world economy changed, the role of the business groups also changed. As markets developed and managers quickly became accustomed to market exchange, uncertainty declined and Chinese firms began to resemble western firms in many ways. In addition, particularly after China's entrance into the World Trade Organization in 2001, both managers and state reformers became much more focused on competition with foreign firms. Although business groups still existed, their role changed and, perhaps more importantly, the effect of business group membership on firm outcomes changed. Indeed, evidence from our second dataset shows that by the middle 1990s, business group membership was negatively associated with firm profits. Table 7.3 includes four GLS models of firm profits: two models for 1994 profits and two models for 1999 profits. In each year, we modeled profits separately for SOEs and non-SOEs. We acknowledge that we are asking a slightly different question here than in the previous section, where we studied the relationship between business group structure and firm performance; however, the dramatically different patterns evident in Table 7.3 indicate that this change in focus is warranted. That is, each model in Table 7.3 shows that business group membership is negatively and significantly associated with firm profits. Cox's proportional hazards models suggest that the apparent increase in strength between 1994 and 1999 is also real. This implies that the negative effect grew over time. Our models control for several other traits that also tend to affect firm financial performance, including the level of subordination (administrative control); firm traits, such as size and age; and manager traits, such as party position, age, and education level. Similar to patterns seen in research on western

Table 7.3 Business Group Membership and Firm Profits: GLS Regression, 1994/1999

	1994		1999	
	SOEs	Non-SOEs	SOEs	Non-SOEs
Business group member	−.247*	−.152*	−.457***	−.165***
	(.140)	(.092)	(.017)	(.061)
Subordination				
City	−.302*	—	−.275	—
	(.130)		(.332)	
County	−.312	−.050	.057	.094
	(.266)	(.095)	(.093)	(.165)
Firm traits				
Assets (logged)	.201**	.205***	1.073***	.095
	(.070)	(.035)	(.185)	(.057)
Age	.002	−.014**	.009	.011
	(.004)	(.006)	(.010)	(.010)
No. workers (thousands)	.063***	−.000	.319***	.109*
	(.017)	(.000)	(.047)	(.048)
Manager traits				
Party official	.025	.027	−.180	−.074
	(.733)	(.089)	(1.862)	(.155)
Age	−.006	−.007	.023	.016
	(.010)	(.007)	(.026)	(.012)
Secondary school	.025	−.003	.245	−.077
	(.113)	(.070)	(.286)	(.121)
Post-secondary school	.141	.050	.817	−.014
	(.193)	(.147)	(.490)	(.256)
Adjusted R²	.145***	.171***	.350***	.224***

Notes: * p < .05 ** p < .01 *** p < .001. GLS estimates of metric regression coefficients; standard errors are in parentheses. N = 433 firms. These are different firms than those included in previous analyses in this chapter. Included in the regression (but not displayed) are dummy variables for industry, province, being foreign-located, and percent of profits remitted to the state.

firms, firm size, measured as either total assets or total number of workers, is the strongest correlate of firm profits. Of course, the relatively small sample size in this data (n = 433) makes statistical significance more rare. Yet the small sample size makes it even more interesting that the indicator of business group membership is statistically significant. Indeed, the business group member variable is comparable in size and significance to firm size measures, albeit in the opposite direction.

What factors might explain the negative effect of business group membership in the 1990s? Reduced uncertainty and growing competitiveness are the most likely causes. As markets became more established, firms no longer needed the protection that business groups provided. Financial markets were more developed by the mid-1990s, and banking reform provided additional certainty and funds that allowed firms to acquire capital outside the business groups. Labor markets were developing rapidly, providing opportunities for hiring from multiple sources that, again, made the business groups less necessary. Managers had also gained considerable experience with markets, and the stronger, more effective managers found that they could function more effectively outside the business groups. Although we do not have longitudinal data on the same firms, it is likely that the more competitive firms left the business groups, leaving their weaker counterparts to reduce the average performance in the group. Finally, because our models compare SOEs and newer, smaller, more nimble non-SOEs, the findings suggest that the newer firms that were not burdened with strong government control and that did not have a history of functioning like bureaucratic entities performed much better than state-connected firms. These findings are not conclusive, and future research could usefully use historical and contemporary data together to explore in more detail the changing role of China's business groups.

Conclusion

We had two objectives in this chapter. First we explored the factors that affected the formation of lending and trade relations in Chinese business groups in the early stages of reform. Second, we examined the effect of business groups in China's transition economy on the financial performance of firms. To study the second issue, we first looked at the relationship between business group structure and the profits of member firms in the late 1980s and early 1990s; we then looked briefly at the relationship between business group membership and firm profits in 1994 and 1999. We started by observing that one of the most profound components of China's industrial reform has been the reorganization of firms into business groups, a process that began in the mid-1980s. We argued that the factors that influenced the formation of ties in these groups are important to understanding the emergent structure of the groups and ultimately China's new economy. We also proposed that using multiple indicators of group structure—including indicators of the presence and predominance of interlocking directorates, informal finance arrangements, and the hierarchical organization of the group—would clarify the role that business groups play in determining firm performance in China and would also inform understanding of the importance of these groups and interorganizational relations more generally. Finally, we drew an important distinction between early and later development in studying the relationship between group structure and firm financial performance. We found that certain elements of group structure benefitted firms early in reform, but as markets became more stable, group membership appears to have become detrimental to firm wellbeing.

Because conditions in China were similar in many ways to those in other transition economies, these results provide important information about the process of economic transformation more generally. Relatively high uncertainty, changing sources of uncertainty, market failure, managers who are not accustomed to markets, and expanding competition were prevalent in China, as they are in many transition economies. The strong but declining role of the state, the continued importance of bureaucratic power, and hardening budget constraints were also typical of a transition economy. Our findings suggest that regional differences in market development during transition may be institutionalized and thus shape economic exchange after transition. Similarly, the continued importance of bureaucratic power during transition may cause the post-transition economic structure to reflect pre-reform advantages. Perhaps most consequential for understanding transition economies, however, is the finding that social ties are important predictors of economic relations. Although the transition context is unique, these results also speak to the process by which interfirm relations emerge, and thus to the general process by which social structures come into being. The somewhat unique transition context required some modifications of existing theory, but much of what we know of organizations from other contexts remained true. Our results highlight the critical role that social relations play in the formation of economic ties, particularly under uncertainty. The results also confirm in a unique setting the notion that external connections decline in salience and internal relations become more important as interfirm networks develop.

Appendix

Research Methods

To study the ideas discussed in this chapter, we used two datasets (described in the introduction to this chapter) and two sets of analyses: (1) logistic regression models of the presence of absence of an interfirm tie using 1988–1990 data on all business groups in non-sensitive industries, and (2) generalized least squares analyses of firm profits using the same 1988–1990 data as above and a second 1994–1999 dataset that includes 800 firms.

Table 7.1 Details: Logistic Regression
Analyses of Interfirm Ties

In analyses of the formation of an interfirm tie, the unit of analysis was the interfirm dyad, that is, the $n = \sum_{i=1}^{40} n_{it} \left(n_{it} - 1 \right)$ ordered pairs of the 535 member firms within the 40 largest business groups (40 separate networks) with every other firm in the same group in each time period. This is equivalent to the n (n–1) = 285,690 dyads minus dyads containing firms in different groups. We included only business group members because our focus is voluntary, repeated relations within these groups. Firms outside business groups did develop lending and trade ties, but the ties they formed seldom coalesced into the close-knit relations that are characteristic of relations in business groups. We included business group members whether they had ties or not; because membership was not defined by having ties, some firms were not connected to any other firms. Our interest was in the off-diagonal cells in a matrix of the 40 distinct networks, or each of 40 (n X n) matrices at five points in time where the rows ($i = 1, \ldots n$) were senders in a relation and the columns ($j = 1, \ldots n$) were receivers. We arrayed these as column vectors (p) such that p = {1,2; 1,3; . . . 1,n; 2,1; 2,3; . . . 2,n; . . . n – 1,1;n – 1,2; . . . n – 1,n} and modeled the likelihood of an (i, j) tie such that:

$$y_{ijt} = \beta y_{jit} + \alpha y_{ijt\text{-}1} + \lambda_i{'}P_i + \lambda_j{'}P_j + \pi_{ij}{'}R_{ij} + \gamma{'}_iX_i + \gamma{'}_jX_j + \rho Wy_{ij} + u_{ijk} + \varepsilon_{ij}$$

where y_{ijt} was a directional tie from firm i to firm j; y_{jit} was a reciprocal tie from firm j to firm i; and $y_{ijt\text{-}1}$ was a lagged tie from i to j. The dependent variable was a dichotomous indicator that firm i sent to firm j in time t. P_i and P_j were column vectors of province-level variables for provinces in which firms i and j were located. R_{ij} was a vector of dyad-level variables; X_i and X_j were vectors of firm-level variables. Wy_{ij} was a dyad autoregressive term included to control bias that might occur because some dyads contained the same firms. $Wy_{ij} = \Sigma_p W_{pq} y_q$ where p and q were dyads and p ≠ q. W_{pq} = 1/n_p if dyads p and q shared a common firm and 0 otherwise. Wy_{ij} was the mean of the dependent variable over all dyads that included firm i or firm j (excluding ij). The terms β, α, λ', $\pi_{ij}{'}$, $\gamma{'}_i$, $\gamma{'}_j$, and ρ were coefficients to be estimated. We used province-level variables and error components to model regional effects; u_{ijk} and ε_{ij} were the region-specific and dyad-specific error terms, respectively. We used fixed effects to control for group-level variation (i.e., 39 group dummy variables), and we estimated generalized linear mixed (pseudo-likelihood) equations that allowed the decomposition of the error term into its fixed and random components.

The dependent variables were dichotomous indicators of the presence of each of four cross-firm ties in the business group in 1990: board member exchange, financial exchange, commercial exchange, and manager exchange. We coded a tie as existing if it occurred more than three times in 1990. Swapping board members was common in the early stages of reform and signaled a degree of social proximity and cooperation between firms. Financial exchange refers to lending or borrowing funds, a practice that was increasingly common in the early stages of reform as firms needed capital and banks were just becoming somewhat independent of the state. Commercial exchange referred to buying or selling any productive inputs or finished products across firms, and manager exchange referred to the movement of directors, supervisors, or other administrators from one firm to another, another signal of interfirm cooperation.

The lagged dependent variable, y_{ijt}, was equivalent to the dependent variable, measured in the prior time period (i.e., 1988). A significant positive estimate of the α coefficient indicated that if firm i sent the resource to firm j in one time period, it was more likely to send that resource in the next period. The reciprocal term, y_{jit}, indicated whether firm j also sent the resource to firm i; a positive estimate of β indicated reciprocity. We measured firm characteristics (i.e., being a core firm or a finance company) for both firm i and firm j. A significant positive estimate of γ'_i indicated that the greater the value of X_i, the more likely firm i was to be the sender in the dyadic tie. A positive γ'_j indicates that the greater the value of X_j, the more likely firm j was to be the receiver. We also controlled regional characteristics as traits of both firm i and firm j. A positive estimate of λ'_i indicates that as the value of P_i increased, i was more likely to be the sender. A positive estimate of λ'_j indicates that as P_j increased, j was more likely to be the receiver. A positive estimate of π_{ij}' indicated that attributes of this pairing made a tie more likely.

We measured market development separately for each dependent variable to capture variations in market expansion for the corresponding resource. In the personnel tie models, we measured labor market development as the number of individuals in the province employed in the private sector as a proportion of those employed in the public sector. In the commodity tie models, we indicated commodity market development as the number of private and collective firms as a percentage of the number of state-owned firms. In the financial tie models, we measured financial market development as deposits of foreign banks as a percentage of total bank deposits. We used province-level indicators because municipal data (often collected by various agencies) are less accessible and less internally consistent. Moreover, given China's size and regional variation, marked province-level differences correspond well to differences in opportunities and constraints (Nee, 1996). We followed Walder (1992) in using an ordinal coding of administrative rank. We used managers' reports to sum within each dyad (1) the number of interfirm (i.e., across the dyad) pairs of managers who were classmates in college, (2) the number of interfirm pairs of managers with family, external professional, or other external social connections, (3) an indicator of whether the firms had a lending or trade relation before the business groups formed, and (4) an indicator of whether the firms were in the same administrative bureau before reform.

Table 7.2 Details: Generalized Least Squares
Regression of Firm Profits, 1990

In analyses of firm performance, the unit of analysis is the firm. To estimate the effects of group structure (in 1988) on firm profits (in 1990), we
used random effects feasible generalized least squares regression equations.
The random effects equations decompose the error term to adjust for auto-
correlation arising from common firm membership in the same group and
inter-temporal correlation of error terms. Because many of the group-level
indicators are present in the same groups (e.g., groups with a finance company often have interlocks as well), the test variables are highly correlated.
Therefore, we display separate equations for each set of test variables (these
are not nested models). The equations are of the form:

$$Y_{1990i} = \alpha + \beta'x_i + \gamma' Y_{1988i} + \lambda'G_i + \varepsilon_{it}$$

where: Y_{1990i} is 1990 profits, α is the intercept, x_i is a vector of group- and
firm-level control variables, Y_{1988i} is a lagged dependent variable, G_i is a
vector of group structure variables that test the hypotheses, and ε_i is the
stochastic error term.

We included a lagged dependent variable (i.e., 1988 profits) in all models;
this facilitated interpretation of other variables in terms of change in the
dependent variable over the two-year period. We measured the density of
ties (i.e., financial, commercial, manager, and board member) as the proportion of potential ties that are actual ties. We included two interlocking
directorates indicators: a dummy variable indicating the presence of interlocks in the business group and a continuous variable indicating the percentage of firms in the business groups involved in the interlocks (both derived
from lists of board members for each firm in 1988). We also included three
variables related to the presence of a finance company: a dummy variable
indicating the presence of a finance company and separate dummy variables
for the core firm in groups with and without a finance company. We also
included an indicator that the group had a branch firm devoted to research
and development (R&D) to indicate investment in future business and forward thinking. We used group-level indicators of the number of second- and
third-tier subsidiaries to control for size and vertical integration. Second-tier
subsidiaries are firms in which a member firm (but not the core firm) has
ownership rights; third-tier subsidiaries are firms in which a second tier sub-
sidiary (but not the core firm) has an ownership interest.

We also controlled total assets and workforce size, whether the focal firm
was the core firm, and total sales to other firms in the group. Eliminating the
core firm from the analyses did not change the results substantively. Finally,
we controlled for having a technology center (i.e., a state-supported research
division), being in a protected industry (e.g., defense), the percent of profits
that were remitted to the state, and location of the focal firm in the same

province as the core firm. A technology center was a subsidized research organization; firms with technology centers (generally those dubbed "high tech") had a portion of their expenses for technological research subsidized and received tax breaks of 30–50 percent. The power, steel, iron, automotive, communications, household appliance, and petrochemical industries were central industries, and firms in these industries received state assistance more readily. Very few firms remitted profits by 1988 and 1990. Approximately 7 percent of the firms were located in the same province as the core firm; this low number is not surprising because there was considerable overlap between group membership and membership in administrative bureaus that existed prior to reform and that were not limited by geography.

Table 7.3 Details: Generalized Least Squares Regression of Firm Profits, 1994 and 1999

To estimate the effects of business group membership on 1994 and 1999 profits, we conducted slightly different analyses. We again used feasible generalized least squares regression, but our models included different variables to reflect the behaviors and processes that were relevant later in reform. The dependent variable was firm profits, and we estimated separate equations for SOEs and non-SOEs because different processes likely operated for these firms. In contrast to the models of 1990 firm profits (Table 7.2), the only business group trait we controlled for in these models was a dummy variable for business group membership. Membership was negatively associated with profits, and no other group traits were significant in these later models. To avoid model misspecification, we did not include the large list of group traits included in Table 7.2. However, we did control for several other firm and manager traits in these models. In particular, we controlled the level of subordination (city or county) for SOEs and county only for non-SOEs to reflect the range of possibilities represented in our data. We controlled for firm assets, age, and number of workers to reflect firm size. We also included dummy variables for industry, province, being foreign-located, and the percent of profits remitted to the state.

This data also included detailed information about managers, and we controlled for relevant traits to hold constant the effect of the manager on firm profits. In particular, we included a dummy variable indicating whether the manager was a party official and a continuous measure of the manager's age. Finally, we included two dummy variables to indicate the manager's highest level of education: a measure that the manager completed secondary school or post-secondary school.

References

Amsden, A. H. (1989). *Asia's Next Giant: South Korea and Late Industrialization*. New York: Oxford University Press.

Bian, Y. (1997). Bringing strong ties back in: Indirect ties, network bridges, and job searches in China. *American Sociological Review*, 62, 366–385.

Clarke, D. C. (2003). Corporate governance in China: An overview. *China Economic Review, 14,* 494–507.

Cook, K. S. (1977). Exchange and power in networks of interorganizational relationships. *Sociological Quarterly, 18,* 62–82.

Dai, J., & Li, G. (1988). *Shanghai Business Groups: Establishment and Development (Shanghai Qiye Jituan: Jianli Yu Fazhan).* Shanghai: Shanghai Kexue Puji Chubanshe.

Fields, K. J. (1995). *Enterprise and the State in Korea and Taiwan.* Ithaca, NY: Cornell University Press.

Goto, A. (1982). Business groups in a market economy. *European Economic Review, 19,* 53–70.

Gulati, R. (1995). Social structure and alliance formation: A longitudinal analysis. *Administrative Science Quarterly, 40,* 619–652.

Guthrie, D. (1997). Between markets and politics: Organizational responses to reform in China. *American Journal of Sociology, 102,* 1258–1304.

Hagen, J. M., & Choe, S. (1998). Trust in Japanese interfirm relations: Institutional sanctions matter. *Academy of Management Review, 23,* 589–600.

Hamilton, G. G. (1991). *Business Networks and Economic Development in East and Southeast Asia.* Hong Kong: Centre of Asian Studies, University of Hong Kong.

Jefferson, G. H., & Rawski, T. G.(1994). Enterprise reform in Chinese industry. *Journal of Economic Perspectives, 8,* 47–70.

Jefferson, G. H., & Xu, W. (1991). The impact of reform on socialist enterprises in transition: Structure, conduct, and performance in Chinese industry. *Journal of Comparative Economics, 15,* 45–64.

Keister, L. A. (1998). Engineering growth: Business group structure and firm performance in China's transition economy. *American Journal of Sociology, 104,* 404–440.

Keister, L. A. (1999). Chinese business groups: The role of conglomerates in the remaking of China's economy. *Journal of Business in Developing Nations, 4,* 215–239.

Keister, L. A. (2000). *Chinese Business Groups: The Structure and Impact of Interfirm Relations During Economic Development.* New York: Oxford University Press.

Keister, L. A. (2001). Exchange structures in transition: A longitudinal analysis of lending and trade relations in Chinese business groups. *American Sociological Review, 66,* 336–360.

Kipnis, A. B. (1997). *Producing Guanxi: Sentiment, Self, and Subculture in a North China Village.* Durham, NC: Duke University Press.

Li, Z. (1995). *Modern Chinese Business Groups (Zhongguo Xiandai Qiye Jituan).* Beijing: Zhongguo Shangye Ban.

Lincoln, J. R., Gerlach, M. L., & Takahashi, P. (1992). *Keiretsu* networks in the Japanese economy: A dyad analysis of intercorporate ties. *American Sociological Review, 57,* 561–585.

Mascarenhas, B. (1989). Strategic group dynamics. *Academy of Management Journal, 32,* 333–352.

Nee, V. (1996). The emergence of a market society: Changing mechanisms of stratification in China. *American Journal of Sociology, 101,* 908–949.

Numazaki, I. (1986). Networks of Taiwanese big business. *Modern China, 12,* 487–534.

Palmer, D. (1983). Broken ties: Interlocking directorates and intercorporate coordination. *Administrative Science Quarterly, 28,* 40–55.

Peng, M. W. (2004). Outside directors and firm performance during institutional transitions. *Strategic Management Journal, 25,* 453–471.

People's Republic of China (PRC), Central Committee of the Communist Party (CPC). (1984). *Regulations of the Central Committee of the Communist Party* of China Regarding Economic System Reform (Zhongguo Zhongyang Guanyu Jingji Tizhi Gaige de Guiding). Beijing: Central Committee of the Communist Party of the PRC.

People's Republic of China, State Council (PRC). (1980). *Provisional Regulations Regarding the Promotion of Economic Alliances (Guanyu Tuidong Jingji Lianhe de Zanxing Guiding).* Beijing: PRC State Council.

Pfeffer, J., & Salancik, G. R. (1978). *The External Control of Organizations: A Resource Dependence Perspective.* New York: Harper and Row.

Powell, W. W. (1990). Neither market nor hierarchy: Network forms of organization. *Research in Organizational Behavior, 12,* 295–336.

Reform. (1993). *Zhongguo Jingji Tizhi Gaige Nianjian (Yearbook of China's Economic System Reform).* Beijing: Gaige.

Shanghai Association for the Study of Business Groups. (1995). *The Shanghai Business Groups (Shanghai Qiye Jituan Fenghua Lu).* Shanghai: Shanghai Kexue Jishu Chubanshe.

Stearns, L. B., & Mizruchi, M. S. (1987). Broken tie reconstruction and the functions of interorganizational interlocks: A reexamination. *Administrative Science Quarterly, 31,* 533–538.

Steers, R. M., Shin, Y. K., & Ungson, G. R. (1989). *The Chaebol: Korea's New Industrial Might.* New York: Harper and Row.

Walder, A. G. (1992). Property rights and stratification in socialist redistributive economies. *American Sociological Review, 57,* 524–539.

Walder, A. G. (2003). Elite opportunity in transitional economies. *American Sociological Review, 68,* 899–916.

Xie, C. (1996). *The Complete Book of Enterprise Property Rights (Qiye Chanquan Shiwu Quanshu).* Beijing: Jingji Ribao Chubanshe.

Yan, Y. (1996). *The Flow of Gifts: Reciprocity and Social Networks in a Chinese Village.* Stanford, CA: Stanford University Press.

8 The State-Owned Asset Management System and the Performance of SOEs

Introduction

China's transition from a centrally planned socialist economy to one with increasing market liberalization has made it the second largest economy in the world. The remarkable economic growth has often led observers to believe that the major momentum of this growth is the rise of private enterprises and to assume that the country's economic system has been transformed into a capitalist economy dominated by private enterprises (OECD, 2000). Proponents of these beliefs can find many facts to support their point. The process of market institution has made steady progress during the past few decades. The contribution of the non-state sector to the nation's GDP has increased dramatically. The factor market, including the markets for financial capital, raw material, and talent, has become more competitive (Fan, Wang, & Zhu, 2011). The product market has been increasingly driven by market mechanisms and the prices of most goods are now set by market forces instead of administrative control. The party's ideological discrimination against private ownership also weakened, and now private entrepreneurs are welcome to join the party (Naughton, 2008). All this evidence leads pro-market observers to conclude that the Chinese government is loosening its control and institutional connection to the economic system and reducing its reliance on state-owned enterprises.

However, such a conclusion is wrong. It is true that much of the growth is driven by non-state-owned enterprises, including foreign-invested enterprises operating in China and China's domestic private enterprises. Despite years of economic reform, state ownership remains significant in the economy. Many of the SOEs are now among the world's largest and most profitable corporations. They are the major entities that carry out the nation's going-global strategy, which aims to enlarge global markets, exploit natural resources abroad, attain higher technologies, and enhance the corporate brand values of Chinese enterprises (Bai, Lu, & Tao, 2006). The size of the state sector remains significant in the entire economy. Despite the significant privatization reform, SOEs still provide a quarter of the employment opportunities in urban areas and contribute more than one third of the nation's

GDP. As of 2013, SOEs controlled 104.1 trillion yuan worth of state assets nationwide. Central SOEs have a total of 48.6 trillion yuan worth of assets, of which, the SASAC controlled 34.9 trillion, the Ministry of Finance managed 12 trillion, and other central ministries controlled an additional 1.6 trillion. Local governments at various levels controlled 55.5 trillion, of which, provincial governments controlled 23.6 trillion, prefecture level governments managed 9.8 trillion, and governments at county and lower levels controlled 22.2 trillion (MOF, 2014). The SOEs are also involved in some of the largest IPOs in recent years, and the state maintained its controlling equity share in many of the companies listed in both domestic and overseas stock markets. When we look at the listed firms, 83.8 percent of the listed firms can be deemed as state controlled, using a minimum of 25 percent of capital to represent control. On average, the state controlled 58.25 percent ownership of the listed firms (Hovey & Naughton, 2007). They are still regarded by the party as the backbone of China's national economy, and the reform of SOEs is still the Chinese government's top priority (Lee, 2009).

In this chapter, we adopted a state-centered approach to study the influence of the state asset management system on China's SOEs. The Chinese SOEs are often connected with the same state owners—i.e., different levels of governments or government agencies (Khanna & Rivkin, 2006)—and share similar structural arrangements as in the conventionally defined business groups. They span multiple industries, maintain associations with different entities, control a substantial fraction of the most productive assets, and often enlist a major share of the largest and most visible firms in a country (Granovetter, 1995; Khanna & Rivkin, 2001). Under such a system, the SOEs are the means to fostering state control and advancing industrial development in the newly industrialized countries, and they are devices that the state uses to achieve its political and economic policy objectives (Yiu, Bruton, & Lu, 2005). Empirical studies suggest that state actors powerfully affect affiliated firms' strategy making so that firms' strategic objectives fit with the government's requirements (Chen, Firth, & Xu, 2009). The state offers institutional support to encourage firms to invest in unrelated industries or focus on a given segment to satisfy the state's political needs (Chung, 2005; Khanna & Yafeh, 2007). Therefore, the management and operation of SOEs and the unique governance system above them are inevitably shaped by the structure of the state political system and by the institutional logic behind state policies (Greenwood, Diaz, Li, & Lorente, 2010; Thornton & Ocasio, 1999). Furthermore, the performance variations of the SOEs are also shaped by the state's controllers and the governance and ownership structures they devised (Yiu, Lu, Bruton, & Hoskisson, 2007).

Building on our empirical analysis of panel data on the firms listed on two Chinese stock exchanges in Shanghai and Shenzhen, we seek to contribute to the current literature on the state's role in affecting firms' management and performance in two ways. First, we focus on examining the de facto federalist state asset management system across multiple administrative levels (i.e., the central, provincial, prefectural, county, and lower levels) and the management practices adopted by state controllers at different levels and across different regions. We suggest that the state's policies and preferences for SOE reforms executed through the state asset management system have powerfully affected firms' investment strategies, governance structures, and ownership structures, which have in turn affected firm performance. Second, we find that the state controllers' strategies, management practices, and affiliated firms' financial performance at different levels have been shaped by differentiated interests among different levels of governments as well as the heterogeneities of market supporting institutions across regions. We thus offer a more sophisticated and comprehensive account for understanding the complicated interconnectedness among state owners, state controllers, and SOEs in large state-owned conglomerates and how such complex institutional and organizational characteristics shape firm performance.

In the next section, we first discuss the evolution of China's state asset management system and the underlying political and economic logics. We then use empirical data to show the complex relational patterns of the state sector. Such analysis allows us to understand how the state extends its control or power to the whole economy. Third, we explore the influence of the peculiar features of China's state asset management system on SOEs' performance.

The Evolution of the SOE Governance System

The reform of SOEs in China is a direct result of a series of market-oriented industrial reforms starting in the late 1970s, which aimed at enhancing the financial performance and efficiency of the nation's enterprises (Keister, 1998; White, Hoskisson, Yiu, & Bruton, 2008). The reformers made important changes to China's economic structure without disturbing the country's socialist political system (Scott, 2002). They believed that large firms were central to the fast growth of Japan and South Korea, and therefore implemented a plan to reform the large state-owned enterprises into modern giant industrial corporations that could compete globally. Following the Japanese state's role in the formation of the *keiretsu*, the Chinese government on the one hand decentralized the control of the SOEs to local governments, and on the other hand allowed firms to acquire ownership stakes in other ventures. The nascent business conglomerates thus formed have certain structural features that are evident in their Japanese and Korean counterparts (White et al., 2008). This new organizational form protected firms from competition, created economies of scale, and enhanced firm performance (Keister, 1998).

The initial reform focused on introducing competition in the marketplace, removing price controls, and increasing managers' responsibilities and rights. However, there were no changes in the ownership of the SOEs and the heavy social burdens on firms. The SOEs became increasingly unprofitable, which created conditions for another round of SOE reforms in the 1990s. In 1997, for example, almost 30 percent of the 22,000 large and medium sized SOEs reported financial losses. This low profitability of SOEs can be largely attributed to an adverse macro-economic environment, such as intense competition from private and foreign firms. Therefore, since the late 1990s, SOE reforms have become a priority for the state and many practical measures were promulgated to improve efficiency and to catch up with market changes that had taken place in other areas of the economy. In particular, the state decided to privatize some of the small money-losing SOEs and convert selected SOEs into modern corporations with state capital and shares from other institutional and individual investors who were independent from the state. More importantly, a fundamentally different characteristic of the reforms starting from the mid-1990s is that, for the first time, measures such as financial support, layoffs, buy-out, and action against corporate insolvency were implemented (Lee, 2009).

Regarding the corporate governance reforms, the state has established a new framework for the SOEs to allow these firms to install a modern enterprise system. The new system changed the internal management system and redefined the relationship between the government and state corporations. The passage of the new company law in 1994 was a significant step toward a better governance structure, which intended to clarify property rights, specify rights and responsibilities, separate bureaucratic control from business operation, and scientifically manage state firms (Lee, 2009).

In addition, all SOEs were strongly encouraged to transform themselves into a corporate entity. Corporatization required a substantial change in the supervisory system within SOEs. Before the reforms, governments acted as both asset investors who held significant equity shares in SOEs and the official entity which took primary responsibility for supervising SOEs. But the Chinese reform is different from the former socialist countries that privatized 100 percent of their SOEs: the Chinese government tried to maintain ultimate control of the economy. Governments at various levels select SOEs to be corporatized and transform them into limited liability companies legally distinct from the state and with ownership represented by share capital (Chen, Firth, & Rui, 2006). After the reform, the government agencies become the representatives of the state and exercise ownership rights, whereas the large conglomerates function as the direct shareholders of the SOEs. Thus, the ownership and management power are separated.

New government agencies—State-owned Asset Supervision and Administration Commission—were established at various levels to represent the state to exercise the owners' rights. The central government's SASAC manages a group of powerful SOEs. Each of these SOEs is in fact a big business conglomerate, which has multiple operation subsidiaries in unrelated or related industries. The executives of these large companies are also politically important in the CPC system. Among the top executives of these central SOEs, more than fifty of them are directly selected and evaluated by the party's organization department. They are considered as having equal political status as the ministers, and the appointment decisions need to be approved by the standing committee of the Politburo. The SASAC appoints the other one hundred or so top executives (Naughton, 2008). This particular HR decision-making process on the one hand enables the state to have tight political control over the SOEs, but on the other hand contradicts the principles of corporate governance and thus leads to serious consequences.

According to China's Company Law (§3, 1993), a Chair is the legal representative of an organization and responsible for the strategic direction of the organization and critical decisions, whereas the GM is often responsible for daily operation of the organization. A Chair–GM dyad structure then gradually takes shape. Stipulated as the sole corporate legal representative, Chairs frequently believe that they are the paramount corporate leaders, which sometimes makes them cross the line and interfere in the firm's daily operations (Rawski, 1999; Schipani & Liu, 2002). The Chinese business culture also regards the Chair as the number one person in a firm, here again the system echoes the Confucian idea of order. Therefore when discussing important issues, most business partners expect to talk directly to the Chair instead of the GM. Otherwise the business partners will feel that they are not gaining full respect from the company (Liu, 2014).

Besides such role ambiguity, in SOEs, both the Chair and the GM are appointed and evaluated by the government (e.g., the party organization department and SASAC) (Schipani & Liu, 2002; Yang, Chi, & Young, 2011). In other words, both the Chair and the GM are state agents or quasi-government officials. They have similar career tracks and bi-directional mobility with government officials (Child, Yan, & Lu, 1996). This means that they have same source of legitimacy of power. To have two leaders with similar status is likely to create a power contest (Zhang & Rajagopalan, 2004). Such role ambiguity/overlap and a similar source of power/legitimacy frequently causes problems of internal conflict between these two most powerful persons, whilst creating confusion among managers, employees, and other stakeholders as to who is the boss (Finkelstein & D'aveni, 1994). Potential conflicts at the top reduce speed and effectiveness in decision-making and create cleavage among employees, which eventually hurts firm performance (Donaldson & Davis, 1991).

A recent incident in the Three Gorges Corporation illustrates this point. On March 25, 2014, the deputy minister of the Organizational Department of the Communist Party of China announced an HR decision in the headquarters of the China Three Gorges Corporation. Guangjing Cao, the Chair of the board, and Fei Chen, the general manager (GM) were transferred out of the company, which is one of the 114 state-owned corporations directly supervised by the State-owned Asset Administration and Supervision Commission (SASAC). The deputy minister urges their successors to uphold the principle of democratic centralism, better communicate and cooperate in the future, and properly define their responsibilities and roles. Dismissing the two most important executives simultaneously is a quite unusual administrative decision. The cause of such a change, according to the correspondent of the Enterprise Observer (Liu, 2014), lies in the poor collaborative relationship between Cao and Chen. The resumés show that Cao and Chen are of similar age and were promoted to the current position in the same year. They both have rich work experience in the hydro power industry and have achieved high rank at early ages, which signals a promising political future. However, this balanced power dyad did not bring benefits to this world's largest hydro-power corporation. Instead, because of the internal competition between them, serious management problems arose. Many middle level managers complained that "when the chair and the GM have disagreements, they will force us to choose sides. This makes our life miserable" (Liu, 2014).

Another important feature of the state asset management system is its decentralization nature. Unlike the state asset management system in eastern Europe or former socialist countries in which the majority of SOEs are organized along the central line ministries, the Chinese state asset management system is more decentralized or federalist in nature (Liu, Sun, & Woo, 2006). Many small- and medium-sized SOEs are lodged under the ownership of a given government jurisdiction ranging from ministries of the central government down to township governments (Walder, 1995). Such a decentralized system makes local governments become the residual claimants in the flow of tax revenues and SOEs become a major source of local government revenue to support local economic development and welfare (Oi, 1992; Wong, 1987). In light of such a close relationship between the local governments and their affiliated firms and the way that government authorities manage industry in cities, towns, and villages in China, many scholars argue that the governments at various levels were in fact comparable to business corporations (Oi, 1992; Qian & Xu, 1993; Wong, 1987).

The decentralized state asset management system is characterized by segmentation among departmental and regional authorities. Using the official phrase, the relations among different state asset management authorities can be characterized by the principle of "state owned but separately represented." It means that the central state maintains nominal ownership, but local governments at various levels represent the state to exercise ownership rights. Local SASACs administer and supervise local SOEs; they are responsible for maintaining and increasing the value of the local state assets. The local SOEs report to and are evaluated by governments at the same level and local SASACs' rights over these firms should not be interfered with by other agencies or governments at other levels (SASAC, 2009). In addition to the separation among different levels of government, the departments at each level or jurisdiction also has relatively independent control over the assets under their purview. This is most evident at the central government level. Centrally owned SOEs include entities managed by the SASAC of the State Council; state-owned financial institutions are supervised by the

China Banking Regulatory Commission, China Insurance Regulatory Commission, and China Securities Regulatory Commission, and state ownership rights are exercised by representatives from the Ministry of Finance. Other ministries also manage some state-owned assets, e.g., the Ministry of Education and the Ministry of Science and Technology.

In addition, a SASAC can establish state asset investment companies, which act as their investment vehicle to expand the reach of state capital and to supervise the operation of other state invested firms. Taking the city of Shenzhen, for instance, the Shenzhen municipal SASAC is the holding entity of these affiliated SOEs; as of 2013 it controlled 23 listed firms. The assets of the SASAC controlled listed SOEs account for 43 percent of the total assets managed by the Shenzhen SASAC (Wang, 2014). Some listed SOEs are directly controlled by the SASAC (e.g., Shenzhen Gas Corporation Ltd., Stock code: 601139). Meanwhile, the Shenzhen SASAC controls other firms through its non-listed investment companies, such as Shenzhen SEZ Construction and Development Corporation. This company in turn controlled listed SOEs (e.g., Shenzhen Yan Tian Port Holdings Co., Ltd., Stock code: 000088) and held shares of listed non-SOEs (e.g., Ping An Insurance (Group) Company of China, Ltd., Stock code: 601318).

Although the arguments in this chapter are not confined to the case of publicly listed firms, we limit our scope to members who are listed companies because, given the difficulty of data collection in emerging economies, data on the listed firms is more accessible, and more importantly, the information on listed firms is more consistent, accurate, and transparent among the information available for Chinese firms.

The Relational Pattern Within and Outside the State Sector

In the 1980s and 1990s, the majority of SOEs reported unsatisfactory economic and financial performance. A study conducted by OECD reported that the SOEs' profit rate after tax was 18 percent in the mid-1980s, but this dropped to 0.9 percent in late 1990s. The proportion of SOEs that posted financial losses has increased from 31 percent in 1994 to 42 percent in 1997 and nearly 50 percent in 1998 (OECD, 2000). Facing this situation, the state initiated the "attaining the larger, releasing the smaller" strategy, which concentrated on restructuring and revitalizing the larger SOEs, whereas smaller SOEs were handled by various privatization methods. Meanwhile, to increase the competitiveness of the large SOEs in the global marketplace and strengthen the state control in major strategic sectors, the state promoted the further growth of selected SOEs by injecting quality assets into these already big corporations (Lee, 2009).

The effects of these reform efforts emerge in the 2000s. The SOEs began to report significant financial returns even though the absolute share of the state sector in the nation's economy was shrinking. The state has given up the labor-intensive and low value-added industries and focused on the strategic sectors, such as banking, telecom, energy, and natural resources. As the state sector gained greater economic strength, it began to extend its influence into other sectors. This trend is especially evident during the late 2000s, when China launched its four trillion yuan economic stimulus plan to overcome the financial crisis. SOEs have struck back in many industries by acquiring assets in steel, airlines, real estate, finance, highway, public transportation, and mining industries. These large-scale structural changes give scholars a good chance to observe the patterns of SOEs' growth strategy and explore the rationale behind their decisions.

In order to understand the expansion of the SOEs, we analyzed the evolution of the cross- shareholding networks among listed firms using panel data on firms listed in both the Shanghai and Shenzhen stock exchanges. Previous studies have used similar approaches to study the interactions among firms (Gerlach, 1992). In these analyses, the listed firms are regarded as the node of the network, and the edge (or ties) between two nodes are often operationalized as equity holding relations, interlock board members, or bank loans. In this study, we used the equity holding relations as the edges. In order to construct the equity holding matrix, we used data from the CSMAR database in which the identities of the ten largest shareholders were listed.

The reason that we focused on the ten largest shareholders while excluding other smaller investors is because most listed SOEs had a highly concentrated ownership structure. For many years, the state shares and the state legal entity shares, which comprise two thirds of SOEs' total shares, had not been allowed to be traded in the stock market. This situation was eventually changed in 2005, when the restrictions on non-tradable shares for state and legal entity shares were relaxed. However, the shares of the listed SOEs are still overly concentrated in the state's hands, which allows the state to exercise continuous controlling rights as the largest shareholder (Lee, 2009).

In order to describe the change in the cross-shareholding network during this period, we calculated four indexes for each year. The first indicator was the number of nodes, which refers to the number of firms who held other companies' shares or whose shares were held by other listed companies. The nodes that had no inward or outward ties were excluded from the analysis. The second indicator was the number of edges (or ties). It was operationalized as directed ties from a shareholding company to the firm whose share are held. For example, if firm A is among firm B's ten largest shareholders, then there is a directed tie from A to B; if B also happened to hold A's share, then there will be another directed tie from B to A. When we count edges, there will be two edges between these two nodes. The third indicator was the number of isolated networks. An isolated network was defined as a network with two or more edges that had no direct connections to any other networks with two or more edges. The forth indicator was the size of the largest network, which refers to the number of nodes in the largest isolated network.

By examining the changes of these four indicators during 1996–2012, we find that first, the number of nodes, number of edges, and number of nodes in the largest isolated network exhibit very similar trends. Significant changes happened in 2002–2003 and 2007–2010. During 2002 and 2003, the state promoted the growth of the national champions, during which firms began to expand their reach to other industries or consolidate their control in their main industries. In addition, the SASAC system was established during this time; one of the impacts of SASAC is to end the segmented SOE management system. The newly established SASACs at various levels became the primary agency that managed the state's assets. The fall and rise during 2007 and 2010 were largely affected by the economic downturn and the subsequent economic stimulus plan, which gave the SOEs more resources to expand. However, it is worthwhile to note that the number of insolated networks has not changed much since 2003, indicating that the number of ultimate owners has been stable over the years. Consider the fact that only a very limited number of private firms has the capacity to control more than one listed firm: the stability observed can be attributed to the stability of the federalist state asset management system.

In the second analysis, we try to explore the driving forces that have shaped the pattern of the networks at different time period. In other words, who reached out and tried to control other firms, and what kind of firms are more likely to be controlled by others? In order to visualize this trend, we first calculated the number of different types of nodes (central SOE, local SOE, or private firms) in the networks, then calculated the average outdegree and indegree of each node. We then subtracted the average indegree from the average outdegree. The resulting index indicates the activeness of different types of nodes, that is, to what extent a node is more likely to control others rather than being controlled by others. Figure 8.1 shows the results; from the figure we see that the state firms are more active in the interfirm networks and private firms are much more passive. Compared with the local SOEs, the central SOEs are even more active in extending their influence in the markets. In particular we find several critical junctures during the study period. The first period was between 1996 and 1998, when the state initiated premarket reform and a large number of SOEs were restructured. This trend was reversed during 2001 and 2003, when the state initiated new reforms and established the new state asset management system. As a result, the listed SOEs began to reach out and control strategic assets in the market. In addition, we can see a significant expansion of the central SOEs after 2009 as a result of the state's economic stimulus plan.

Figure 8.2 further shows the relational pattern between state and private sectors. Before 2002, SOEs rarely held private firms shares. In particular, compared with local SOEs, central SOEs held even less private firm shares. Since 2002, the SOEs began to make considerable investments in private sector firms. This trend was reversed in 2008, but the SOEs struck back again in 2010 when state control over private firms reached its historical

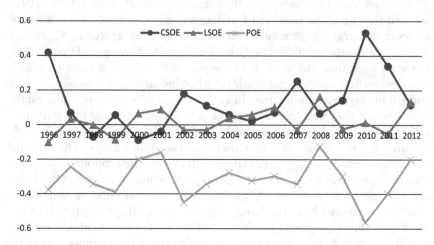

Figure 8.1 The Difference Between the Average Outdegree and Indegree

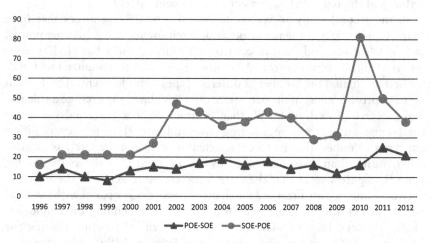

Figure 8.2 Number of Directed Ties Between Different Types of Firms

peak. This is exactly the time when the state advances and private retreat phenomenon became the hot topic in public discussion.

The SASAC and Affiliated Firm Performance

In this section we explore how structures of the state asset management system affected firms' performance. We view the federalist state asset management system as a governance structure in which the political status of the ultimate owners, i.e., the SASACs or government agencies, the hierarchical structure above the member firms, the degree of diversity of firms that a SASAC manages, and the connection between the state and private sectors have significant influence on firms' strategies and financial performance.

Decentralized SASAC System and Firm Performance

Scholars studying the economic transition of the former socialist countries often attributed the cause of SOEs' poor economic performance to the bilateral monopoly relationships between the state and the SOEs, which led to soft budget constraint problems (Kornai, 1992; Naughton, 1992). It is argued that in these economies, governments have other objectives besides profitability, such as supplying scarce inputs for other enterprises, maintaining a high level of employment, and providing various social services to employees and the communities. These nonfinancial preferences of the planning officials add operational costs to the SOEs. Whereas from the SOEs' perspective, because they helped governments fulfill their social service responsibilities, they can use these services as excuses for their poor performance and then demand bailouts and subsidies from the governments (Kornai, 1992). This created a mutual dependence between a government and enterprises.

However such analysis relies on a simplistic view of the structure of the state and the motivations of governments at different levels. As Walder (1995) pointed out, the soft budget constraint analysis is usually based on the assumption that there is only one owner in the economy, i.e., the state. But in fact there potentially are as many owners of public enterprises as there are government jurisdictions. This is especially true in the Chinese case because, as we described above, the nation adopted a decentralized state asset management system. Local governments at various levels are de facto owners of the SOEs and enjoy exclusive management rights over these assets. In addition, the dual monopoly (or mutual dependence) relations that lead to soft budget constraints are not invariant. The strength of such relations tends to vary according to the scale and organization characteristics of government jurisdictions and their industrial bases (Oi, 1992; Walder, 1995; Wong, 1987).

From the central government down to the township government, the scale and diversity of the government's industrial base change dramatically. The SASACs and other government agencies of higher-level governments must manage more SOEs, which usually span multiple industries and are often larger in scale. Therefore, compared to state asset management officials at higher-level government agencies, their counterparts at lower-level government agencies face less complex management issues, are closer to the firms they supervise, and are more likely to have a clearer understanding of the opportunities and challenges that firms face. Moreover, the fiscal reform in the 1990s dramatically changed the distribution of revenue and allocation of expenditure responsibilities among different levels of governments. Whereas more tax revenue is centralized in the hands of higher-level governments, the assignment of expenditure responsibilities is largely intact. This mismatch makes lower-level governments face greater financial challenges.

Under such a situation, lower-level governments have more financial interests in their SOEs and greater incentives to improve the SOEs' profitability so that they can collect more revenue. In addition, compared to the lower-level governments, higher-level governments have greater non-financial interests in their firms. During our field interview, an executive of a state SASAC controlled firm mentioned that the central government often asks the firm to help it realize some policy goals, such as renovation of the inner city old residential communities. However, the funds given by the state are not enough to cover the basic construction costs. As a result, this firm, China's largest construction corporation, has to use its own funds to subsidize this policy project. In the executive's view, this is part of their social responsibility, i.e., their responsibility to their major shareholder—the central government. These observations suggest that compared to higher-level governments, lower-level governments have more financial interests and less non-financial interests in their SOEs; meanwhile, the managerial tasks they face tend to be less complex because the firms they manage are smaller in scale, less diverse, and fewer in quantity.

One method of distinguishing ownership of listed companies is to track the ownership hierarchy of the largest shareholders to identify the ultimate owners. Using this method, the state-owned companies can be divided into local SOEs (owned by local SASACs or government agencies) or central SOEs (owned by the central SASAC and other central ministries). Although most SOEs have multi-hierarchical ownership structures, there are a few firms that are directly owned by their ultimate owner. This is more often seen among local SOEs, whose incorporation reforms have lagged behind other forms of owners and whose ultimate owner has relatively fewer firms to manage and thus has no need to set up intermediary levels of management. We constructed an ordinal variable to measure the political status of the state asset management agencies. As we discussed, China's state asset management system is highly decentralized; therefore each level of government has considerable autonomy in managing their firms. There are five major levels in the state political structure; from the highest to lowest, they are central, provincial, prefecture, county, and township levels. Because the sample includes firms that are not controlled by local states, their political status value equals zero.

In addition, to operationalize firms' performance, we rely on two measures that are widely used in the management and financial literature. The first measure is firms' return on asset (ROA), which is an accounting indicator of firms' profitability. A high value of ROA indicates that a firm gained more profits relative to its total assets. It helps us to understand how efficient management is at using its assets to generate earnings. The second indicator is Tobin's Q, which is a measure of the market value of a firm. It is calculated as the sum of the market value of equity and book value of debt over the book value of total assets. It indicates the firm's expected cash flows and risks and more generally firms' future performance. Although these two measures are often strongly correlated, they do have important differences. The major divergence between Tobin's Q and ROA is that, under certain circumstances, even though firms are efficient at a point in time, i.e., having a high ROA, external shareholders fear that the gains will not accrue to them, and hence discount the value of the firm (Khanna, 2000).

We used multilevel mixed effects models to conduct the data analysis. We first regressed the independent variables against ROA. The status of the asset management agencies was used as both a categorical and continuous variable. It shows that in general there is a negative and significant relationship between political rank and firms' profitability. Specifically, we find that compared to the centrally controlled firms, firms controlled by private owners, township level governments, and provincial level governments are significantly more profitable during our study period. However, we find such a relationship does not exist when using Tobin's Q as a dependent variable. By using political status as a categorical variable, we find that compared to centrally controlled firms, those controlled by prefecture and county level governments have significantly lower Tobin's Q.

These results reveal a more complex picture of the relations between the political status of the leading state agencies and member firms' performance. We borrowed insights from the literature on market transition of former socialist countries and argue that the existence of the dual monopoly relationship between the state and the SOEs is one of the primary causes of the soft budget constraint problem, which led to the poor financial performance of SOEs (Kornai, 1992). But the strength of this dual monopoly relationship is not homogeneous among governments at different levels. Previous studies argue that as the administrative level decreases, government nonfinancial interests in SOEs will decline, which helps SOEs harden their budget constraints (Walder, 1995). We therefore predict that firms affiliated with lower-level state asset management agencies will have stronger performance. When we look at member firms' profitability (as measured by ROA), we find the results are consistent with the theoretical prediction. That is, as the controllers' administrative level decreases, the costs incurred by firms' policy burdens will be reduced, which contributes to firms' profitability.

To strengthen this finding, we also used Tobin's Q as an alternative measure of firms' financial performance. However, our finding is opposite to the direction that we specified in the earlier part. Firms affiliated with higher-level state asset management agencies receive higher (instead of lower as predicted) market valuation than their counterparts controlled by lower-level agencies. Our interpretation of these seemingly contradictory results is that the leading agencies' political status may have different implications regarding firms' probability and firms' market value. As previous literature suggested, investors' perceptions of a firm's value can be affected by signaling effects of the state owner's political status. The emerging context is characterized by high institutional uncertainty and volatility (Peng, 2003). In this context, investors need to find ways to mitigate the risks associated with institutional imperfections. Equity retention by a state agency lowers the ex-ante uncertainty of domestic investors because investors tend to interpret equity retention by the state as the government's confidence and a business guaranty (Mok & Hui, 1998; Sun, Tong, & Tong, 2002). That being said, retention by higher-level governments tends to be a stronger signal to the investors, which leads to more confidence in the firms they controlled.

The Limitation of the Temasek Model

In addition to the controlling state agencies' political status, another important structural feature that affects firms' performance is the overhead governance structure, which functions as a command chain along the hierarchy from the dominant owner to individual firm management. In the Chinese case, the state asset management authorities play a leading role in management. They obtain administrative authority over individual firms typically through a hierarchical ownership structure, in which a unit at the upper level holds stock in other units at the next lower level. With the existence of the holding state agency, this state asset management system differentiates itself from network form business groups in which the vertical authoritative structure is weak, and individual firms in the groups are connected more by social relations and cross-shareholding, rather than vertical ownership. They are more like partners rather than subordinates or subunits of a hierarchy (Yiu et al., 2007).

In China's decentralized state asset management system, the SOEs and their actual owners have complicated but strong relationships. For the local and central governments, the listed firms are their valuable assets. This is not only because these firms tend to have superior economic performance, but also because in the Chinese financial market, gaining the listing license is a challenging task. Having a listed firm means that the owner can obtain access to the financial market. In order to get listed on the market, most governments will restructure their assets under the slogan of "state assets optimization" (Naughton, 2008). Such policies basically refer to the process in which the state owner transfers the most valuable assets of a business corporation to one of its core companies to allow this core company to meet the listing requirements. Although this practice allows the core company to have superior assets and performance, other assets managed by the same owner remain in the nonlisted shell company, which has inferior performance. Therefore, behind most listed SOEs there exist similar related companies that have been sacrificed for the benefit of the listed companies. Because the core and the shell companies are often managed by the same owner, the performance of the entire corporation is easily manipulated.

Previous studies have shed some light on the performance implications of the hierarchical management structure. It is argued that some Chinese business groups employ highly centralized management styles in which the core firm is actively involved in the day-to-day operations of its subsidiaries. It makes the production and personnel decisions in addition to directing more typical matters such as corporate strategy. Although there are other business groups that are more decentralized, the core firm is reduced to that of a shareholder once the group is established; it can only encourage certain types of management structures to develop in the groups and does not control member firms' operation. Empirical evidence suggests that the decentralized management structure is more beneficial to member firms' financial performance (Keister, 1998).

Since the establishment of the tax sharing system in 1994, the state-owned firms were no longer required to remit their after-tax profit to the government. From then on, the centrally managed state-owned enterprises had not paid any profits to the Chinese government. However, during this time, many of the SOEs did remit profits to their administrative superiors, but those superiors had been transformed into holding companies of various kinds, and these companies become the final beneficiaries of the SOEs' profit (Naughton, 2008). In other words, they will not pass the remitted money to the government anymore. This allows the holding company or in many cases the shell company to have the capacity to use the profit generated from the listed firms to subsidize the operation of the inferior subsidiaries. For example, big corporations like Sinopec and Petro China have various assets: some of the assets are of public interest, some are monopolistic in nature, whereas others are in competitive industries. These corporations thus need to reallocate the profit generated within the corporation and make the less profitable but essential firms viable.

In fact, choosing between a centralized and a decentralized management structure is also a hotly debated issue among the policy circles. In many places the SASACs maintain strong control over their member firms. They have heavy influence in terms of the appointment of the top executives of member firms; they often use administrative orders to influence member firms' business operations or strategic choices. Whereas in other places, the governments set up a few state asset investment companies below the SASAC and use market means to control their affiliated firms. This governance structure is also known as the Temasek model. Singapore's Ministry of Finance owns Temasek and is responsible for supervising the operation of Temasek. The MOF only retains the rights to nominate key executive members and audit the financial details of the company, whereas the Temasek board has full autonomy in making various detailed business decisions.

Experimenting with the Temasek model is one of the four policy measures of the latest round of SOE reform. The plan calls for transferring control of state equity to state-owned holding companies that focus more on capital management. The goal of this plan is to reduce the political interference in the management of SOEs by the state asset management agencies. It thus aims to design and establish the holding companies to focus primarily on shareholder value maximization rather than on realizing the policy goals set by the state or its agencies (Xinhua, 2015).

However, for a long time there were two different voices in the policy making circle regarding how to change the overhead governance structure of the state sector. The Ministry of Finance favors the Temasek model. In 2013, officials from the MOF visited Singapore's Temasek and the Bureau of State Asset Management of Israel. In their study report, they mentioned that the experiences of these two countries have important implications for China's SOE reform. They argued that the state asset management agencies need to immediately change their roles and transform from multi-role actors who manage personnel issues, decisions, and assets to professional regulators. They proposed new reform measures in which the existing 120 largest central corporations should be classified into those in competitive industries and those in industries that are of great strategic, public, and national security interests (Feng, 2014). Multiple state asset investment and management companies should be established who represent the state to exercise the shareholders' rights.

The closest example to the Temasek model is the Central Huijin Investment Ltd, which was commissioned by the State Council in 2003. The company represents the state to exercise shareholders' rights among the state-owned financial companies. Similar to the Temasek, Huijin is supervised by the Ministry of Finance. The Huijin model is different from the SASAC model in that the former is a marketized state asset management model, i.e., is commissioned by the state and follows market principles. Its role is strictly limited to a shareholder not the traditional administrator. More importantly, Huijin is a company whereas SASAC is an administrative agency. Huijin gets a dividend from its firms and sends directors to the boards of affiliated firms, whereas the SASAC does not take a dividend and does not send directors to affiliated firms. Huijin will not influence the directors' decisions, whereas SASAC still uses administrative oversight to manage firms (Feng, 2014). Due to these advantages, the Temasek/Huijin model has received much attention in the policy making circle and has begun to be experimented with in major corporations and municipalities.

However, the SOE reform is driven by both market and political considerations. On the one hand, the state fully understands the need to improve SOEs' financial performance and increase the strength of the state sector; on the other hand, the state also needs to maintain effective political control over the SOEs so that they can appropriate these resources for political purposes. For instance, during the 2015 market stabilization process, the state mandated the 21 largest security firms to contribute 15 percent of their net assets to a newly established emergency fund to stabilize the market. In addition, the central SASAC and local SASACs all issued directives to their affiliated firms and asked them to initiate stock repurchase plans to stabilize their stock price. It would be very difficult for the state to effectively control the situation if the state relinquished its political control over SOEs.

That being said, concerns over the effective political control of SOEs made it difficult for the state asset management authorities to clarify the power division between the government and the intermediate agencies. Although the state appeared to demonstrate a commitment to a declining presence in the SOEs through creating these asset management or investment companies, in practice few substantive changes were made to the way the state manages its subsidiaries (Wang, Guthrie, & Xiao, 2012). Because of the lack of a thorough, substantial power reallocation, the newly added intermediate agency could not function effectively; in most situations it even increased the organizational costs and thus adversely affected SOEs' performance. For example, the Shenzhen city adopted the three-level Temasek model ten years ago, but it caused many conflicts and frictions among various affiliated entities (Feng, 2014). No firms want to have another superior above them or be pulled in conflicting directions by their higher-level management bodies.

To empirically test the impact of the governance structure on affiliated SOEs' financial performance, we constructed a dummy variable, which indicates whether a listed SOE is managed directly by the SASAC or indirectly managed by a state investment management company. Our model results show a significant and negative relationship between this variable and firms' performance, indicating that firms' performance (as measured by both ROA and Tobin's Q) will be weaker when they are indirectly managed by state-owned investment companies.

Previous studies on the conventional Chinese business groups argue that member firms' financial performance will be positively associated with a less decentralized group structure, in which the controlling firm only maintains rights such as the nomination of top executives but does not exercise operation control over member firms (i.e., the Temasek Model) (Ang & Ding, 2006). However, we find that firms in a more centralized management structure perform better than those in a decentralized structure. Empirical evidence shows that in the Chinese context, when following the Temasek model and adding another governance body between the leading state agency and the member firms, firms will be adversely affected because such an arrangement will generate conflicting demand from the upper-level management bodies. Moreover, when further partitioning affiliated SOEs into different blocks led by separate state asset investment companies, interest conflicts will arise among the investment companies, which may weaken the coordinating capacity of the leading state agency (Feng, 2014). This in turn diminishes the benefits of group affiliation.

The Impact of Alternative Ownership

Another pilot program in recent SOE reform proposals is to attract private investment and improve corporate governance. The State Council has issued a document encouraging SOEs to adopt the mixed ownership model and improve their governance through this practice. The policy makers realized that SOEs are facing increasing intense competition in both domestic and international markets. SOEs in industries with a high level of market competition should actively accept non-state investment. Foreign capital is welcomed in restructuring through a variety of methods, including overseas mergers and acquisitions, cooperation in investment and financing, and offshore financing. Although the state relaxed the barriers for private and foreign investors into state-owned assets, it does highlight the importance of maintaining the state capital's absolute controlling position, especially in fields relating to national security (Xinhua, 2015).

For a given state asset management authority, the SOEs are no doubt the majority of affiliated firms. However, there are also some non-SOE firms in which the state asset management authorities have stakes. Local SASACs and other agencies can acquire shares of private or foreign companies through the state asset investment companies and become one of their major but not controlling shareholders. Such connections facilitate the communication among firms with different ownerships. Previous studies show that connections with firms with alternative ownerships, such as foreign-invested firms, function as important sources of information for firms in developing countries (Carney, Gedajlovic, Heugens, Essen, & Oosterhout, 2011). Information regarding technological innovations, market trends, and best management practices can flow from the participating firms to the SOEs. Such beneficial information can then be passed to all members of the group through one or more of the formal or informal connections that exist among affiliated firms (Keister, 1998; Ma, Yao, & Xi, 2006).

Meanwhile, affiliating with the SOEs or the state asset management authorities also brings benefits for the non-state firms. An affiliated firm can share the state firms' reputation capital simply by being associated with the prestigious and influential SOEs (Peng, Lee, & Wang, 2005). Moreover, like in many other emerging economies, China's financial intermediaries are either absent or not fully evolved, which makes insider lending a substitute for formal financial services. When firms are affiliated with SOEs or state asset management authorities, they are more likely to get access to otherwise scarce capital (Keister, 2001); this logic also applies to the acquisition of raw material and intermediate goods (Carney, 2004; Khanna & Rivkin, 2001; Yiu et al., 2005). In addition, affiliated firms can also receive considerable external support from the government, which may spill over to the affiliates and generate higher financial returns (Ma et al., 2006; Peng et al., 2005).

Our empirical results strongly support this point. The dummy variable we created indicates whether a state asset management authority also controlled or invested in non-state firms. We find that when foreign or private capital is included in the SOEs' network, then SOEs connected to this network will benefit from this mixed ownership structure.

Conclusion

The role of the state during economic development has long been the focus of the market transition literature. Studies on the Chinese transitional context frequently pointed out that governments at various levels are de facto owners of the SOEs they manage; they resemble market-oriented firms, which closely monitor and coordinate the economic activities of their affiliated firms. Taking these ideas as a starting point, we bring the state asset management authorities at different levels into the analysis and explore how characteristics of the controlling state asset management agencies, the governance structure, and the composition of alternative ownership forms affect the financial performance of firms affiliated with a state asset management agency. By examining the impacts of the structure features of the state asset management system on their member firms, we seek to develop a fuller, deeper account than what the current literature shows for understanding the importance of the linkage between the state and the firms it controls. We place the state and state actors at the center of our theoretical framework and define China's decentralized state asset management system as the state's "long hand," which extends and grants the central government's power and control over SOEs to local governments at multiple administrative levels. Such a "long hand" of the state has given rise to some crucial structural features of the state asset management system, where the member firms share same state ownership but respond to different state controllers. In conducting our empirical analysis, we have traced the actual controllers of China's publicly listed firms and investigated how different administrative levels to which the firms are affiliated as well as other structural characteristics affect affiliated firms' financial performance.

Our study is in line with and goes beyond the current literature on SOEs in transitional economies by offering more evidence for the impact of China's de facto federalist structure on the performance of the state-controlled economy. We support and confirm the widely held argument that the mutual dependency between the state and the SOEs would cause the SOEs "soft budget constraints" and relevant problems, which would lead to these firms' inefficiency and poor financial performance (Kornai, 1992; Kornai, Maskin, & Roland, 2003). Furthermore, we argue that the strength of such mutual dependencies between the state and the SOEs varies across the government's multiple-level administrative system; the motivations and interests of state actors at different levels are not homogeneous. As the administrative level goes down to localities, the governmental agencies' nonfinancial interests in SOEs decline, which according to Walder (1995) helps SOEs harden their budget constraints. However, our results reveal a more complex picture regarding the administrative hierarchy's influence on firms' performance. We find that the political capital of the state owners can benefit firms. As the previous literature suggested, investors' perceptions of a firm's value can be affected by signaling effects of the state owners' political status (Sun et al., 2002), and higher-level governmental agencies are commonly regarded to have higher, more important political status. Equity retention by state agencies lowers the ex-ante uncertainty of domestic investors, because investors tend to interpret such a retention as the government's confidence and thus business guaranty (Mok & Hui, 1998; Sun et al., 2002). Thus, retention by higher-level governmental agencies tends to be a stronger signal to the investors that the government has more confidence in the firms involved.

Our study sheds some light on understanding the institutional and organizational outcomes originated from and shaped by China's gradualist reform approach. The Chinese state has chosen to reduce its control over the economy and simultaneously cultivated market-oriented infrastructures and institutions in a piecemeal fashion. In reforming the SOEs' governance structure, the government has intended to guide and incentivize economic agents to pursue efficiency and profitability by decentralizing the central state's ownership and control down to localities. However, as our findings suggest, the expected benefits of decentralization are difficult to achieve, mainly due to unclear power division between the government and the SASAC system. Our results show that the firms suffer from the conflicting commands made by multiple governance authorities; the firms suffer more when more layers are added to the governmental hierarchy, a situation similar to what has been found in Singapore's Temasek model. Moreover, when further partitioning affiliated SOEs into different blocks led by separate state asset investment companies, interest conflicts will arise among the investment companies, which may further weaken the coordinating capacity of the leading state agency (Feng, 2014). This in turn diminishes the positive benefit.

The interplay between political and market considerations has shaped the ownership structures of the state asset management system. We find the partnership between state and other types of owners can bring benefit to both parties, allowing them to exchange valuable resources that are crucial to business successes. More specifically, the SOEs are likely to receive useful technological, entrepreneurial, and market information from their private or foreign partners. The private and foreign firms can benefit much from their connections with the SOEs, which would enable or broaden their access to financial capital and restricted markets. For China's SOE reform, the current "talk of the town" is the idea of "mixed ownership," which is defined as a type of ownership featuring "crossholding by, and mutual fusion between, state-owned capital, collective capital and non-publicly owned capital" (Central Committee of the Communist Party of China, 2013). Our findings in this regard thus have significant practical implications for both state and private investors who may be doubtful about the prospects of mixed ownership reforms.

It is important to acknowledge that our study is limited to Chinese listed firms that are directly or indirectly controlled by state asset management agencies. In the Chinese context, the assets in listed SOEs account for around

40 percent of the total assets managed by various state asset management agencies, and they tend to be the most productive and profitable assets controlled by state asset management agencies at various levels. It is thus important to conduct further studies to see whether our argument or findings can be generalized to the nonlisted SOEs. Moreover, the construction of major independent variables is based on limited information available in listed firms' annual reports. Due to the variation in the data disclosure efforts, we are unable to systematically collect the desired information that allows us to construct better measures of the latent construct we intended to study. Therefore the validity and reliability of the measures need to be improved in future studies.

References

Ang, J. S., & Ding, D. K. (2006). Government ownership and the performance of government-linked companies: The case of Singapore. *Journal of Multinational Financial Management, 16*, 64–88.

Bai, C.-E., Lu, J., & Tao, Z. (2006). The multitask theory of state enterprise reform: Empirical evidence from China. *The American Economic Review, 96*, 353–357.

Carney, M. (2004). The institutions of industrial restructuring in Southeast Asia. *Asia Pacific Journal of Management, 21*, 171–188.

Carney, M., Gedajlovic, E. R., Heugens, P. P. M. A. R., Essen, M. V., & Oosterhout, J. V. (2011). Business group affiliation, performance, context, and strategy. *Academy of Management Journal, 54*, 437–460.

Central Committee of the Communist Party of China (2013). "Decision of the central committee of the communist party of China on some major issues concerning comprenensively deepening the reform." Retrieved from http://www.china.org. cn/china/third_plenary_session/2014-01/16/content_31212602.htm

Chen, G., Firth, M., & Rui, O. (2006). Have China's enterprise reforms led to improved efficiency and profitability? *Emerging Markets Review, 7*, 82–109.

Chen, G., Firth, M., & Xu, L. (2009). Does the type of ownership control matter? Evidence from China's listed companies. *Journal of Banking and Finance, 33*, 171–181.

Child, J., Yan, Y., & Lu, Y. (1996). Ownership and control in Sino-foreign joint ventures. *Research Papers in Management–University of Cambridge Judge Institute of Management Studies*. Retrieved from http://hdl.handle.net/10068/427417

Chung, C.-N. (2005). Beyond Guanxi: Network contingencies in Taiwanese business groups. *Organization Studies, 27*, 461–489.

Donaldson, L., & Davis, J. H. (1991). Stewardship theory or agency theory: CEO governance and shareholder returns. *Australian Journal of management, 16*, 49–64.

Fan, G., Wang, X., & Zhu, H. (2011). *NERI Index of Marketization of China's Province 2011 Report*. Beijing: Economic Science Press.

Feng, Y. (2014). Managing capital versus managing people, operation, and assets. *Southern Weekly*. Retrieved from http://www.infzm.com/content/102558

Finkelstein, S., & D'aveni, R. A. (1994). CEO duality as a double-edged sword: How boards of directors balance entrenchment avoidance and unity of command. *Academy of Management Journal, 37*, 1079–1108.

Gerlach, M. L. (1992). The Japanese corporate network: A blockmodel analysis. *Administrative Science Quarterly*, 105–139.

Granovetter, M. (1995). Coase revisited: Business groups in the modern economy. *Industrial and Corporate Change, 4*, 93–130.

Greenwood, R., Diaz, A. M., Li, S. X., & Lorente, J. C. (2010). The multiplicity of institutional logics and the heterogeneity of organizational response. *Organization Science, 21,* 521–539.

Hovey, M., & Naughton, T. (2007). A survey of enterprise reforms in China: The way forward. *Economic Systems, 31,* 138–156.

Keister, L. A. (1998). Engineering growth: Business group structure and firm performance in China's transition economy. *American Journal of Sociology, 104,* 404–440.

Keister, L. A. (2001). Exchange structures in transition: Lending and trade relations in Chinese business groups. *American Sociological Review, 66,* 336–360.

Khanna, T. (2000). Business groups and social welfare in emerging markets: Existing evidence and unanswered questions. *European Economic Review, 44,* 748–761.

Khanna, T., & Rivkin, J. W. (2001). Estimating the performance effects of business groups in emerging markets. *Strategic Management Journal, 22,* 45–74.

Khanna, T., & Rivkin, J. W. (2006). Interorganizational ties and business group boundaries: evidence from an emerging economy. *Organization Science, 17,* 333–352.

Khanna, T., & Yafeh, Y. (2007). Business groups in emerging markets: Paragons or parasites? *Journal of Economic Literature, 45,* 331–372.

Kornai, J. (1992). *The Socialist System: The Political Economy of Communism.* Princeton, NJ: Princeton University Press.

Kornai, J., Maskin, E., & Roland, G. (2003). Understanding the soft budget constraint. *Journal of Economic Literature, 41,* 1095–1136.

Lee, J. (2009). State owned enterprises in China: Reviewing the evidence. *OECD Occasional Paper,* 6–7. Retrieved from http://www.oecd.org/corporate/ca/corporategovernanceofstate-ownedenterprises/42095493.pdf

Liu, G. S., Sun, P., & Woo, W. T. (2006). The political economy of Chinese-style privatization: Motives and constraints. *World Development, 34,* 2016–2033.

Liu, Q. (2014). Personnel earthquake of the three gorges corporation questions the executive management system of the central managed state-owned firms. *The Enterprise Observer.* Retrieved from http://ccnews.people.com.cn/n/2014/0416/c141677-24901936.html

Ma, X., Yao, X., & Xi, Y. (2006). Business group affiliation and firm performance in a transition economy: A focus on ownership voids. *Asia Pacific Journal of Management, 23,* 467–483.

MOF. (2014). The accounting report on the nation's state-owned enterprises (2013). In M. o. F. o. China (Ed.). Beijing. Retrieved from http://www.mof.gov.cn/preview/qiyesi/zhengwuxinxi/gongzuodongtai/201407/t20140728_1118640.html

Mok, H. M. K., & Hui, Y. V. (1998). Underpricing and the aftermarket performance of IPOs in Shanghai, China. *Pacific-Basin Finance Journal, 6,* 453–474.

Naughton, B. (1992). Implications of the state monopoly over industry and its relaxation. *Modern China, 18,* 14–41.

Naughton, B. (2008). SASAC and rising corporate power in China. *China Leadership Monitor, 24,* 1–9.

OECD. (2000). *Reforming China's Enterprises.* Paris: OECD Publishing.

Oi, J. C. (1992). Fiscal reform and the economic foundations of local state corporatism in China. *World Politics, 45,* 99–126.

Peng, M. W. (2003). Institutional transitions and strategic choices. *Academy of Management Review, 28,* 275–296.

Peng, M. W., Lee, S., & Wang, D. (2005). What determines the scope of the firm over time? A focus on institutional relatedness. *Academy of Management Review, 30,* 622–633.

Qian, Y., & Xu, C. (1993). Why China's economic reform differ: The M-form hierarchy and entry/expansion of the non-state sector. *Economics of Transition, 1,* 135–170.

Rawski, T. G. (1999). Reforming China's economy: What have we learned? *The China Journal*, 139–156.

SASAC. (2009). *Guidance on Further Strengthening the Supervision and Administration of Local State-Owned Assets ([2009]286)*. Beijing: State-owned Asset Supervision and Administration Commission.

Schipani, C. A., & Liu, J. (2002). Corporate governance in China: Then and now. *Columbia Business Law Review*.

Scott, W. R. (2002). The changing world of Chinese enterprise: An institutional perspective. In A. S. Tsui & C. M. Lau (Eds.), *The Management of Enterprises in the People's Republic of China* (pp. 59–78). Boston, MA: Kluwer Academic Publishers.

Sun, Q., Tong, W. H. S., & Tong, J. (2002). How does government ownership affect firm performance? Evidence from China's privatization experience. *Journal of Business Finance and Accounting, 29*, 1–27.

Thornton, P., & Ocasio, W. (1999). Institutional logics and the historical contingency of power in organizations: Executive succession in the higher education publishing industry, 1958–1990. *American Journal of Sociology, 105*, 801–843.

Walder, A. G. (1995). Local governments as industrial firms: An organizational analysis of China's transitional economy. *American Journal of Sociology, 101*, 263–301.

Wang, J., Guthrie, D., & Xiao, Z. (2012). The rise of SASAC: Asset management, ownership concentration, and firm performance in China's capital markets. *Management and Organization Review, 8*, 253–281.

Wang, Z. (2014). The reform direction of Shenzhen's 619.9 trillion yuan State-owned Asset. In *21st Century Business Herald*. Retrieved from http://finance.sina.com.cn/china/dfjj/20140402/023618684331.shtml

White, R. E., Hoskisson, R. E., Yiu, D. W., & Bruton, G. D. (2008). Employment and market innovation in Chinese business group affiliated firms. *Management and Organization Review, 4*, 225–256.

Wong, C. P. W. (1987). Between plan and market: The role of the local sector in Post-Mao China. *Journal of Comparative Economics, 11*, 385–398.

Xinhua. (2015). China urges SOE modernization through mixed ownership reform. In *China Daily*. Xinhua News Agency: Beijing. Retrieved from http://www.chinadaily.com.cn/business/2015-09/25/content_21979076.htm

Yang, J., Chi, J., & Young, M. (2011). A review of corporate governance in China. *Asian-Pacific Economic Literature, 25*, 15–28.

Yiu, D. W., Bruton, G. D., & Lu, Y. (2005). Understanding business group performance in an emerging economy. *Journal of Management Studies, 42*, 183–206.

Yiu, D. W., Lu, Y., Bruton, G. D., & Hoskisson, R. E. (2007). Business groups: An integrated model to focus future research. *Journal of Management Studies, 44*, 1551–1579.

Zhang, Y., & Rajagopalan, N. (2004). When the known devil is better than an unknown god: An empirical study of the antecedents and consequences of relay CEO successions. *Academy of Management Journal, 47*, 483–500.

9   Conclusion
The Chinese Experience

Thirty-eight years have passed since China started its economic reform in the late 1970s. Today China has already spent a longer period in building a market economy than the time under Maoist socialism. During this period, the country has embraced market mechanisms and become an active player in promoting economic globalization. By the mid-1990s, China had successfully moved away from the command economy and adopted a functioning market economy (Naughton, 2007). The gradual establishment and improvement of the market system, and the decentralization of fiscal as well as economic decision-making power to local levels and once tightly government controlled SOEs, make observers believe that this movement toward marketization may have represented a transitional phase through which China would gradually move away from its command economy structure and toward a market structure or a form of capitalism that is consistent with the conventional liberal capitalist system (Nee, 1989, 1996).

However, as many observers also noticed, despite the remarkable achievement in market building, the market transition process in China is far from complete (Lin, 2011; Meyer, 2011; Nee, Opper, & Wong, 2007). It was expected that the second phase of reform would witness even more profound and thorough reforms that will eventually introduce an institutional system that is compatible with a market economy, a dramatic shrinkage of the state sector, and the creation of conditions enabling fair competition among all market participants (Naughton, 2007). But much of the evidence in the latter period has cast doubt on the previous transition-based conjecture (Meyer, 2011). It was argued that maybe the Chinese government has determined to maintain its one-party political rule and explore a new model of development in which the party and its apparatus will unite various economic forces under its leadership so that the nation can advance economically and socially with efficiency and stability. The goal of the reform is clear, that is to reach the other bank of the river, which symbolizes wealth and happiness, and the method to reach the goal is to cross the river by feeling the stones. "What was left unsaid is that finding the next stone and coordinating the next movement are commanded by the party, not by free-market mechanism" (Lin, 2011: 72).

Some thus contended that instead of conceptualizing the Chinese reform as a transition process, the essence and future direction of China's reform can be better interpreted if we treat it as a transformation that forges a new way to produce economic growth (Fligstein & Zhang, 2011; Lin, 2008, 2011). Lin viewed the Chinese model as centrally managed capitalism, a variant of state capitalism. It differs from liberal capitalism (Dutch-British-American model), which is a form of economic activity dominated by private firms. Private firms compete in markets for goods and services and in markets for capital. Ideally, under capitalism the role of the state is limited. The state sets the rules, limits excesses, and intervenes in markets as a last resort. Although the state may operate infrastructure enterprises like postal systems, railways, and utilities, state-owned and private enterprises rarely compete because the latter are hopelessly disadvantaged (Meyer, 2011). In contrast, centrally managed capitalism is a form of state capitalism that takes on the capitalistic form with the essential elements of capitalism: it promotes calculating capitalists, a free market, wage labor, and an expansive system. The degree of variation of state capitalism can be characterized by two dimensions: the extent to which the state owns the means of production, and the extent to which the state dictates or coordinates with big firms and unions in the marketplace. In the Chinese system, the state plays an active role as a capitalist who exercises much freedom in creating and maintaining enterprises through ownership, holding a majority of the shares, and direct control over critical personnel decisions and supply of capital (Lin, 2011).

However, other scholars feel it is difficult to put China in any existing typology. Through a comparison of China's current system with other capitalist systems, Fligstein and Zhang find that the French system is most proximate to China, but it is also evident that many of the institutions, such as independent labor unions, do not exist in the Chinese system. They thus argue that every transition to capitalism has produced a new variety of capitalism, and in each transition, a set of common problems has had to be solved (Fligstein & Zhang, 2011: 47). Gao (2009) highlights the challenges that existing theoretical perspectives, such as structural views and agency-centric perspectives, have encountered when explaining Chinese reform. He then proposes that the Chinese system may be a combination of multiple institutional elements that emerge and persist as the state adapts or responds to domestic and international challenges. Walder (2011) maintains that the future state of Chinese capitalism depends on the relative potency of four economic sectors: state-owned, transitional, privatized, and entrepreneurial sectors. If the former two are consolidated and grow, then China will evolve into a highly statist form of corporate capitalism, which joins political and economic power, whereas if the latter two sectors triumph, then power and wealth will be less closely linked. In addition, there are still others who believe China is not capitalistic, at least as capitalism is ordinarily conceived. The current system may be just a combination of an institutionalized GDP growth machine with a resulting centralized governance structure (Meyer, 2011).

All these divergent views show the difficulties in establishing a singular theory that accounts for the cause and direction of this fundamental social change. Instead of taking a paradigm-driven approach to develop a grand theory, many authors have suggested a mechanism-based theorizing, which provides an intermediary level of analysis in between pure description and storytelling and universal social laws. The mechanism-based theories, such as environmental mechanisms, cognitive mechanisms, relational mechanisms, diffusion, network cultivation, and strategic leadership, allows us to make sense of social change processes and is broadly applicable to management and organization phenomena in times of economic transition (Davis & Marquis, 2005).

Many past studies have taken this approach to explore how the spread of markets or the transfer of property rights from the state to private interests has led to different social stratification outcomes. Although these studies yield fruitful results, the scholarship on how legal, financial, and cultural institutions change, and how such institutional changes affect the evolution of organizational forms, the governance structure, and organizations' strategies is still limited (Keister, 2009). Just as Nee and Opper (2009) argued, the revitalization of the market transition literature would require a focus on firm-level analysis, which provides an alternative approach to examining the association between institutional evolution, the shift of social and economic power, and the change of actors' coping strategies. Davis and Marquis (2005) hold similar views and believe that organizational theory can provide a natural history of the changing institutions of contemporary capitalism. The organizational theorists have developed a distinctive toolkit for addressing puzzles such as how societies diverge, how specific ecosystems of institutions change, what accounts for the widely disparate performance characteristics, and have developed a well-elaborated set of theoretical mechanisms that can illuminate how macrolevel changes, e.g., government policies, impact organizations.

Therefore, it is important to continue scholarly investigation of the management and organization phenomena that emerged during China's reform process. The several studies incorporated in this volume represent our recent attempt in advancing this line of inquiry. Although the substantive topics expand to multiple different research fields, the central focus of these studies has been very clear. We aim to relate the distinctive institutional characteristics of the Chinese context to the behaviors and strategies of individual entrepreneurs, firms, as well as crucial entities with other organizational forms. We inherited the central questions embedded in the previous market transition and Chinese capitalism studies and paid special attention to the mechanisms through which government intervention and intergovernmental interactions shape the trajectory of economic development, and the question of how the state and the business community interact to promote further evolution of the business as well as the political system. These intervention and coordination mechanisms, we believe, are important elements of China's emerging economic order.

The first set of studies we conducted investigates how firms in different economic sectors handle relationships with key stakeholders in the environment. Much of the literature on transition invokes ideas from network analysis indirectly, but few studies have effectively applied contemporary ideas and methods from network analysis to understand transition. Walder (2011) pointed out that exploring how personal ties link the concentrations of corporate power to the top reaches of the political system is potentially very important for us to understand the patterns of current and future systems, even though this is the most obscure and difficult of research topics. Social ties of this kind can provide entry to the highest reaches of political power, and in turn, they can benefit those in the business world who are known to have such ties. It will come as no surprise to observers of China that such ties serve an important function in an emerging market economy. Yet we have only a vague sense of the extent of such ties and their potential importance. To examine these networks in a systematic way rather than through anecdote and scandal presents a major challenge (Walder, 2011).

In the first analysis (Chapter 2), we borrowed insights from institutional theory, network theory, and literature on stakeholder management. We proposed that as the market expands the institutional environment will evolve, which changes the resources allocation mechanisms and strengthens the influence of market mechanisms. These institutional changes have redefined the power, legitimacy, and urgency of different stakeholders to firms. In order to adapt to this change, firms may adjust their networking strategies accordingly in order to figure out who are the salient stakeholders in their environment and the ways to strengthen relations with these salient stakeholders. In the early phase of reform, firms tended to consider networking as necessary in almost every process of economic transactions and thus tended to use social relations comprehensively, whereas in the later phase, a more codified institutional environment emerged. Firms can then better understand the utility of certain stakeholders to their operation, and are more likely to give different weight to the stakeholders in the environment. In other words, as the market system becomes more established, firms are more likely to base their networking strategy on objective indicators, such as firms' industry, local environment, and firms' market status.

Our study advanced the literature on network capitalism by shedding light on the relationship between the use of a network-based strategy and the expansion of market institutions. Following institutional substitution logic (Xin & Pearce, 1996), when resource allocation is more market driven, and barriers to trade and market entry are eliminated, the importance of a network-based strategy to business growth and financial performance will decline. However, contrary to their prediction, networking investments still matter in the changed market environment. The continuing relevance of networking with market actors suggests that impersonal and formal market transactions will not automatically follow when the market becomes competitive. Market competition might reduce the benefit brought by the utilization of the social network, but market competition alone cannot eliminate networking in business transactions. The market economy depends heavily on the development of various market supporting institutions, such as rule of law, free press, accountable government, well-governed and transparent economic entities, and business norms/ethics.

Our second analyses (Chapter 3) focused on the adoption of network-based strategies in the foreign-invested economy sector. We introduced new theoretical mechanisms to investigate the relationship between institutional conditions and the use of social networks in the business fields. We adopted institutional duality theory in the international business context (Kostova & Roth, 2002; Kostova, Roth, & Dacin, 2008) to examine how, why, and who as well as where and when foreign firms use corporate political strategies in establishing their legitimacy or gaining advantage in a new market. In so doing, we also paid close attention to the impact of sector and region specific intuitional conditions on FIEs' strategic choices. Our study addressed Walder's (2011) concern regarding how social ties link the concentration of corporate power to the top reaches of the political system. Whereas most extant studies focus narrowly on firm-based political tactics, our study extends the scope of research on how firms engage governments by examining multiple firm-based political tactics simultaneously, and more importantly, by investigating the adoption of collective-oriented associational activities.

This study also advances the existing literature by examining the intricate relationship between firm-based and collective-oriented CPS. We find that trade associations have important political functions and serve as a communication channel between FIEs and the host government. The affiliation with domestic or foreign business associations enhances an FIE's activeness in taking extensive political tactics to engage the host government. However, the functioning mechanism of foreign and domestic organizations may differ to some extent. Whereas the foreign business associations can create more interactive opportunities between firms and the state to strengthen their relationships, they can significantly improve the bargaining power of foreign business in the host country by initiating collective action. This external pressure may result in changes in the existing institutions, which may further facilitate or limit the operation of foreign businesses. Compared with foreign trade associations, Chinese domestic trade associations function as an important corporatist institution, which allows the state to effectively coordinate the interests of newly emerged economic groups. There is evidence indicating that the organizational form of the domestic business associations have undergone significant changes. The emerging types have different institutional distance from the state, which may raise new challenges to the existing corporatist institutions.

Our study highlights the importance of a thorough understanding of an FIE's specific institutional environment at various levels to make strategic choices. Our findings suggest that FIEs scrutinize their specific institutional environments and linkages with both foreign and local sides when choosing different approaches in CPS rather than blindly emulating others. Meanwhile, practitioners consider both firm-based and collective-oriented political activities as complementary and interconnected strategies. As associational activities can further promote interactions between firms and the host government, it should receive considerable attention. Moreover, domestic trade associations exert a greater impact on strengthening firm–government ties and enhancing firm-based political tactics; practitioners may move beyond their comfort zone in foreign business associations and more actively engage local business associations to better overcome environmental uncertainties, gain legitimacy in the emerging markets, and secure institutional support from the host government.

Our third analysis (Chapter 4) focused on the entrepreneur sector, which constitutes an important institutional force that may redefine the future of Chinese capitalism. To determine the potential of the entrepreneurial sector, a better understanding is needed as to the microsocial processes that influence the quality and quantity of resources that entrepreneurs can mobilize toward the exploitation of an entrepreneurial opportunity (Casey, 2012; Kotha & George, 2012). Structural and relational properties of entrepreneurs' social networks have often been quoted as important factors that affect their resource-seeking behavior; however, much less attention has been paid to the effects of the resource properties of such networks. This study fills the gap by employing new measurements to simultaneously explore the effects of three types of network embeddedness on entrepreneurs' financial ambidexterity. We found that the institutional resources embedded in entrepreneurs' social network, as measured by upward-reaching connections, can help entrepreneurs overcome constraints in accessing formal sector resources. Entrepreneurs are more likely to receive financial support from banks and other formal financial institutions when they have connections to those that hold important positions in the state bureaucratic system. Moreover, we also see the impact of social stratification outcomes on entrepreneurs' capacity of mobilizing financial resources. We find the proportion of urban ties affects firms' financial ambidexterity through two means. For one thing, because urban residents tend to be more affluent then rural residents, when entrepreneurs have more urban contacts, they have a greater pool of financial resources which they can utilize to meet their urgent financial needs. For another, urban residents are more likely to have more financial knowledge, which can help entrepreneurs apply for formal financial resources. In addition, entrepreneurs from disadvantaged social groups make more effort and are more successful in activating their private-network resources. Similarly, the higher ambidexterity of some entrepreneurs may be attributed to their higher socioeconomic status, which is often regarded as creditworthiness by the formal financial institutions rather than the effect of network embeddedness. We incorporated both explanations into the same model and the results indicate that although these two factors are often closely associated, their effects are largely independent and function through different mechanisms.

China's economic reform is characterized by the expansion of market mechanisms in many economic fields. However, the phrase "market growth" is a process that is more complex than it seems to be. It involves the establishment of market-oriented management systems within firms and the cultivation of a market system at the macrolevel and in fields that used to be restricted to non-state capital. Therefore, examining the diffusion of managerial practices and pro-market policies became our second goal in this volume. We believed such analysis will help us to further understand the mechanisms that led to the introduction and spread of market mechanisms in China's economic system. These understandings directly addressed the question of what factors have helped the capitalist order and liberal capitalist system gain a foothold in this then-command economy system.

Studies of diffusion across individuals, organizations, and social movements have a long tradition in organizational sociology. Since the late 1970s, sociologists have studied public policy diffusion through the lens of constructivism, coercion, and economic competitions. For instance, it was argued that the spread of neoliberal economic policies is closely associated with the intensified economic competitions among nations. When countries compete for capital and export markets, governments have little choice but to choose market-friendly policies to attract global investment and keep exports competitive so that they will not fall behind their direct competitors. Borrowing insights from previous diffusion literature, our first analysis on this theme investigated how managers adopted two important innovative management practices in the early transition period. We showed that the spread of piece wages and buying/selling producer goods on markets had been facilitated by market development, workers' support for managerial decisions, and managers who were market-oriented. We showed that as managers and firms got more experience with the new market-oriented practices, the motivation behind their adoption decisions also changed. As reform progressed, workers' support of managers and market development became less important factors that affected firms' adoption decisions. Instead, simple imitation gave way to imitation of specific, usually profitable others.

More importantly, our study goes beyond previous literature on managerial practice diffusion. We highlighted that when making strategic decisions, firms not only consider their firm-specific capabilities but also consider the incentives or disincentives originating from the institutional environment. Our findings suggest that, in the Chinese case, the state has been an important factor that determined the relative salience of internal and external influences. The state seldom enters strategic choice analyses and it enters most institutional analyses as an afterthought. However, our study indicates that the state has the capacity to define the context, i.e., to determine what factors will be relevant and when they will matter. The state can determine which firms are essential to its survival and thus will continue to be under its control and which can be decentralized to local government, or jointly controlled with non-state investors, or simply privatized. Such discretion defined the relative mix of internal and external constraints that firms faced in the short run. In the long run, the central state's decisions about which firms to protect initially is likely to influence which firms are adept at negotiating market exchange and which remain weak dinosaurs. Of course, there are some industries that are protected in nearly all economies (e.g., defense), and the mere presence of state control does not necessarily imply reduced competition.

Our second diffusion analysis (Chapter 6) aims to explain how market institutions emerge and grow in once highly restricted sectors. In this study, we chose a hotly debated issue in current Chinese policy making and academic circles—the spread of public–private partnerships. We noted that in the past 20 years, the wide spread liberalization of the formally state-controlled infrastructure sectors has redefined the role of the state in the economy (Izaguirre, 2005; Simmons, Dobbin, & Garrett, 2007). State monopolies in major infrastructure sectors have been abolished or restricted, and private capital has participated in a wide range of projects through schemes such as concession, greenfield projects, and divestiture. During China's rapid urbanization and industrialization process, the private sector has played a crucial role in mobilizing financial resources for key urban services, such as urban roads, public transportation systems, municipal solid waste management, and water and sanitation. Despite widespread adoption of the pro-market policies, cities differ greatly in the extent to which they allow the private sector to participate in these sectors. And the temporal distribution of different liberalization schemes reflects the state's intricate balance between market liberalization and effective state control over the economy.

Our results highlighted the state's role in establishing a neoliberal economic order in this urban infrastructure sector. We argue that similar to other diffusion processes, the spread of public–private partnerships was initially driven by internal conditions of cities. Cities with a stronger economy, a higher industrialization rate, a larger scale investment in fixed assets, and a bigger and floating population are more likely to require greater infrastructure service capacities. This high demand will positively affect a city's propensity to adopt the privatization policy. Moreover, a local state's fiscal and political capacity is crucial to the implementation of private participated projects.

What makes our study distinctive is that we abandoned the approach that treats the state as a singular entity; rather we treat the state as a complex system with many interdependent political actors whose decisions are heavily influenced by their structure positions in China's political system and the vertical as well as horizontal intergovernmental relationships among different governments. Our results show that along the vertical dimension, the central and provincial governments exert strong influence on local policy making through the specification of macro policy guidelines or direct administrative order. However, the effectiveness of such pressure is not homogenous across cities; it is conditioned by resource dependence relations among different levels of governments. Regarding the horizontal intergovernmental relations, we find that geographic proximity facilitates the social learning process and promotes interjurisdictional competition for capital, labor, as well as other production factors. In highly competitive environments, local governments are keen to their neighbors' policy innovations, and try to institute similar policies that may increase their competitor's competitiveness. In addition to this form of competition, local governments are also competing with peer cities that are subordinate to the same higher-level government. The leaders of these cities compete with each other for better local economic performance, which is closely related to their future promotion prospective. In addition, we also paid attention to the role of policy research communities in the liberalization process. We argue that the theorization efforts of the policy research professionals are significant in promoting the marketization of the urban infrastructure and utility sectors.

This study also speaks to the question of whether the states will support the privatization reform to its full extent, or will stop at some point, at which the state maintains a balanced relation with the private sector. Previous studies have discovered a privatization–nationalization cycle in many different settings (Gomez-Ibanez & Meyer, 1993). In this cycle, private investments are introduced to improve the efficiency of the public sector. Private firms' power and market share then expand and take over the inefficient facilities in neighboring cities. The private firms may consolidate and possess significant monopolistic power over a greater service area, which then triggers pressure for monopoly regulation. Regulation aims to reduce the prices and profitability, which discourages maintenance and new private investments. The subsequent decline of service quality will encourage the state to nationalize the firm and subsidize it. The provision of subsidy again causes inefficiency, which paves the way for the next round of privatization (Dailami & Klein, 1998).

However, in addition to the reasoning of the privatization–nationalization cycle model, the Chinese case shows that the fluctuation in the degree of privatization may also reflect the changing balance between state power and private power. When the power of the state sector increases, it may expand its control over more economic sectors and squeeze out private investments. As in many other cases, the adoption of the public–private partnership model is largely due to the lack of available financial resources of the local states for maintaining or improving local infrastructure services. The quick increase of private participation in the late 1990s and the revival of the PPP discussions are partially driven by the capital needs of the local states. However, during the early 2000s, the fiscal power of both central and local states improved significantly. Together with the fast growing economic power of the state firms, the state sector expanded their control in many fields, especially the infrastructure sectors. As the public sector has the incentive and financial power to take back its turf, the degree of private participation may therefore stagnate or even decrease.

Another major issue in this book is to map the enterprise ownership structure by documenting whether the ownership and control exercised by state owners over corporations are diminishing, strengthening, or transforming (Walder, 2011). The study of the ownership and the governance structure helps us to understand how the state controls and manages firms while allowing them to compete in the marketplace. Specifically, we can partially explore how the features of China's emerging system are similar or dissimilar to the models specified by previous scholars (Lin, 2008; Walder, 2011). We explored how the state controls and manages the top managers of the firms beyond the usual market oriented rewards and incentives. The state-owned or affiliated enterprises compete with other enterprise in the marketplace, and its elites enjoy the rewards and benefits largely consistent with other capitalists. However, the elites ultimately answer to the dictates of the state rather than boards of directors, shareholders, or stakeholders. The market is asymmetric in favor of state-owned and affiliated enterprises in accessing loans and resources (land, raw materials, and so on) and operating in both domestic and foreign markets. Some state-owned and affiliated enterprises become 'national champions' as the state restricts their competitors and encourages their mergers and acquisitions.

Our first analysis on this theme examined the influence of business groups in China's transition economy on the financial performance of firms. We explored factors that affected the formation of lender and trade relations in Chinese business groups in the early stages of reform. We argue that one of the most profound components of China's industrial reform has been the reorganization of firms into business groups, a process that began in the mid-1980s. Investigating the mechanism that led to such formations is important to understanding the emergent structure of the groups and ultimately China's new economy. We proposed that using multiple indicators of group structure—including indicators of the presence and predominance of interlocking directorates, informal finance arrangements, and the hierarchical organization of the group—would clarify the role that business groups play in determining firm performance in China. More importantly, we drew an important distinction between early and later development in studying the relationship between group structure and firm financial performance. We found that certain elements of group structure benefitted firms early in reform, but as markets became more stable, group membership appears to have become detrimental to firm wellbeing.

The results of our study also provide important information about the process of economic transformation more generally. Relatively high uncertainty, changing sources of uncertainty, market failure, managers who are not accustomed to markets, and expanding competition were prevalent in China, as they are in many transition economies. The strong but declining role of the state, the continued importance of bureaucratic power, and hardening budget constraints were also typical of a transition economy. Our findings suggest that regional differences in market development during transition may be institutionalized and thus shape economic exchange after transition. Similarly the continued importance of bureaucratic power during transition may cause the post-transition economic structure to reflect pre-reform advantages. Perhaps most consequential for understanding transition economies, however, is the finding that social ties are important predictors of economic relations. Although the transition context is unique, these results also speak to the process by which interfirm relations emerge, and thus to the general process by which social structures come into being. The somewhat unique transition context required some modifications of existing theory, but much of what we know of organizations from other contexts remained true.

Our second analysis (Chapter 8) described the recent changes in the state asset management system, which arises as the results of China's de facto federalist economic management system. We adopted a political economy perspective in the study of the impact of the structure features of the state-led business groups on their member firms (Khanna & Fisman, 2004; Yiu, Lu, Bruton, & Hoskisson, 2007). We argue that previous studies on Chinese business groups were not able to fully appreciate the importance of the linkage between the state asset management agencies and the SOEs they controlled. This omission prevented us from seeing the interconnectedness above the conventionally defined business groups, or understanding how such higher order group structure affected the financial performance of its subsidiaries. We therefore brought state actors back to the center of business group studies and defined the state-led business groups, which is a reflection of China's decentralized state asset management system. By tracing the actual controller of China's publicly listed firms, we identified the members of state-led business groups at various levels. We then further explored how group structures and characteristics of group controllers affected member firms' financial performance.

We borrowed insights from the literature on market transition of former socialist countries and argue that the existence of the dual monopoly relationship between the state and the SOEs is one of the primary causes of the soft budget constraint problem, which led to the poor financial performance of SOEs (Kornai, 1992). But the strength of this dual monopoly relationship is not homogeneous among governments at different levels. Previous studies argue that as the administrative level decreases, government nonfinancial interests in SOEs will decline, which helps SOEs harden their budget constraints (Walder, 1995). We find that on the one hand, the profitability of SOEs will increase as we move down to the lower levels, whereas the political capital brought by high-status state owners helps firms gain market recognition (as measured by Tobin's Q).

In addition to the leader's status, we further investigated the influence of group governance structure and group composition on firm's performance. We noticed that previous studies on the conventional Chinese business groups argue that member firms' financial performance will be positively associated with a less decentralized group structure, in which the controlling firm only maintains rights such as the nomination of top executives but does not exercise operation control over member firms (i.e., the Temasek Model) (Ang & Ding, 2006; Keister, 1998). Our findings do not support this relation; instead, we find that firms in a more centralized group structure perform better than those in a decentralized structure. Empirical evidence shows that in the Chinese context, when following the Temasek model and adding another layer of governance body between the leading state agency and the member firms, firms will be adversely affected because such an arrangement will generate conflicting demand from the upper level management bodies. Moreover, when further partitioning affiliated SOEs into different blocks led by separate state asset investment companies, interest conflicts will arise among the investment companies which may weaken the coordinating capacity of the leading state agency (Feng, 2014). This in turn diminishes the benefits of group affiliation.

Our findings also advance our understanding of how group diversification affects member firms' performance. We differentiated the policy and market driven diversification and argue that the unrelated diversification of the state-led business groups are primarily driven by state policies (Chung, 2005; Khanna & Yafeh, 2007). Our findings indicate that a high degree of group diversification negatively affects member firms' financial performance because having firms in many unrelated industries greatly increases the complexity of management tasks and increases the coordination costs at the group level. In addition, we argue that the impact of diversification is contingent on the institutional environment; a more diversified organization is more likely to survive the coarse grained environment, whereas a specialist, i.e., an organization with a low degree of diversification, is more suitable to a fine grained environment (Hannan & Freeman, 1977). We noted that the existence of different types of ownership forms is an important institutional feature of the emerging economy. We find that the presence of an alternative ownership form is beneficial to both state and non-state firms. On the one hand, a fair amount of non-state firms may allow SOEs to receive helpful technological, entrepreneurial, and market information from their private or foreign fellows in the group. Meanwhile, the private and foreign firms can benefit much from their connections with the SOEs, which greatly improve their access to the scarce resources.

Taken together, our approach in this volume has been consistent with Nee's (2009) argument that in order to determine whether the prediction of a decline of state power in the emerging market context is accurate, empirical tests need to focus on discrete economic transactions linked to well-defined institutional domains of the transition economy. In this way, it is possible to discern with greater reliability whether the state relaxes or loses its direct control over the transactions in market exchange or, alternatively, maintains or possibly even gains advantage in such transactions. The empirical evidence presented in this volume and those reported in previous studies have cast doubt on the original predictions of the market transition thesis. Much evidence suggests that China does not seem to be moving toward a western liberal capitalist model; however it is also difficult to rule out the possibility completely that the indigenous growth of the domestic private sector and the interaction between this newly emerged power and the state institutions can lead to further growth of the neoliberal economic system, a more open and inclusive political system. In response to early evidence contrary to the predictions of market transition theory, Nee and Cao (2004) reconsidered the theory's early prediction. They acknowledged that market development is indeed slowed down, but they argue that the "discontinuity stemming from market forces most frequently commences from small beginnings through changes at the margins, which are often difficult to discern in empirical studies, especially in the early stages of transitions from state socialism. By contrast, continuity is more readily apparent because the processes that sustain equilibrium conditions embedded in long-standing formal and informal institutional structures are more resilient than many assume" (Nee & Cao, 2004: 4). It takes a significant amount of change before emergent patterns reach a tipping point, and empirical investigations are still needed to shed more light on this profound transformation process (Keister, 2009).

References

Ang, J. S., & Ding, D. K. (2006). Government ownership and the performance of government-linked companies: The case of Singapore. *Journal of Multinational Financial Management, 16*, 64–88.

Casey, C. (2012). Low-Wealth minority enterprises and access to financial resources for start-up activities: Do connections matter? *Economic Development Quarterly, 26*(3), 252–266.

Chung, C.-N. (2005). Beyond Guanxi: Network contingencies in Taiwanese business groups. *Organization Studies, 27*(4), 461–489.

Dailami, M., & Klein, M. U. (1998). Government support to private infrastructure projects in emerging markets. *World Bank Policy Research Working Paper*, 1868.

Davis, G. F., & Marquis, C. (2005). Prospects for organization theory in the early twenty-first century: Institutional fields and mechanisms. *Organization Science, 16*(4), 332–343.

Feng, Y. (2014). Managing capital versus managing people, operation, and assets. *Southern Weekly*. Retrieved from http://www.infzm.com/content/102558

Fligstein, N., & Zhang, J. (2011). A new agenda for research on the trajectory of Chinese capitalism. *Management and Organziation Review, 7*(1), 39–62.

Gao, B. (2009). The Rubik's cube state: A reconceptualization of political change in contemporary China. *Research in the Sociology of Work, 19*, 409–438.

Gomez-Ibanez, J. A., & Meyer, J. R. (1993). *Going Private: The International Experience with Transport Privatization.* Washington, DC: Brookings Institution.

Hannan, M. T., & Freeman, J. (1977). The population ecology of organizations. *American Journal of Sociology, 82*(5), 929–964.

Izaguirre, A. K. (2005). Private infrastructure: Emerging market sponsors dominate private flows. *Public Policy Journal, 299*, 1–4.

Keister, L. A. (1998). Engineering growth: Business group structure and firm performance in China's transition economy. *American Journal of Sociology, 104*(2), 404–440.

Keister, L. A. (2009). Organizational research on market transition: A sociological approach. *Asia Pacific Journal of Management, 26*(4), 719–742.

Khanna, T., & Fisman, F. (2004). Facilitating development: The role of business groups. *World Development, 32*, 609–628.

Khanna, T., & Yafeh, Y. (2007). Business groups in emerging markets: Paragons or parasites? *Journal of Economic Literature, 45*(2), 331–372.

Kornai, J. (1992). *The Socialist System: The Political Economy of Communism.* Princeton, NJ: Princeton University Press.

Kostova, T., & Roth, K. (2002). Adoption of an organizational practice by subsidiaries of multinational corporations: Institutional and relational effects. *Academy of Management Journal, 45*(1), 215–233.

Kostova, T., Roth, K., & Dacin, M. T. (2008). Institutional theory in the study of multinational corporations: A critique and new directions. *Academy of Management Review, 33*(4), 994–1006.

Kotha, R., & George, G. (2012). Friends, family, or fools: Entrepreneur experience and its implications for equity distribution and resource mobilization. *Journal of Business Venturing, 27*, 525–543.

Lin, N. (2008). Emerging Chinese capitalism and its theoretical and global implications. *Social Transformations in Chinese Societies, 3*, 13–62.

Lin, N. (2011). Capitalism in China: A centrally managed capitalism (CMC) and its future. *Management and Organization Review, 7*(1), 63–96.

Meyer, M. W. (2011). Is it capitalism? *Management and Organization Review, 7*(1), 5–18.

Naughton, B. (2007). *The Chinese Economy: Transitions and Growth.* Cambridge, MA: MIT Press.

Nee, V. (1989). A theory of market transition: From redistribution to markets in state socialism. *American Sociological Review, 54*, 663–681.

Nee, V. (1996). The emergence of a market society: Changing mechanisms of stratification in China. *American Journal of Sociology, 101*, 908–949.

Nee, V., & Cao, Y. (2004). Market transition and the firm: Institutional change and income inequality in urban China. *Management and Organization Review, 1*, 23–56.

Nee, V., & Opper, S. (2009). Bringing market transition theory to the firm. *Research in the Sociology of Work, 19*, 3–34.

Nee, V., Opper, S., & Wong, S. (2007). Developmental state and corporate governance in China. *Management and Organization Review, 3*, 19–53.

Simmons, B. A., Dobbin, F., & Garrett, G. (2007). The global diffusion of public policies: Social construction, coercion, competition or learning? *Annual Review of Sociology, 33*, 449–472.

Walder, A. G. (1995). Local governments as industrial firms: An organizational analysis of China's transitional economy. *American Journal of sociology*, 263–301.

Walder, A. G. (2011). From control to ownership: China's managerial revolution. *Management and Organization Review, 7*(1), 19–38.

Xin, K. K., & Pearce, J. L. (1996). Guanxi: Connections as substitutes for formal institutional support. *Academy of Management Journal, 39*(6), 1641–1658.

Yiu, D., Lu, Y., Bruton, G. D., & Hoskisson, R. E. (2007). Business groups: An integrated model to focus future research. *Journal of Management Studies, 44*(8), 1551–1579.

Index